ACCLAIM FOR CATHERINE WEST

"Seamless and elegant, yet brimming with raw and robust emotion, this trip to wine country pulls out all the stops on the scenic route of great fiction. West has cultivated another poignant story of hope and healing all tangled in the vines with a second chance love story you won't want to miss. One to be breathed and sipped and savored to the last drop!"

—AMY LEIGH SIMPSON, AUTHOR OF *WHEN FALL FADES* AND *FROM WINTER'S ASHES*, ON *THE MEMORY OF YOU*

The Memory of You is a multifaceted story of family relationships that are hindered by secrets shrouded in regrets. Author Cathy West's realistic writing shines once again as she weaves together several compelling storylines, with each one pointing readers to the need for God's grace. West also reminds us that truth sets us free from past mistakes, allowing us to embrace the future God has for us.

—BETH K. VOGT, CHRISTY AND CAROL AWARD-WINNING AUTHOR

"Overall, it's an engrossing and ultimately moving novel, filled with mystery, romance and drama."

—*RT BOOK REVIEWS*, 4 STARS, ON *THE THINGS WE KNEW*

"A beautiful exploration of the bonds that tie us together as family and the secrets that sometimes unravel those threads. Catherine West builds a world worth entering and characters that linger long after the last page is turned."

—JULIE CANTRELL, *NEW YORK TIMES* AND *USA TODAY* BESTSELLING AUTHOR OF *THE FEATHERED BONE*, ON *THE THINGS WE KNEW*

"Smartly written and highly engaging, Catherine West's *The Things We Knew* dazzles, piercing the shadows of a family's tragedy with the light of love."

—BILLY COFFEY, AUTHOR OF *THE CURSE OF CROW HOLLOW* AND *WHEN MOCKINGBIRDS SING*

"Displaying an understanding of the conflicting dynamics of family relationships, Cathy West deftly weaves together the tumultuous story lines of the Carlisle and Cooper families. In *The Things We Knew*, she wrestles with how secrets can hide the truth of the past and cloud the future."

—Beth K. Vogt, 2015 RITA Finalist, author of *Almost Like Being in Love*

"A poignant, multi-faceted novel that pulled me in deeper with every turned page, *The Things We Knew* so adeptly explores the power of truth and its ability to set us all free. I can't wait for readers to fall as hopelessly in love with Nick and the Carlisle family as I did. Well done, Catherine West!"

—Katie Ganshert, award-winning author of *The Art of Losing Yourself*

"Catherine West's debut, *The Things We Knew*, is a beautifully readable exploration of family secrets and their continuing effects on both those who know and don't know them."

—Christa Parrish, award-winning author of *Still Life* and *Stones for Bread*

"*The Things We Knew* is a remarkable story, and author Catherine West is truly a wordsmith."

—Kathi Macias, award-winning author of *Red Ink*

"Intriguing setting, realistic characters with all-too-familiar tensions, and a tangle worth tracing to its source make *The Things We Knew* as satisfying as a Nantucket sunrise."

—Cynthia Ruchti, author of *As Waters Gone By* and *Song of Silence*

"Dynamic and lovely. This is a story that will capture your heart from the first page."

—ALICE J. WISLER, AUTHOR OF *RAIN SONG* AND *UNDER THE SILK HIBISCUS*, ON *THE THINGS WE KNEW*

"Integrally woven, fast-paced, and hard to put down. Loved the setting and loved the characters. Great book!"

—CELESTE FLETCHER MCHALE, AUTHOR OF *THE SECRET TO HUMMINGBIRD CAKE*, ON *THE THINGS WE KNEW*

"Winner! Cathy West's latest novel takes us on a journey into the heartache of aging parents, regrets, and sibling issues in ways that are both penetrating and infused with hope. Well-written, painted with emotional battles, addictions, and romance, West gives us poignant moments that stay long after the final page is turned."

—JAMES L. RUBART, BESTSELLING AND AWARD-WINNING AUTHOR OF *THE FIVE TIMES I MET MYSELF*, ON *THE THINGS WE KNEW*

The Memory of You

OTHER BOOKS BY CATHERINE WEST

The Things We Knew

The Memory of You

CATHERINE WEST

THOMAS NELSON
Since 1798

Published in Nashville, Tennessee, by Thomas Nelson. Thomas Nelson is a registered trademark of HarperCollins Christian Publishing, Inc.

Published in association with the Books & Such Literary Management, 52 Mission Circle, Suite 122, PMB 170, Santa Rosa, California 95409–5370, www. booksandsuch.com.

Thomas Nelson titles may be purchased in bulk for educational, business, fundraising, or sales promotional use. For information, please e-mail SpecialMarkets@ ThomasNelson.com.

Scripture quotations are taken from the Holy Bible, New International Version®, NIV®. Copyright © 1973, 1978, 1984, 2011 by Biblica, Inc.® Used by permission of Zondervan. All rights reserved worldwide. www.zondervan.com. The "NIV" and "New International Version" are trademarks registered in the United States Patent and Trademark Office by Biblica, Inc.®

Publisher's Note: This novel is a work of fiction. Names, characters, places, and incidents are either products of the author's imagination or used fictitiously. All characters are fictional, and any similarity to people living or dead is purely coincidental.

Library of Congress Cataloging-in-Publication Data

Names: West, Catherine (Catherine J.), author.
Title: The memory of you / Catherine West.
Description: Nashvillle, Tennesse : Thomas Nelson, 2017.
Identifiers: LCCN 2016042630 | ISBN 9780718078768 (softcover)
Subjects: LCSH: Family-owned business enterprises--Fiction. | Family
  secrets--Fiction. | Wineries--Fiction. | Domestic fiction. | GSAFD:
  Christian fiction.
Classification: LCC PR9680.B43 W476 2017 | DDC 813/.6--dc23 LC record
available at https://lccn.loc.gov/2016042630

Printed in the United States of America

17 18 19 20 21 LSC 6 5 4 3 2 1

For my beautiful daughter, Sarah.

You are experiencing one of God's greatest blessings as I write this. A precious new life will soon join our family and you will become a mother. As you begin this amazing adventure, I pray you will cherish the daily joys of motherhood and truly know what a great gift and blessing you have been and continue to be to me.

One

THE WOOD-PANELED WALLS OF THE BOARDROOM WERE CLOS-
ing in.

Natalie Mitchell fiddled with the strand of pearls around her neck and took deep breaths, painfully aware that every pair of eyes in the room were fixed on her as she stood to the side of the large screen and tried to make sense of the flowchart she had been describing succinctly only moments ago.

"And as you can see, our charitable donations last year gained significant notice in the . . ." Natalie tried to untangle her thoughts. She avoided Peter's intense gaze and wished for the thousandth time for her ex-fiancé to find employment elsewhere. "In . . ."

Was it sweltering in here? Even as cool air blew from the vents above her, Natalie felt a drop of perspiration slide down her back. She adjusted the collar of her silk blouse and scanned her notes. *Come on, think!*

"I'm sorry, I . . ." Natalie glanced up and caught her father's stare. The papers she held slipped from her shaking hands. She bent to pick them up off the floor, straightened, and cast about for one friendly face seated around the long table. Vague expressions and awkward silence forced a final attempt to pull it together.

Somehow she found her voice and made it through the presentation. It wasn't her best moment. Her father's frown confirmed it. One of the downsides of working in the family business was constantly having to prove herself. She'd only been head of PR at Mitchell Enterprises for a few months, so the pressure was on.

"Thank you, Natalie." Her father cleared his throat and raised a brow. "I hope you're not coming down with that nasty bug going around."

He didn't expect an answer. Not here. Natalie managed a weak smile and sat in miserable silence through the rest of the meeting. The minute it was over she gathered her things and fled the room.

She barely made it to the bathroom before the nausea overtook her.

The screeching of tires and the sickening thud that followed played over and over in her mind, no matter how hard she willed the memory away.

How was she supposed to live like this?

She'd been doing so well the past few years. This regression had to be temporary. Natalie shook her head and glared at her flushed face in the mirror. Weeks ago she could have believed that. But this had been going on too long. It was time to do something about it.

She also knew one thing her father didn't. This was no bug.

⌒

That Friday night she finally agreed to join her parents for a weekend away from the city. She loved New York, but lately the noisy, crowded city set her on edge.

Natalie sat on the porch of their Yarmouth, Cape Cod home after dinner, hoping the fresh, early September sea air would revive her shattered spirit. After the fiasco of a meeting on Tuesday, she'd given in and seen her doctor that afternoon. And the news wasn't good.

Sleepless nights, lack of appetite, nausea, and flashbacks. All the familiar signs were there. He was concerned about the possibility of another breakdown. Started her on new meds and wished she'd come in sooner.

Now she sat in semidarkness, debating with herself. She couldn't tell her parents what was really going on.

There was no quick fix for this.

"Nat-a-lie? Are you out here?"

Natalie pulled the colorful patchwork quilt tight around her shoulders and waited.

Her mother's succinct steps drew closer.

The screen door squeaked open and banged shut.

Heels tapped out an unbroken code on the one-hundred-year-old wooden planks as Jane Mitchell marched across the upper porch with purpose. "There you are. For heaven's sake! It's freezing tonight, you'll catch your death."

Natalie swiped her cheeks and sent the white rocker into high gear.

Her mother gripped the arms of the chair and brought it to an abrupt halt. "Natalie!"

The moon escaped the clouds and illuminated her wide, worried eyes. "What's going on? Your father says you almost lost it at a meeting the other day."

Natalie huffed and averted her gaze. "I did not almost lose it. I was fine."

"Like you've been fine ever since June when you and Peter called off your engagement?"

"Mom, if you invited me out here for the weekend to rehash all that, I'd rather not."

"I'm worried about you. We both are."

"You needn't be. I just had a bad day. That's all." A bad few months.

"Come downstairs to the study. Your father wants to talk to you."

"Talk or lecture?"

Her mother backed up, smoothed her crisply creased linen trousers, and patted her sleek bottle-blond chignon. The salty breeze would coax a few stray curls out of confinement any minute. "Are you coming?"

"Yes." No use refusing. She extricated herself from the rocker, dragging the quilt along.

In her father's study on the first floor, a fire danced and beckoned her over to wiggle her cold fingers before the yellow and orange flames. Strains of Vivaldi filtered through speakers hidden somewhere in the ceiling.

Her mother scoured the area like a sergeant on patrol, picking dead bits off her prize-winning violets and straightening magazines already stacked in perfect piles along the gleaming cherry wood coffee table.

Bill Mitchell held court behind his desk. The lines that creased his brow said whatever he planned to discuss was serious.

"You wanted to see me?" Natalie shuffled across the rich red-toned Persian rug and stood before him, thirteen years old again.

We're sending you away, Nat. It's a lovely school. You'll be happy there. You can move on, put all this behind you . . .

Her mother positioned herself in one of the burgundy leather armchairs across from him and waved Natalie toward its twin. "Sit, Natalie."

Natalie sat and tried to shove off apprehension.

Dad leaned forward and studied her. "I'm concerned about the way you've withdrawn since June. We haven't been able to get you out here all summer. Natalie, I have to ask. Are you . . ." He blew out a breath and sat back, unable to say it.

Are you having another breakdown?

Natalie sank a little lower in her chair.

That awful night at the beginning of June when she'd shown up at Peter's apartment unannounced, only to find him with another woman, had flicked some invisible switch. Since then, she'd been battling the past and all its demons 24/7.

"Don't worry. I'm totally fine."

"I don't think you are fine." Her father sounded perfectly calm, as though a maelstrom wasn't brewing. But his eyes told a different story. He was a highly respected businessman, but known as someone you did not want to cross. Unfortunately, she often felt the same.

"Dad, I said I'm—"

He held up a hand. "One moment you're giving a presentation at a board meeting, the next you can't finish a sentence. You're working long hours, but frankly, the last two presentations haven't been what I expect from you. And from what we can surmise, you spend far too much time alone in your apartment." He paused, letting each volley of words reach their intended target. "Is it just the breakup with Peter or is there more going on?"

She couldn't find the courage to tell her parents the truth. Couldn't admit that, once again, she had failed to meet life's challenges with the stoicism modeled by them.

Dad exhaled and downed dark liquid from a crystal tumbler. The storm in his eyes abated, but he still didn't look pleased. "Natalie, you can talk to us." He took on a kinder tone. "We only want to help."

"You want to help?" Natalie echoed, the irony mind-numbing. She dug her fingernails into her palms and stared at the marks they left. She remembered the last time her parents had tried to "help" and shuddered at the thought.

What could she say now?

A shutter banged against the side of the house and shook her. The evening's predicted storm was rolling in.

"You're not pregnant, are you?"

"Bill!" Her mother's horror was almost humorous.

"What, Jane? It's a logical question, is it not?"

Natalie watched them shoot sharp, swift, and silent arrows at each other.

When had they chosen sides, turned into opposing teams?

"No, Dad. I'm not pregnant." If she remembered those high school health classes correctly, you actually had to have sex with someone for that to happen.

"Well, that's a relief." Color crept back to his cheeks. "In any event, I think you need some time to get yourself together. I'd like to suggest you take a leave of absence."

"A what?" Natalie stared at her father and tried to mentally swerve around the hairpin turn in the conversation. He was cagey. Brilliant, really. You never knew when he was trying to catch you out until after the fact.

"We think you need a break. So I'd like you to go to California."

He really needed to stop throwing verbal knives in her direction. "California?"

The return of her nightmares had already sent her world careening off course, chaining her to a roller-coaster ride she couldn't stop.

No. Going west was not an option.

Aggravation niggled the corner of her father's mouth. "Well?"

"I can't take time off now. I've got important meetings all next week. I . . . are you actually serious?" Natalie tossed the quilt off her shoulders.

"Quite." Dad set down his glass. "We've got people to cover for you. I want you to go to Sonoma. To see your grandfather."

"Grandpa Hal?" Natalie tried to tear her thoughts from the multitude of scenarios about what would happen at work in her absence, pulled fingers through her tangled mess of hair, and searched the photographs on the bookcase behind her father's desk.

Silver frames encased the images of their childhood—school portraits, Christmas dinners, Natalie's brief foray into show jumping, her high school grad photo—and tucked between the bigger moments of their lives sat a small black-and-white image of Hal Mitchell holding a chubby two-year-old Natalie on his knee.

She hadn't seen her grandfather in years.

But going back to Sonoma . . . the place she'd tried to ignore for so long . . . until the memories barged back in and refused to retreat. Images of that dark night never really went away. Thirteen years had passed since Nicole's death, yet it could have happened yesterday. There were other places she could go if he insisted on her taking a vacation.

Natalie laced her fingers together to keep her hands from trembling. "I don't think I can."

Her mother gave a wisp of a sigh and placed a hand on Natalie's arm. "Well, then. Bill . . ."

"Jane. Enough." Dad pushed a worn looking leather photo album toward her. "I hadn't looked at these in years." He sat back and massaged his jaw. "I'm well aware how difficult this is, Natalie, but I'd like you to consider it."

"You always said that was your favorite part of summer, going to California." Mom leaned in to look at the pictures.

"Yes, for some reason, you loved Maoilios." Dad's mouth puckered, as though the name of her grandfather's winery was bitter on his tongue, like a sour grape.

"I did love it." Perhaps it wouldn't be so bad. And it would certainly provide the opportunity to get over this latest setback alone, without their interference.

"Such an odd name for a winery." Her mother peered at a tattered photograph. "Oh, Nat. You were a little pudgy back then, darling."

Natalie reached for the album and stared at the image.

The memory sprang to life. She was maybe six or seven, stuffed into an old tire swing, her sister Nicole pushing her.

"Pudgy" was being kind.

Natalie studied another photo. Two little girls looked up at the photographer with identical grins. Both with curly brown hair tied in pigtails, sporting red ribbons. Nicole had a dimple in her right cheek. Natalie didn't. Fraternal twins. As they got older it was easier to tell them apart. Nicole possessed a natural beauty, a sparkle that seemed to draw people to her. Natalie simply stood in her sister's shadow.

She put down the photo and picked up another. Scrunched her nose and stared at the castle-like structure.

Maoilios—a place she'd once loved more than anything.

The magic of it made her free. Free to do what she wanted, free to be herself. Free from overbearing parents who would often go off on side trips of their own, leaving the girls in the care of their grandparents.

Natalie enjoyed those times most.

And then, the year they turned thirteen, on a perfect star-lit August night, in one screeching, skidding, sickening moment, everything changed.

She sat back again and shook her head. "Why are we doing this?"

The unanswered question joined the silent choir of things her parents refused to discuss. "Why now?" She searched her father's face. "I haven't been there since the accident. We haven't seen Grandpa Hal more than a couple of times since Grandma died."

Dad suddenly looked uncomfortable. "We probably should have told you earlier, but your mother didn't want to upset you." Deep grooves privy to untold secrets furrowed his brow.

"Told me what?"

"Your grandfather had a heart attack, Natalie."

"A heart attack?" The words squeaked out. "When?"

"Last week."

"What? How could you not tell me? Mom, come on . . ." Natalie watched her mother fiddle with the large rings on her fingers and knew she was on her own.

"Don't be so dramatic," Dad growled. "We're telling you now."

Natalie stifled the argument, still treading water, trying to keep from going under. "Why didn't you go to see him?"

"He told me not to bother." His jaw tightened and he nailed her with his classic don't-dare-defy-me look. "So. I would like you to go. See how he's doing." The space between his eyes got smaller. "And actually, he's asked for you."

"For me?" She tapped her worn deck shoes together and watched a few grains of sand fall onto the rug. "I don't want to go back there." She could only whisper the words.

But part of her longed to.

Longed to return to the place she'd once loved so much, to see her grandfather again, to hear his laugh and bask in the smile that always made her feel like the luckiest girl in the world. With Grandpa, there was no competing. No trying to pretend. He loved her for who she was.

Dad took another swallow of Scotch. "I understand your reasons, God knows. But you can't hold on to those memories forever. Maybe if you go back and face it, you'll let it go."

Let it go.

Natalie startled as the fire cracked and hissed along with the pointed words.

Somehow he'd known. Seen right through her with hardly any effort at all.

"My sister died there, Dad. I could have—" She made fists and shut her eyes against the scene.

"I know." He cleared his throat and sat in silence for a long, painful moment. "But I think you need to go, Natalie." He was as unrelenting as the wind that now battered the trees outside.

You have to go away to school, Natalie. You're failing every class. It's time you learned to buckle down and stand on your own two feet.

"Natalie." Her mother's flawless face seemed strangely lined and pinched. "Your father and I really would like you to go." They were a team again. It worked when it suited them.

Natalie picked at stray threads on the quilt and watched a section of stitching unravel. "Is Grandpa in the hospital?"

"No. He's home now. He sounds well enough, insists he's fine, but who knows." Uncharacteristic worry laced her father's tone. "But he's going to drive himself into an early grave with that confounded vineyard. Another reason I want you to go, see what's going on. Perhaps it's time to shut the place down."

"Shut it down?" Surely things weren't that bad.

"Should have been done years ago," Dad started in again. "Regardless, it will do you good to get away, clear your head. Your flight is booked. You'll arrive early Friday morning."

So she didn't have a choice. Typical. "I can't just leave. I can't . . ." Her final attempt to find a way out fell flat. He was right. She was more of a hindrance at the office and they would survive without her. And if Grandpa Hal wanted her . . .

"Natalie? Are we in agreement?"

What if, in some way, this was just the reprieve she needed?

"All right. I'll go."

"Good." He rubbed his eyes, looking tired. "So, you're really okay? Because if you need to see another doctor or—"

Natalie's mother lifted her head. "Bill, really, she said she's fine. I don't think that's—"

"Jane." Dad held up a hand and shut her down.

Her mother sighed and began to twist her rings again.

Natalie never knew what her mother was thinking, never knew how she felt. And couldn't imagine what it must be like to live a life marked in half-finished sentences.

"Well." Mom stood, smoothed her hair, and gave a tight smile. "I'm going up. Good-night, dear. Good-night, Bill." She stalked across the carpet, closed the door quietly behind her with a definitive click. Jane Florence Harris Mitchell never slammed a door.

Natalie wrestled with relief, watched sheets of rain wash the windows, and willed her stomach to quit heaving. She could go out to California, deal with this latest emotional setback there and they'd never be the wiser. "How bad are things with the vineyard?"

"Now you're talking." Her father put aside the images of the past and pushed a folder her way. "Take a look at these numbers."

Natalie opened the file, curiosity overriding stubbornness, and studied the latest financials for Maoilios. "They bottomed out the year after Grandma died."

"Yes." Her father leaned back and put his hands behind his head. "I thought perhaps, since your grandmother foolishly left you her 50 percent of the place, that might concern you just a tad."

Natalie hadn't given much thought to her share in the winery over the last few years.

"Does Uncle Jeffrey know about this?" A grin caught her unaware. "Where is he these days?"

Dad's eyes narrowed. "Haven't heard from him since your grandmother's funeral. And he washed his hands of Maoilios years ago."

"How has Grandpa been managing?"

"I don't know. He's got some boy not much older than you running the place. I've no idea how he ended up in charge, but your grandfather seems to think he's Jesus."

Natalie laughed. "Well, if you want out, sell your shares to him, whoever he is. If he really is Jesus, you stand to make quite a profit." She turned the file toward him and pointed out a few dates. "This isn't a total loss. Just the past few years, and even then they had some good months. Perhaps a new business model, fresh marketing." Natalie wished the numbers weren't quite so blurry. The new meds she'd started were already wreaking havoc with her system. "Are you sure shutting the place down is the solution?"

Her father sighed. "My instincts say it's time to fold. Hal won't listen. If anybody can convince your grandfather to get rid of that winery, Natalie, it's you."

"Assuming *I* want to get rid of it." *Where had that come from?*

"And what would you do with a winery?"

"What would Grandpa do without Maoilios?"

"He would still own the house, the land. We're only talking about getting rid of the winery, the vineyards, and the label."

"So just getting rid of Grandpa's whole world then?"

"Natalie." Her father rolled his eyes.

"And what if the business is salvageable?" Did she really want to take this on?

"Are you going to argue about this? I want the place closed, and that's that."

"What if I can prove you wrong?" A sense of purpose and determination she hadn't felt in months blindsided her. Almost made her smile.

Dad shook his head, his mouth drawn. "You won't."

And there it was.

Because no matter how hard she worked, how well she did, her father would always find a flaw.

Even her best was never good enough.

Two

The flight from JFK to San Francisco International was smooth for the most part, and Natalie even managed to get some sleep.

Finally seated in her rental car, a shiny silver Jaguar convertible her father had arranged, she dialed her mother's cell, not surprised when it went straight to voice mail.

"Hey, Mom. Just letting you guys know I'm here. I'll call you later from Grandpa's."

Natalie adjusted the air-conditioning, set the satellite radio to classic oldies, and set her course for Sonoma. As she was about to pull out, her cell phone rang.

Not her mother though. Laura.

Of course.

Laura Johnson, her best friend since high school, was the only person Natalie hadn't managed to completely alienate in recent weeks.

"Hey, Lars. I just landed."

"I figured. Just wanted to make sure you got there safe and sound."

"Safe. Not sure about sound."

"Nat." Laura giggled. "How are you feeling, being there?"

"I'm not there yet." During the flight, Natalie pulled snippets from her memory of times in California. Barbecues out on the deck. Trees and landmarks, and journeys north along a winding coastal road that led to the beach.

"Um, I saw Peter yesterday. Gave him his ring back." Natalie turned the AC higher.

"How was that?"

"Okay. He wasn't surprised, of course. I didn't stay long."

"Good. I'm glad it's over."

"Like you didn't see it coming." It was impossible not to smile at her friend's insight. "But, better to know what kind of man he is now, right?"

"You'll find someone else, Nat. Someone who will love you the way you deserve."

Natalie scrunched her nose. "I won't be looking for love in Sonoma."

"You know what they say, sometimes when you least expect it—"

"Hey, Lars, I gotta go."

"Okay, hon." Laura's wistful sigh filled her ear. "Take care."

"Thanks. Talk to you later." Natalie hung up, took a few deep breaths, and eased the car out of the parking bay.

As she crossed the Golden Gate Bridge, bright shards of light split the clouds and the California sun began to warm the car's interior.

Her smile broadened as the scenery changed.

Rolling brown hills ran into rows upon rows of lush vines that hid clusters of purple and gold treasures under green foliage. The sight unwrapped feelings she thought she'd long put aside. The sweet smell of grapes permeated her senses, and the joy found in simply being here surprised her.

As she navigated the highway and sang along with The Beach Boys, memories trickled back like a slow-moving stream. Once the small town of Sonoma came into view, she didn't need the GPS anymore. Somehow she remembered the right turn that led her through the open metal gates and over a gravel road lined with tall Italian cypress trees. She couldn't recall the acreage of Maoilios, but what she saw impressed her. Vineyards spread out on either side of the road as far as the eye could see. As she made the last turn, she spied her grandfather's house.

The place resembled a French château, like something out of a travel magazine. Sunshine bounced off sparkling glass windows. Apricot-colored walls covered with ivy, a terra-cotta-tiled roof, and green wooden shutters complemented the layout, adding to the impression that she might indeed be in another country entirely.

Smooth lawns snaked around the property and stretched down to the vineyards. A large stream ran between the garden and the grapes. Somewhere along the way she knew there was a bridge. Nicole used to jump across the two-or three-foot wide expanse of rushing water, but Natalie always used the bridge.

Her gaze shifted back to the house and landed on the rounded structure to the left. The turret. A rebellious grin tickled the corners of her mouth. Sometimes she and Nic would sneak up there with their dolls and pretend to be princesses. Other days the neighborhood boys they'd become friends with hijacked it and threatened to dangle the girls from the window by their hair if they didn't retreat. Nicole always stood up to the boys.

The house now soothed and scared her. Bade her welcome like an old friend, but held a warning like a long-forgotten journal, tattered pages filled with too much pain.

She gathered up her thoughts and memories and drove around the fountain, parked, and stepped out onto the gravel drive. The thought of her sick grandfather living in this big house all on his own was not comforting.

She walked up the front steps and rang the doorbell. Somewhere off in the distance, dogs barked. Something that sounded like an intercom crackled and beeped.

"Yeah, come on down to the end of the road. Park the truck off to the side and we'll unload her there." A male voice competed with several loud pops and crackles. Natalie searched the wall, parted a few leaves to reveal a small speaker, and pressed the button.

"I . . . um." She glanced at her rental car and shrugged. "I don't have a truck. I'm here to see Hal Mitchell."

"What?" Whoever was on the other end sounded a million miles away.

Natalie pressed the button again. "HAL MITCHELL. I'm his granddaughter." She bit her lip and waited.

Nothing. Not even a tiny crackle. Just white noise that faded into ominous silence.

"Fine, then." She marched down the steps and scanned the area. A dirt road wound downward to the right of the house and she spied several buildings at the bottom of it. She remembered her mother telling them never to go down there.

Too many trucks.

Too much dirt.

Too much Hal.

Natalie set off, glad for the flat soles she'd chosen for her journey. As she walked, she told herself it was all going to work out, that she'd made the right decision coming. Her grandfather would be happy to see her. Sure, it had been years and she hadn't kept in touch, but still. She was family. And he'd asked for her.

Unless her father had made that up to get her out here.

As she approached the buildings, three black and white dogs shot up from their prone positions and raced toward her. They circled her legs and sniffed around, giving the occasional whine. No growling.

"Okay, hi. Friendly, are you? Good." She held out her hands and allowed the moderately sized beasts to check her out. She passed inspection and was rewarded with licks and wagging tails. Bravery got the better of her and she bent to pat their soft heads. "So where is everyone, huh?"

Shielding her eyes against the sun, Natalie looked toward a building where several men moved around, busy with their tasks. A forklift moved large plastic containers filled with grapes to a long stainless-steel contraption with a big corkscrew-like thing in the middle of it that looked a little scary. She inhaled and wrinkled her nose as the distinct smell of yeast hit hard. Her stomach lurched and her already dry throat threatened to toss out the last meal she'd eaten several hours ago.

"Can I help you?" A long shadow fell across her path.

A man stood at the entrance of the building. The dogs left her side and jumped around him. He promptly sent them off to a corner where they flopped down in the shade.

Natalie squinted up at him. "Yes. I . . . I hope so. I'm looking for Hal Mitchell. I'm his granddaughter."

He pushed his hands into the pockets of his jeans and peered at her. The barest of smiles raced across his face. "Hello, Mouse."

Natalie stepped back, not sure if she'd heard correctly. Nobody had called her that in years. And the only person who had was . . .

Standing right in front of her.

"Tanner?" Natalie lifted her shades, blinked, and squelched a squeak of surprise and the temptation to hurl herself at him. "Tanner Collins?"

He stepped out of the shadows. "You remember."

Natalie nodded and readjusted her sunglasses. She wanted to say "wow" but managed to swallow the word as she studied the object of her first crush.

Tanner's mother was the housekeeper at Maoilios, and they had lived on the property. Close in age, she and Nicole had become friends with him and the other employees' children who lived on the grounds. She'd often thought of Tanner over the years, wondered what he'd done with his life.

That last year, fifteen-year-old Tanner Collins had been heart-throb material. Tall and lanky, with just the beginnings of facial hair cresting a handsome upper lip. Dark brown hair kissed by the summer sun, hazel eyes flecked with gold were often filled with mischief and found company in the dimple in his left cheek whenever he smiled.

"You want to say hi or just stare?" His deep tenor brought heat to her cheeks and Natalie looked at the dogs instead.

Watchful eyes regarded her from almost identical black and white faces. One of the animals raised a paw, as if to say hello. Natalie was tempted to wave back. She'd never had a pet of her own. Her mother wouldn't hear of it. Dogs and small children were always kept at bay around Jane Mitchell.

Natalie faced Tanner Collins again, the more than five-hour flight still doing a number on her synapses. "I had no idea you were still here, Tanner."

"How would you?" His tone definitely hovered near the lower end of the barometer. Fine lines creased the corners of his eyes. Light stubble grazed his jaw and there was no dimple in sight. His tan bore testimony to working outdoors, the tip of his nose a light pink where the skin had started to peel.

"Well. I . . . um . . . came . . ." Heat and cold battled each other, making her stomach do somersaults and she closed her eyes. "I'm sorry. Jet lag, I guess."

"Get out of the sun." He grabbed her elbow and steered her toward a door on the side of the building, into a small air-conditioned office. "Sit." He pretty much pushed her onto the nearest chair but if he hadn't, she'd have been on the floor. A minute later he held a glass of cold water in front of her face.

"Thanks." Natalie took small sips, waiting for her stomach to settle. The dogs flopped at her feet. Natalie reached down to pat the closest one, grateful for a friend.

"That's Gwin," Tanner told her. "She belongs to me. The other two, Millie and Roscoe, belong to Hal."

"I see." Did he want to make small talk about dogs? "I'm surprised you remember me, Tanner." She switched her shades for glasses, and let the room come into focus.

He backed up against a metal desk. "Of course I remember you, Mouse."

A feeble laugh slid from her. "Nobody's called me that since the last time I was here."

He folded his arms, tipped his head. "I suppose not."

She took another sip of the cool liquid, the haze beginning to clear. Years rolled backward, revealing memories she'd almost forgotten.

Tanner was the first boy she'd been able to talk to without sounding stupid.

After that final, awful summer, he'd tried to keep in touch. Wanted to know if she was all right, how she was doing in school. After a few pathetic attempts at trying to describe her muddled feelings through e-mail, Natalie gave up. Partly because she just didn't know what to say, mainly because he was a reminder of Nicole—and the accident. Eventually the contact stopped.

Not that extricating him from her life had helped.

Nothing helped three months later when she wound up in the psych ward.

Tanner pulled a cell phone from his pocket and glanced at it, then back at her. "So what's it been? About fourteen years?"

"Thirteen." She wondered what his life looked like now. At twenty-eight, he was probably married, might even have kids. Natalie studied her blue canvas shoes, startled by the thought and the disappointment that tagged behind it.

"What are you doing here, Natalie?"

Alarm coursed through her, made her feel woozy again. "My

grandfather didn't tell you I was coming? I thought my father called."

"Hal didn't mention it to me." Tanner tugged at the collar of what was probably once a white T-shirt, now streaked with stains, his hands colored the same deep purple. "I spoke to your father about a week ago. I told him not to bother sending you all the way out here. It's kind of a busy time. Harvest, you know. I did get the feeling he wasn't taking me seriously."

"Don't take it personally. The only person my father takes seriously is his stock broker." Natalie swatted a fly and pushed hair off her face, trying to gauge Tanner's cool expression. "How is my grandfather doing?"

Tanner gave that annoying shrug again. "He's not dead."

"Well, that's a relief." What was his problem?

She let out her breath and glanced around the office.

Photographs of the vineyard hung everywhere. A huge white-board covered one side of the wall, almost illegible writing merging together in what she surmised was some sort of schedule. The surface of the small metal desk was covered in files and piles of papers that didn't look like they'd been touched in years. Shelves on the far side of the room overflowed with more files, binders, and paper-work. Whoever was responsible for this mess needed some lessons in office management.

"So, Tanner . . . you're working here?"

The corner of his mouth twitched as he glanced down at his grape-stained shirt. "No. I stopped in to see your grandfather on my Avon route. We were just about to have a cup of tea and discuss the new fall lipstick line."

His sarcastic reply hit its target like a well-placed serve. Natalie trained her gaze on the terra-cotta tiles. The grout was moldy. Stale coffee and that infernal stench of rotten eggs launched another attack, but she pushed to her feet.

"Speaking of my grandfather, I should go and say hello." And find out if he was indeed expecting her. She glanced at her watch. "What is the correct time?" In her hurry to gather her things and bolt off the plane as soon as humanly possible, she hadn't bothered to adjust her watch.

"Gotta be around lunchtime, I guess." Tanner strode to the door and yanked it open.

"That's helpful, thanks." She ignored the scowl he tossed her way as he moved ahead of her out of the office. He stalked toward the building he'd come out of when she arrived.

The friendly, kind Tanner Collins from her youth was clearly just a figment of her imagination. "Hey, wait a sec!" Natalie had to yell to get his attention.

He stopped, turned, and faced her. "Something else I can do for you, Miss Mitchell?"

Miss Mitchell?

Natalie took a few quick steps toward him. "Yes, please, *Mr. Collins*." Start acting like a human being. "You could tell me which room my grandfather is in. Is the front door of the house locked? I don't want to disturb him if he's sleeping."

Lazy laughter loosened his features and Natalie caught a quick glimpse of the boy she remembered. "He's not up at the house." He tipped his head toward the long warehouse-like structure. "He's over there."

"You could have just said so," she muttered, trying to keep up as he marched along a row of large stainless-steel tanks. Natalie placed a hand over her nose and mouth. Getting out and about was probably good for her grandfather, but she didn't know how anyone could stand this putrid smell for long.

"Something wrong?" Tanner came to an abrupt halt and she almost ran into him.

"It stinks in here."

Tanner revealed a flash of perfect white teeth. "Fermentation process. Yeast. It mixes with the sugars in the juice and gives off . . . well, never mind. You didn't come all this way to get a lesson in wine making." He swiveled and pointed down the row. "Hal's over there."

Natalie squinted, expecting to see a frail-looking man sitting down someplace. "I don't . . ."

He tapped her shoulder and indicated a little higher. "Up there."

A white-haired man stood on the top rung of a ladder that reached to the very top of one of the huge vats of fermenting wine. He peered over the rim and looked almost ready to dive in.

"That's your grandfather."

Natalie blinked and shook her head. Surprise swallowed speech. "What is he doing up there? Isn't that dangerous?"

A word she couldn't catch slipped from Tanner's tongue. "Look. We're in the middle of harvest. The last of the grapes will come in over the next week or so and I don't have a minute to breathe, let alone worry about why you're here. I don't have time for games."

"Games?"

"Please," he scoffed. "Drop the act. I know what your father wants, and I assume he's sent you here to do the job." He stepped closer, eyes flashing under the stark overhead lighting. "Far as I can tell, Hal isn't on his deathbed or anywhere near it. So if your plan was to come out here, play nice, and nurse him back to health, then sell Maoilios out from under him while he napped, you might want to reconsider."

"Excuse me?" Natalie was unprepared for the sparks of anger that flew from him.

"Just so we're clear, Hal might be happy to see you, but I'm not. You make one false move, do one thing to hurt him, and I'll run you out of town faster than a wildcat can run down a rabbit. Got it?"

Natalie exhaled, backed up against his assault, and bit back tears of exhaustion. "If you're done, I'd like to let my grandfather know I've arrived."

"Suit yourself." Tanner turned toward the back of the room and yelled. "Hey, Hal! Someone here to see you."

Three

At Tanner's yell, the man at the top of the enormous stainless-steel tank looked up. "Who is it?" He clambered down the ladder as easily as a boy. A minute later Natalie stared into an older version of her father's face. Except this version was smiling. "Well, I'll be."

"Hi, Grandpa." She waved as he approached.

"Natalie!" He took her arms and peered at her through sparkling blue eyes.

"Yes. It's me."

"Goodness, saints preserve us! I'd forgotten you were due today." He enfolded her in a warm embrace. "Welcome back to Maoilios, my dear. Here you are, all grown up. A sight of beauty to behold." The rumbling tenor she remembered cloaked her like a blanket, pushing aside the unpleasant altercation she'd just experienced.

When her grandfather released her from his bear hug, Tanner Collins was nowhere in sight. Relief unwound the cords of tension in her neck.

"You did know I was coming?" Natalie held her breath.

"Of course. Your father phoned and barked something about putting you on a plane, you checking up on me, me taking care of you. He always did talk too fast."

"I usually find it best to nod and smile." Natalie laughed at the sparkle in his eyes. "It's good to see you. Really."

"Likewise, my dear. It's been a long while, hasn't it?" He guided her out of the building. "We had some fun, didn't we?"

"Yes." Snatches of days gone by began to bob to the surface like apples in a barrel of water. "You took us to the ocean. Every summer."

"That's right." He nodded, pulling at his bristly cheek. "I'd forgotten that. Still allergic to clams, are you?"

"Probably." Natalie grimaced. "I haven't had one since." She'd ended up in the emergency room that night, swollen and barely breathing.

"Thought your mother was going to have my hide over that." Rough laughter shook him and brought him to a halt. "You and your sister sure did get up to some tricks." He smoothed a hand over a shock of thick almost-white hair. "But we won't talk about that yet, will we?"

"No." She managed a thin smile. Not yet.

Maybe not ever.

He nodded. His leathery skin was tanned and bore a healthy glow. His blue eyes overflowed with untold tales of the life he'd lived. First-generation American born to Scottish immigrants, he had embraced the American dream. He had to be in his late seventies, but he could pass for younger.

Tanner's words rang true. Hal Mitchell certainly didn't look like he was about to drop dead anytime soon.

"You look great, Grandpa." Natalie was completely convinced the man was healthier than she was. "From what I heard, I expected you to be in bed."

"Nah." He waved a hand and took her by the elbow as they approached the hill. "The old ticker had a little hiccup and everyone overreacted. Kept me in the hospital a week, but between you and me"—he leaned in and gave her a wink—"I think it was indigestion."

"Grandpa." Laughter rushed from her before she could do a thing about it.

"Come on now, let's get you up to the house. You're looking a little green around the gills, my girl."

The dirt road was steep, and she still felt a bit dizzy. After a while, he stopped walking, the two dogs doubling back to wait at his heels.

"Are you all right?" Natalie had to ask, but she was breathing more heavily than he was. He could probably run a half marathon before she made it to the door.

"I am, but you look as though you could take a breather." He smiled, stepped a little closer to put a hand under her chin. "You're every bit as beautiful as your grandmother was at your age, Natalie Grace."

She felt her cheeks flush with the compliment. "I never thought I looked like Grandma. Everyone always said Nicole favored her."

He nodded and shoved his hands into the pockets of his dirty jeans. "To be sure, your sister had some of Grace in her. But you have more than just her look. You have her poise, her charm, that certain something in your eyes that says I'm in the presence of a great lady." His smile made her feel she was the most important person on earth. But then, he always had.

Natalie waved off his words. "I think you're just being your old charming self, Grandpa." Her voice hitched and she took a minute to categorize her scattered thoughts. "You know, before I arrived, I only remembered bits and pieces. Things we did, Nic and I. As soon as I hit the gates it all started to come back. Like a dream I'd just forgotten. Weird, huh?"

"Not at all." He slipped his arm through hers and picked up his pace again, leaving her no choice but to keep up. He let out a low whistle as they approached the house and her rental car came into view. "Now that's a car."

"Dad rented it for me." She squinted as the afternoon sun bounced off the silver exterior.

"Won't have much use for it out here. May as well return it if you're planning on staying a spell."

"Well . . ." What was a *spell*, exactly? "I've got a few meetings lined up in San Francisco. Think I'll hold on to it for now." Natalie popped the trunk and went for her suitcase, but her grandfather snatched it up before she had a chance.

"Whoa, girlie, what have you got in here?" He marched up the stairs, chuckling. Natalie grabbed her purse and briefcase and followed him into the big house.

Inside, she stopped and stared at her surroundings. Her mouth inched upward.

Shadows danced across the gleaming mahogany floor of the foyer. Paintings hung on dark wood walls and colorful woven rugs ran the length of the hall ahead. A long staircase to the left led to upstairs bedrooms.

Wood polish and the perfume of roses pulled back the curtain of memory again.

Nothing was different.

But everything had changed.

She walked to a long table set against the wall and studied a bronze statue of two horses captured in full canter and ran a finger across the back of one of them. "I used to help Grandma polish these. Wednesday was cleaning day."

Nicole would never lift a finger. Claimed to be allergic to dust. But Natalie didn't mind helping. She liked having her grandmother all to herself for a few hours.

"Sure was. Still is." He thumped her bag down at the foot of the stairs and coughed. "Don't look at me like that, I'm fine. Just a bit winded."

"I can get you some water." Natalie glanced down the corridor toward the kitchen.

"Come on. You must be famished. I'll make us some sandwiches and tea." He took off at a clip.

Natalie rushed to catch up.

They passed a large formal dining room, ornate pocket doors closed halfway, went through what they used to call the mess room because it was the only room in the house that they'd been allowed to make a mess in, and finally entered the farm-style kitchen.

Her throat constricted against a wash of unexpected emotion.

It was just as she remembered.

Organized clutter that welcomed visitors, no matter the hour.

Butter-colored walls with green ivy painted along the border displayed framed photographs of the vineyard, family photos, along with a few paintings by their favorite local artists. An old bookcase buckled under recipe books, magazines, and more photographs. Dried sunflowers and lavender sat in ceramic vases along the windowsills.

The copper hood shone brightly over the big stovetop. Empty wine bottles with the Maoilios label lined up like soldiers along the top of all the cupboards, some dating back to the opening of the vineyard in the '70s. The old fridge was plastered with faded photographs and postcards and receipts.

In a flash of memory, her grandmother stood there, waiting with something sweet right out of the oven.

Grace Mitchell's presence still filled the room and sent Natalie into a chair.

"You all right?" Grandpa waggled his eyebrows.

"Yes. It's just strange." She took off her glasses, wiped her eyes, and watched him gather items from the fridge. "It feels like she's still here. Like she's going to walk through that door any minute."

Along with Nicole.

He fumbled with a jar of mayonnaise and set it on the counter, turned to face her with a sad smile. "I've had a few years to adjust to the fact that she's not."

Five years ago, the phone rang in the middle of the night.

Natalie went to see what was wrong, because phones didn't ring at that hour unless it was bad news. She'd found her father and mother in their bedroom, locked in a tight embrace. The sight was so startling that a small cry escaped, announced her presence, and they pulled away from each other at once.

It was the first time since Nicole's death that she'd seen tears in Dad's eyes. And the first time in what felt like forever that she'd seen her parents show any kind of affection toward one another.

"You must miss her a lot, Grandpa."

"Every day. But she's in the better place."

"I'm sorry I didn't come to the funeral." She'd given it little consideration, the thought of returning to California too overwhelming. In fact, as she remembered, her parents insisted she not go.

Don't want to go down that road again, heaven help us, Dad had muttered. He'd grown fond of the saying over the years.

A year away from graduating college with finals approaching, Natalie didn't argue. In the end, only her father went.

"Not to worry. Funerals aren't my cup of tea either." Grandpa tipped his head toward the bread box on the counter. "Grab us some slices and help me out here. I'm not very skilled in the kitchen, and Sarah doesn't work on Fridays."

Since her world collapsed in June, she hadn't prepared a proper meal for herself, preferring to order out or make-do with scrambled eggs or soup.

Perhaps she'd cook for Grandpa next week, as long as she promised not to burn down the kitchen. They'd almost done exactly that one summer. Nicole forgot to set the timer and they went outside to play and forgot about the cookies in the oven. An hour later the kitchen was full of smoke and the cookies resembled black lumps of coal.

"Sarah?" Natalie pulled out a few slices of whole wheat bread and went to work fixing the sandwiches while he made tea.

"You must remember Sarah," Grandpa said. "Tanner's mother. She's worked here for years."

"Oh. Mrs. Collins." Natalie nodded. She was always friendly and interested in hearing about Natalie's life in New York.

They took their lunch out through the French doors onto an expansive patio.

To the left, large oaks provided shade. Lush green hills rolled downward to the stream that stretched along the property to the small lake where a few trout used to swim for them to catch and throw back. Eventually the tended garden gave way to rows and rows of grapes.

"Remember this?" Her grandfather lowered himself into a comfortable lounger and gave a contented sigh.

"It's so beautiful." And so peaceful.

Incredibly, blessedly, peaceful.

Perhaps she could deal with things here. Perhaps she'd found a place to rest.

And maybe, to heal.

"I didn't tell Tanner you were coming," Grandpa confessed with a sly grin. "Wanted to surprise him."

"I'd say you succeeded." Natalie pulled up a chair and sank onto the soft blue-striped cushion. "He was surprised all right. And not pleasantly, I don't think."

Grandpa huffed. "Tanner's a little rough around the edges, but he's got a good heart."

"Are we talking about the same man?" Natalie put her sun-glasses on and leaned back against the cushions. "Because the Tanner Collins I just met was rougher than sandpaper and didn't seem to have much resembling a heart."

"Well . . ." He leaned over and pulled at the laces of his brown work boots, kicked them off, removed red socks, and wiggled long gnarled toes toward the sun. "He'll warm up." He took a huge bite of his sandwich and wiped his mouth with the sleeve of his plaid shirt.

"What exactly does he do here?" She'd been too concerned with ducking the darts shooting from Tanner's eyes to ask.

"Tanner?" He chuckled at the question. "Why, he runs the place."

Ah. Tanner Collins was the Jesus character her father referred to. Which meant she'd probably be seeing more of him.

Her smile faded fast.

"So, Natalie Grace." Grandpa put down his tea. "What have you been up to since I last saw you?"

Natalie took her time talking as she ate. Somehow she didn't think the burly man would be interested in homecoming dances, the debutante balls she'd been forced to attend, her graduation from Harvard Business School, but he wanted to hear everything. And he had an uncanny way of knowing when she was hedging, leaving stuff out and avoiding the truth.

"Last I heard there was a wedding being planned," he remarked, peering at her hand. "I don't see a ring."

Natalie crossed her legs and tried to ignore the way her chest tightened. She pulled fresh air into her lungs and shied away from unpleasant thoughts. "We called off the engagement at the beginning of the summer. It hasn't been an easy few months."

"I can see that. You've hardly smiled since you said hello."

She stared across the shimmering pool at the rows of grapevines. Off in the distance men moved amongst the vines, the dogs racing down the lanes, following a tractor. A cooling breeze curled around her face.

"I've upset you."

"No." She reached out and squeezed his arm. "Not at all. I was just thinking how glad I am to be back here."

"Well, that's good then." He folded his arms and smiled. "I

never did know how to mind my own business. But I'm here to listen if you ever need an ear."

"Thank you, Grandpa. I appreciate that."

He tipped his head and studied her for a long moment. "Now comes the hard question. Did your father really send you to California because I asked him to or are you here to shut down my business?"

"Grandpa." Natalie tried to laugh, but her pulse began to race. She slid her gaze from his inquiring expression and studied the ground again.

"You won't deny it."

"Well, I've heard things aren't great, but . . ." Natalie fidgeted in her chair. Why had she agreed to this again? "Grandpa, it's just that—"

He put up a hand. "I was expecting it."

Natalie flinched at his dejected expression. "You know how he is. Don't worry."

His wrinkles deepened with his frown. "Well, if you must know, I asked you out here to prove him wrong. So that you can see for yourself things aren't as bad as he thinks."

Natalie registered a hint of smoldering embers in his eyes, ready to ignite. Tight laughter lodged in her throat. "If that's the case, then I'll be happy to relay the message. As he reminded me, it's my winery too."

"Indeed it is." That seemed to please him. Grandpa Hal's eyes twinkled in the afternoon sun.

Natalie studied a small chip on the rim of her china plate, looked back at him, and finally asked what she'd wondered for years. "Why did Grandma leave her shares to me?"

Her grandfather's smile was slow, as though he'd been waiting for the very question. "That, my dear, is something you are going to have to discover for yourself."

Not helpful, Grandpa.

"But you don't have any power, you have no say in your own business."

"Oh, I have a say." He wiped his mouth, surveyed the landscape around them with a satisfied smile. "I own this house and the land around it. Trust me, my dear, the decision to bequeath your grandmother's shares to you was made with my blessing." He rolled up the sleeves of his shirt, eyeing her carefully. "Maoilios has taken a few hits, but we're far from being done. I suspect you'll figure that out. As would your father if he'd bother to study any of the spreadsheets I've been sending him. For whatever reason, he's got it in his head that I'm too old to be running a winery. Which is far from the truth. And I have Tanner."

"Okay." Natalie studied the view instead of her grandfather. How would she convince her father he was wrong, if indeed he was? "You're not getting any younger, perhaps he's just concerned for your well-being."

"Hogwash." Hal threw crumbs to the birds and drank his tea. "Natalie, as you may remember, I've always been forthright. I'm sorry to say so, but I don't trust my son. He's always been too bull-headed for his own good. For whatever reason, he wants to see the doors close on this place. But I'll tell you this." As he sat forward, she recognized her father's steady gaze and obstinacy. "The day they shut the gates on Maoilios will be the day they lower my body into the ground."

Four

Tanner noticed a bulb had gone out in the small chandelier above his mother's dining room table. Added it to the long list of things that needed doing around the house.

Like he'd have time.

He poked holes in his mashed potatoes and glared at his untouched food. Natalie Mitchell had a lot of nerve, showing up at the worst possible time of the year. Having her nosing around was not something he needed to deal with right now.

Not that he'd have a choice. She'd bat those thick eyelashes at Hal, have him at her beck and call in ten seconds flat.

He probably already was.

For the first time, Tanner felt his future at Maoilios was suddenly in jeopardy.

"Don't play with your food, Tanner."

He looked up and found his mother watching him. Jeni and Jason began to giggle from across the table.

"If he gets to play with his food, do we?" Jason sounded hopeful, but his grandmother's raised eyebrow wiped the grin off the ten-year-old's face at once. Tanner always envied his mother's ability to speak loudly without ever opening her mouth.

"No. You don't." Tanner made some effort to eat. Didn't have the appetite though. He ended up feeding most of his meat to Gwin, who hid under the table out of sight. Of course Mom knew the dog was there, she just chose to ignore it.

Later, after the dishes were done and homework finished,

checked, and put into backpacks, Tanner padded down the hall to say good-night to the kids.

Jeni's room first. The Pepto-Bismol room, as he liked to call it.

"Hey, Pink Girl." He stepped over Barbie dolls and picked up Kaya, Jeni's favorite American Girl doll. He placed the Native American doll beside the doll from the '60s, whatever her name was. Jeni's collection was growing. The books that came with them were cool. He even liked reading the stories with her. A far cry from the Captain Underpants books he'd enjoyed in early childhood.

"Hey." Swallowed up by fluffy pink blankets, her eyes heavy with sleep, Jeni gave a tired smile. Gwin jumped onto the canopy bed for their nightly snuggle. She grinned and hugged the dog's furry neck.

Tanner eased down on the edge of the bed and smoothed her blond mop of curls. "Did you have a good day at school?"

"No." Jeni rubbed her nose and stared up at him through soulful pools of blue, deeper than the Pacific, and filled with questions he didn't have answers for.

"How come?" He shooed Gwin off over Jeni's protests, pulled the blankets up again, and retrieved her teddy bear from the floor. One pajama-clad arm snuck out from under the covers and wrapped the bedraggled stuffed animal in a vise grip.

"We had math. I hate it."

"Ah." He could relate. "Well, how's your new teacher? You like her, right?"

"She's okay. But she has stinky breath." Jeni yawned, her snub nose inching into her face until it threatened to disappear altogether. She let out a sigh and studied him like he could tell what she was thinking. He wished. What he wouldn't give to know what was going on inside that seven-year-old mind. "We have to do a family project."

"Oh." Tanner's gut twisted. Just when he thought he might

get through one day without being reminded of everything they'd lost.

"With pictures."

Of course.

"Okay. Well, I'm sure Nan can help you out with that, Jeni."

"Can you?"

"Can I what?"

"Help me." She huffed out her answer and handed him the Doofus Award with her eyes.

"I can try, Jeni Bear." Try to get through the rest of this conversation without you ripping my heart out, but after that, sure.

"Okay. I love you." She rewarded him with a smile and stretched her arms out.

Tanner eased into them, wrapped her in a tight squeeze, and counted.

One . . . two . . . three . . .

Maybe tonight the question wouldn't come.

Maybe tonight he'd finally get a reprieve.

Four.

Maybe tonight . . .

"When's Mommy coming home?"

Tanner exhaled, tucked her back in, nice and tight the way she liked, and planted a kiss on her forehead. "I don't know."

"Soon?"

"Probably not soon."

"Is Grandpa going to come back and visit soon?"

Tanner stared at the bookshelf. "You'll have to ask Nan."

"Why does he live so far away? What's it called again?"

"Seattle." A day's drive away. Not far enough. "Jeni Bear, you need to get some sleep. No more questions. Nan will come in for your prayers."

"You could listen."

Tanner pinched the bridge of his nose. Sighed. "Not tonight."

"Okay. But . . ."

He waited. She hadn't asked lately. But she was about to. He could tell by the hope shining in her eyes.

"Mommy will come home, right? One day?"

Tanner shoved fingers through his hair and glanced across the girly room. When they'd first moved in, he'd painted it pink, not really knowing if she even liked the color.

Turned out he could have painted it black and she would have liked it.

It wasn't okay to lie. He knew that.

"Sure she will."

"You promise?"

"I promise." The words popped out before he'd had a chance to think. And he couldn't take them back.

Tanner shut his eyes.

He could still smell Marnie in here. That perfume she'd always worn permeated the places she'd spent her time. He couldn't catch a whiff of it now without drowning under a tsunami of emotion.

Her photographs were everywhere. She stared down at him from the silver-framed portrait on the dresser. In the picture she was smiling, almost laughing. But her eyes held secrets he hadn't always known. Secrets he wished now he'd never discovered.

Mom said it was good for Jeni to keep the photographs. To look at them. To remember the way things were. Before. Because, despite everything, there had been good times.

"Time to sleep, princess." Time to get out of here before he started blubbering like a baby.

"Okay." As always, she accepted his word as gospel. Never questioned. Never argued. "I love you." She said that a lot. More now than she had before. She held on tighter when she hugged, cried harder when she got hurt. His mother said that was normal. Tanner didn't exactly agree.

Nothing about any of this was normal.

"Love you too, baby. Sweet dreams." He tweaked her nose and tried not to choke on a mouthful of guilt. He called Gwin out and turned off the light.

Tanner leaned against the wall and sucked air. Would it ever get easier? Something told him no. Told him he deserved every bit of pain the kids served him. His eyes landed on the sliver of light emanating from under Jason's bedroom door, and Tanner steeled himself against that pain, ready to receive another slice.

He knocked once before entering. "Lights out, buddy."

Jason sprawled across his bed, reading a copy of *Sports Illustrated*. The swimsuit edition.

"Hey!" Tanner strode across the room and grabbed the magazine. "Where'd you get that?"

"From your bathroom." Jason flipped onto his stomach and laughed. Or cackled. "It's sorta gross."

Sorta? Tanner rolled up the glossy magazine and tapped Jason on the head with it. "Yeah, well. You're ten years old. You don't need to be looking at stuff like that." He made a mental note to burn the magazine pronto. Search his room for any others and burn them too.

"Actually, I'm almost eleven." Jason scrambled under the blankets and flashed a grin that managed to peel away another layer of Tanner's heart.

"Yeah, yeah. I know how old you are. Okay, listen . . . I got this a long time ago. We . . . uh . . . guys . . ." Oh, he was so not ready for this kind of conversation. "Women are, well, they're not—"

"I know, I know." The kid actually rolled his eyes. "Miss Kline gave us the big lecture in health class. Women aren't sex objects and guys need to respect them."

"Right." Heat prickled Tanner's cheeks but relief ran down the embarrassment. "That's where I was headed."

"It's cool. I got it." Jason yawned and stretched. Tanner noticed a few hairs sprouting under his arms.

"Okay." Tanner shoved the magazine under his arm. He'd make a hasty exit before Jason decided to ask any questions. "See you in the morning, bud."

"Did you remember about my soccer game tomorrow? I'm goalie. Coach said if I—" Jason narrowed his eyes and scowled. "You forgot."

Tanner rocked back on his heels and tried to come up with a viable excuse. "Jase, I have to work, buddy."

"But it's Saturday. You always have to work." Jason pouted. It was actually a good look for him. "Why can't somebody else stomp some grapes for a while?"

"The grapes don't get stomped. They're crushed. By the crusher." Sometimes Tanner wished they still did things the old-fashioned way. An hour or two of taking his frustrations out on a bunch of grapes might do wonders for his soul. But all he had to do was flick a switch and let the machine do the work.

"Can you please come?"

Jason didn't ask for much. In fact he never asked for anything. Tanner ran his tongue over his teeth and did some mental calculations. "What time?"

"Nine. Or maybe ten."

"You don't know?"

"I forgot." Jason inched down in the bed.

"Well, that doesn't help me much, does it?"

"Forget it." Jason rolled over and squished his face into his pillow. "You wouldn't have come anyway."

Tanner turned and headed for the door. "I'll ask Nan about the time and see what I can do. 'Night, Jase."

"Whatever."

Later, after his mother'd gone in to say good-night to the kids, they sat out on the back porch. She took up her usual position in the old rocker, a Mexican blanket around her legs, fingers flying as she worked on whatever latest creation she was knitting. Something for Jeni, if the varying strands of pink were any clue.

"Rough day?" Sparkling brown eyes studied him over the rim of silver spectacles. Her hair was swept into a ponytail tied at the nape of her neck. Tanner swore she didn't look a day over thirty, though she was in her fifties.

"You could say that." He tromped across the porch to the small table beside her chair. Picked up a wine bottle and examined the label. "How is it?" Two thousand nine. A good year. Should just be coming into its own.

"Lovely, as usual." She picked up her glass and swirled the red liquid around. "Gwin, leave the cats." The pup whined, but settled at her feet obediently. Tanner picked up a glass, poured a splash, and stuck his nose in. A bouquet of flavors pleased his senses and produced another smile. "Not bad." He set it down and backed off. "How does she taste?"

"Full-bodied. A little oaky, but what I would expect from a Cab. Just a hint of chocolate. I like it."

"Good." He lowered himself onto the empty rocker across from her, leaned his head against the cushion, and closed his eyes. "Jeni has to do a family project."

"Yes, she told me."

Tanner rubbed his face. "This isn't getting any easier."

"It's not your fault, Tanner." His mother's voice took on the tone that bordered on challenge.

He wouldn't take her up on it. The argument was old. One he was tired of losing. "Jase wants me to go to his game tomorrow. What time does it start?"

"Nine. You should go. Leave Leo in charge for a change."

"Please." Tanner's clenched his fingers, his jaw tight. Leo Kastner still goaded him, even after two years. Riled him up with that cocky half smile and shifty eyes. Tanner couldn't imagine why Hal hired him in the first place, but he'd yet to come up with a viable excuse to fire the man. "We're in the middle of picking and sorting. This week is going to be nuts."

"So you still won't be getting much sleep then?"

"I hear it's overrated." He couldn't remember when he'd last slept through the night anyway. Being out amongst the vines was better than staring at the ceiling. "Did you see Marnie today?"

"I go to see her every day, Tanner. You know that."

Tanner tilted his head and studied the stars. Not so long ago, he would have identified each of the various shapes and patterns. These days he couldn't care. What did names of stars and constellations matter when life could be snuffed out in an instant?

"How was she?" He asked because it was expected, not because he needed to know the answer. Barring a miracle, which he now highly doubted would happen, his sister's condition would not change.

"The same."

"I figured."

Click, clack, click. And then a sigh. "Tanner, I think it's time."

All air left his lungs. He squeezed the edge of the chair, pushed his toes onto the warm wood planks, pushed her words away. "Mom. No."

"Sweetheart, I know how you feel. I do. But—"

Tanner sat forward. "You kept saying not to give up. Right? That God would heal her? So where is your God now, Mom?"

"He's your God, too, Tanner Michael Collins, and don't you forget it."

Tanner flinched and looked away. Used to be.

But his mother's sharp words warned he'd already said too much.

He picked up the wine glass again and sniffed, satisfied that the formula he'd played with for so long would deliver the results he hoped for.

Tanner put the glass down. The temptation to relieve a little tension with a wine buzz was strong tonight. He couldn't afford to do that.

"I talked to your father today." She let the announcement ferment. "He wants to be here, of course. He's going to tell Rance."

"Great." Tanner glowered at the bottle of wine, now wanting to down the entire thing. "Should we start packing their stuff now or wait until Rance gets here?" Not that he knew whether the kids' father would have the slightest interest in them. Up until now he certainly hadn't. Tanner stood, strode across the porch, his breath coming hard and fast, like he'd just come in from a long run.

"You're angry."

"Of course I'm angry, Mom!" He paced until he could think and talk without shouting. The last thing he needed was Jason coming outside to see what the noise was about. "I won't give up the kids. No way."

"Tanner, you may not have a choice. You're only their uncle."

"He doesn't deserve them. Where has he been all this time? How many years, five?"

"Tanner, please. This is hard enough." Her voice trembled with tears. "You know why Rance hasn't come. And it's not like you would have welcomed him anyway." She swiped at her cheeks. "I'd like you to talk to your father this time."

"I talked to him last time." Said hi and took off to the mountains for the weekend. Tanner bent over his knees and let out a low curse. "I can't deal with this right now."

"There are things you don't know, Tanner. Things you need to know about why your father left."

Why was she being so insistent tonight?

"It's ancient history." He took slow steps back to where she sat. Pulled up a chair close to hers and took her hand. "Mom. I'm sorry. But promise me you won't make any final decision about Marnie, not yet." Her tears were almost enough to send him crashing down the cliff of self-righteousness he'd just climbed.

"I don't know what else to do, sweetheart. How long are we supposed to wait?"

"As long as it takes." Meaningless words. They both knew the truth. Marnie wasn't coming back. Ever. "Christmas. We wait until after Christmas."

"Tanner. That's almost three months."

"Yep. Won't make a difference to her, will it?"

"We can't wait. You have to accept this, sweetheart." Her voice shook and she took a few deep breaths. "I told the doctors we'd make the final decision soon."

Tanner shook his head, but didn't argue. There was no point.

Mom resumed her knitting, and Tanner retreated to the two-seater swing. Pushed off and rocked, back and forth, willing his brain to slow down.

Accept it?

The Lakers losing three in a row he could accept. Jason being mad at him for forgetting about his game, he could accept. This? Planning his sister's death?

No. This was not acceptable.

Somewhere out in the scrub-covered dark hills that presided over the vineyards, a wildcat screamed. He wanted to scream back, but that would definitely wake the kids.

"So what else is going on?" Mom asked. "You barely touched your food." She knew him too well.

Tanner sighed. She'd find out sooner or later, probably tomorrow, if she didn't already know.

"Mouse is here."

"Who?"

Tanner opened his eyes and found her watching him. He let go a sudden grin and shook his head. "Sorry. Natalie. Natalie Mitchell? Hal's granddaughter."

"I know who she is." Her needles clicked against one another in rapid rhythm. "Natalie. Well, well. I suppose she's come to see Hal?"

"That's her excuse." Hal rarely talked about the family back East and Tanner minded his own business. But when Bill Mitchell called last week, Tanner smelled trouble in the air. And it drove through the gates of the winery this afternoon in a rented Jag that probably cost more than what he currently had in his bank account. "Hal didn't tell me she was coming. It's weird."

"Actually, he did ask me to make up the room she used to use. Didn't say why and I didn't ask. Maybe he wanted to surprise you."

"I don't like surprises."

She laughed and tossed him a smile. "How is Natalie?"

Tanner crossed one leg over his knee and picked at a hole in his jeans. "We didn't have a long conversation."

"I hope you weren't rude."

"I was cordial." Long nights and lack of sleep were getting to him. Natalie Mitchell's arrival was all he needed to push him butt first onto the rocks.

"Tanner."

"What, Mom?" He blew out his irritation. "I haven't seen the girl since we were kids. I barely remember her." Not true. The minute he'd laid eyes on her again a truckload of memories pulled up and parked right beside him.

Natalie had always been shy, Nicole the talker. But over the years, he'd seen Natalie come out of her shell. At least around him, when her sister wasn't with them. As a kid she'd been a little on the chubby side, but the last summer the family came, she'd lost the weight and was inching toward pretty. And, he had to admit, the grown-up Natalie had captured his attention almost at once.

He'd tried not to study her for changes the years had brought. Tried not to notice the way her eyes sparkled behind her glasses. Eyes his favorite color of deep iris blue.

"If I remember rightly, I think you were a little sweet on Miss Natalie."

"I was not." He almost bolted out of his chair, tempted to check the alcohol count on that bottle of wine. "Your memory must be fading in your old age."

His mother laughed. "My memory is better than yours most days."

"Well, whatever. Mouse was . . ." Tanner stopped midsentence as a memory snuck up on him. A memory he hadn't realized he still possessed.

One he did not care to dwell on.

And one he definitely would not be discussing with his mother.

Natalie Mitchell was no longer his childhood friend. It was entirely possible she was about to ruin his life. What was left of it.

"Of course, her sister had her sights set on you and left Natalie in her dust."

Tanner swallowed a grin. "Seriously, Mom? We were kids. It was a crazy summer all around. I'm actually surprised she came back. I can't imagine it's easy being here."

"No, I don't suppose it would be." Mom sighed and dabbed her eyes. "I still can't believe it happened. Such a tragedy."

"Yup."

"I suppose she's only here because of Hal's heart attack," Mom mused. "She hasn't been back since Nicole died."

Tanner balled his hands into tight fists. He tried not to think about that night.

"I thanked God for days afterward that I'd grounded you that weekend. I don't know what those two girls were thinking, taking Hal's Jeep out in the middle of the night."

"It was Nicole's idea and she was the one driving. I doubt there was any thought involved." He still remembered the haunted look on Natalie's face when he'd gone to see her afterward. She'd tried to convince him it was all her fault, that she should have talked her sister out of it. Of course she wasn't to blame. He'd told her that, over and over again as she lay there, tears streaming down her face.

He wondered if she'd ever believed it.

"How long is she staying?" Mom wanted to know.

"Didn't say." Not that he asked. "Hal was pleased to see her." A yawn snuck out of him and he glanced at his watch. Just after nine and he was ready for bed. Pathetic. "I should have seen this coming. Hal's son called after Hal's heart attack. Did I tell you? Got all riled up with me."

"What?" She put down the bundle of wool and sat forward. "You talked to Jeffrey?"

"No." Tanner took in the anxious look in her eyes. "I talked to Bill."

She picked up her needles again. One of his mother's many outdoor cats snuck out from the shadows, stretching to bat the ball of wool on the ground. "And what did Bill have to say for himself?"

Gwin growled and Tanner glared at the orange-striped nuisance through a sneeze. "Sounds like you already know the answer."

"He threatens to shut this place down every year, Tanner. I wouldn't worry."

Tanner pushed off again, his nose itching. Stupid cats. "I think he's serious this time. Why do you think Natalie's really here, Mom? We haven't recouped our losses from the last two years. I'm hoping we might break even this year but—" Another sneeze shook him.

"Shoo! Go on." Mom slapped her slipper-clad feet together and the cat scooted off into the darkness. Gwin shot after it with a delighted bark. "But Hal is a stubborn old coot who refuses to keep up with the times."

Tanner laced his fingers together so he wouldn't rub his stinging eyes. "I wish he'd listen to me. There are so many things we could do. The wine isn't the problem."

"No. But you're not a shareholder, Tanner. You may think you run things around here, but—"

"You don't have to tell me what I already know." Tanner walked across the porch again. Whistled for Gwin and she came charging back, flopped at his feet with a huff.

Tanner stared up at the sky. Clouds had moved in but the forecast predicted it would remain dry, which was good news. A few stars blinked through the blackness, trying to convince him there was still a little hope to hold on to. He wasn't so sure.

He took his seat again. "Bill seems more adamant than ever. He'll use Hal's health issues to full advantage. If you think Natalie came all the way out here just to see how her grandfather was doing, think again."

"So, he's sending his daughter to do his dirty work for him."

"Looks that way. She's the major shareholder."

"Poor Natalie." His mother tut-tutted. "She was always the quiet one. I remember her sister used to push her around like no tomorrow. I suppose her father does the same, not completely unexpected, knowing Bill Mitchell."

"Poor Natalie, nothing. She knows exactly what she's doing. She's no slouch in the business world. I Googled her."

"You Googled her? Tanner!" Her shoulders shook with sudden laughter. "For pity's sake, if you wanted to know what she did, why didn't you just ask her?"

"Because I don't trust her." The words hissed out, surprising him with their venom. He could validate them easily enough if she called him on it.

His mother's eyes narrowed and she crossed her arms. "You don't know her. Not anymore."

"My point exactly." So there. "Let's see, since we last saw each other she's attended some snotty girls prep school, spent a year in Europe, graduated from Harvard School of Business, and now she's head of PR at Daddy's company back East." He wouldn't mention the broken engagement. Mom would be all over that like flies on rotting grapes. "His shipping company. One of five across the globe. Maoilios is a blip on their radar, Mom. They don't need it. If they want to shut us down, they can do it tomorrow."

"That would be just like Bill. Go in guns blazing with little thought to anybody else."

He grinned, picked up the cork from the wine bottle, and sniffed. "Bill thinks Hal's too old to be running a winery."

"He obviously doesn't know his father as well as he should." Her eyes took on the troubled look he'd grown used to the past few months. She held her glass toward him.

He gave her a refill and set the bottle down. "Hal does need to take it easy, but he'd go crazy if he left this place." Trying to keep the man in bed for two weeks was all Tanner could handle. Eventually he'd given up, and Hal had ambled on down the hill the next morning like he'd never landed himself in the hospital.

"Same goes for you."

"I'm not going anywhere." Tanner inhaled and pushed away the possibility. Rubbed the sore spot in the small of his back. "Neither is Hal. The sooner his family accepts that, the better."

"You don't know for sure that's why Natalie's here. They could be genuinely concerned about him."

"The only thing the Mitchells are genuinely concerned about is their bank account." He shifted in his chair and listened to the cicadas singing themselves to sleep in the olive trees that surrounded their small garden. "If sales don't pick up soon, we're done."

"It's been a hard couple of years. Things will improve. Stay positive."

"I'm trying." Trying not to go crazy or broke in the process.

"There's no harm in being nice to Natalie, you know. A little civility goes a long way."

"Uh-huh." Time to change the subject. "So. Was it my imagination or did you just freak out a little when you thought I'd talked to Jeffrey Mitchell?" Tanner could only recall meeting the man a couple of times. Hal's younger son rarely called. Never visited. He must have come for his mother's funeral, but Tanner had been away at the time, on a well-earned vacation that Hal insisted he continue rather than coming back to California two weeks early. Tanner had said his good-byes to Grace before leaving; he had no regrets.

His mother made that singsong noise that came out whenever she had something she wanted to say but didn't quite know how. Tanner watched her put down her work again, pick up her glass, and finish the remainder. Her eyes glimmered under the glow of the porch light. "I suppose it's about time I talked about this."

"Talked about what?" Tanner's voice skipped an octave. Her small smile did nothing to soothe the sense of trepidation that settled over him.

"Jeffrey and I have a history."

"A history?" Tanner sat forward. "Like a romantic history?"

"We were young. And I was foolish." She met his stare with a frown. "I've never talked about it because I didn't see the point."

"So what happened?" Tanner folded his arms against an uncomfortable knot in his stomach. "If you're about to tell me that Jeffrey Mitchell is my real father, I gotta say, I'm really not up for that kind of revelation tonight."

"Oh, for heaven's sake, Tanner!" Laughter caught in her throat and lit her eyes. "Don't be silly. I met your father two years after Jeffrey. You are Brian Collins's son, through and through. You know that. No, Jeff hightailed it out of here long before you were born." Her sigh was sad, but she pushed her shoulders back and settled her gaze on him again. "Jeffrey left me the day he and I were supposed to get married."

Five

NATALIE WATCHED THE SUN RISE THROUGH THE CURTAINS OF her bedroom windows. She lay very still, took deep breaths, and savored the moment before coming fully awake, the few minutes in the day when she actually felt like maybe she could cope after all. Soon reality would crash in and shove her back to the point of barely being able to survive it.

She stretched and waited, wondering what her first full day in California would bring. The room she and Nicole always stayed in had not changed. Their grandmother let them pick the color. Light mint green. Spearmint, to be exact, according to the label on the paint can. They'd chosen white poplin material for the curtains and Grandma had them sewn and hung in two days. The large canopy bed they'd shared was as soft as she remembered, and she'd enjoyed a full night's sleep. The first she'd had in weeks. Maybe months.

Perhaps coming here had been a good idea.

Natalie got up, found her pills, and took them with a few sips of water. She padded over old floorboards and stopped at the bureau, opened a few drawers, not surprised to find them empty. She'd unpack later. The small writing desk in one corner bore scratches and doodles they'd marked it up with over the years. She poked through those drawers for remnants of years gone by and pulled out a yellowed piece of paper, hidden way in the back of one of them.

Natalie unfolded it and stared at the two words scrawled across the page.

I'm sorry.

She glared at the writing, crumpled the note into a ball, and tossed it into the wastebasket. Something she should have done that summer. She doubted he'd been sorry at all. Refused to discuss it with him. And it hardly mattered now.

A framed photograph of herself and Nicole sat on a shelf above the desk. Natalie stared at the image of her twin and swallowed acid.

Oh, Nic.

Would there ever come a day when it wouldn't hurt when she thought about her sister?

Not quite ready to shower and head downstairs, she sat in bed, thumbed through the magazines she'd bought at the airport and not read on the plane, and avoided touching the small Bible Laura had given her a few years ago. She didn't read it much, hardly at all, but for some reason always carried it with her.

When things exploded with Peter, Natalie spent a weekend at Laura's, unable to face her parents' questions and phone calls. She'd gone to church with the family, out of politeness really, but wondered at the things she'd seen and heard. Wondered at the authenticity of the relationship they talked about having with God.

And wondered if maybe . . .

She tossed those thoughts aside and fiddled with her iPad, then her laptop, and quickly came to the conclusion that there was no Internet connection in the house. Great. Her phone worked though, so she checked e-mails, nothing from work, and confirmed her appointment in San Francisco on Tuesday.

Her doctor back home had been helpful in making the referral and ensuring she would receive proper care in California. It had been one of Natalie's concerns with coming out here. But everything had fallen into place.

Almost as though her being here was meant to be.

By the time she went downstairs, dressed in light coral capris and a white cotton blouse, it was close to lunchtime. Natalie stopped at the doors to the long living room as a middle-aged woman came toward her.

"Hello, Natalie."

Natalie squinted, recognition tapping at her brain. "Good morning. Mrs. Collins, right?"

"Good memory." Sarah smiled. "Did you sleep well?"

Natalie rolled her eyes. "Longer than I intended to. Woke early and fell back to sleep."

"Not to worry, I'm sure you needed it. It's good to see you again." The woman was dressed casually in beige trousers and a turquoise top, and she wore a friendly smile. "If you're ready for some food, I've set the table for you on the patio. Your grandfather won't be able to join you for lunch, but he'll see you at dinner tonight." She recognized Tanner's smile. Not that she'd really seen it yesterday.

"Okay. Thanks, Mrs. Collins." Natalie crossed the room.

"Of course. And call me Sarah." She waved a hand toward the set of French doors on the far side of the room. "Go on, it's a beautiful day to be outside. I'll bring a fresh pot of coffee, unless you'd like something else?"

"Coffee is fine. Thank you." Natalie ventured toward the doors and pushed them open. A cooling breeze hit her face as she stepped out onto the stone patio. The vista was breathtaking.

The house rested on a hill, and she looked down over the fields of lush green vines, some still heavy with their bounty of dark grapes. Towering oak trees provided shade for the rambling garden. A long swimming pool sat at the far end of the patio, sparkling in the midday sun. A massive wisteria vine curled around a white arbor trellis, thick foliage giving needed shade, the cascading lavender-colored blooms permeating the air with their perfume.

Sunlight filtered through the branches and warmed her cheeks.

Natalie kicked off her sandals and wandered over to check out the water. She bent and trailed her fingers through it, tempted to dive right in.

"You'll find it a little chilly." Tanner Collins's low voice almost sent her in headfirst.

Natalie scrambled to her feet and caught her breath. "Do you make a habit of creeping up on people and scaring them half to death?"

He quirked a brow, placed a tray down on the table. "Not generally, no. But that was amusing."

His dog . . . what was her name? . . . Gwin . . . wandered over and Natalie burrowed her fingers in the animal's soft fur a moment before surveying the spread Tanner was setting out.

"That looks good." An assortment of cheeses, crusty bread with olive oil for dipping, and a bowl of olives stirred hunger and almost made her forget the pills she'd taken that morning and the affect they might soon begin to have. A large round of salami sat on another plate, along with a hearty slice of liver pâté and a selection of pickles.

"The bread is just out of the oven. Whole wheat with nuts and raisins. Mom's special recipe." He went about opening a bottle of white wine. "And I thought you might like a taste of what we do here."

Natalie dropped into her chair and stared. "Well, I was going to have coffee," she told him, eyeing the silver carafe on the tray, "but okay. Just a little."

Dressed in jeans, a faded denim shirt rolled at the sleeves and untucked, Tanner looked completely relaxed. His dark hair waved around his face and settled just above the nape of his neck. His eyes held a certain sparkle that definitely hadn't been there when she'd arrived.

The sudden one-eighty in his behavior was interesting.

"This Chardonnay is our best seller." Tanner poured a bit of the gold liquid into two glasses, offered one to her, and stuck his nose in the other. "A reliable offering I like to call Gwin."

Natalie smiled as she studied the meniscus. "You named a wine after your dog?"

Tanner swirled his glass. "Gwin is intensely loyal and totally dependable. But treat her the wrong way and she could come back to bite you." He held up his glass with a nod. "It's also the Welsh word for *wine*."

"How clever of you."

"I thought so. Cheers."

Why not? It was lunchtime here. And she was in wine country. "Cheers." Natalie sniffed and took in the rich aroma. "Nice." She took a small sip and pushed the liquid through her teeth, waiting for the flavors to settle.

Tanner sat opposite her and put his glass down. "You know what you're doing."

She swallowed with a nod. "My father. You can take the boy out of vineyard, but you can't take the vineyard out of the boy."

"Is that so?" A shadow of something close to consternation crossed his face. He lifted his glass again, sniffed, took a sip, and promptly spat into a small silver spittoon. "Does your father buy our wine, Natalie?"

She took another sip, too aware of his scrutiny. "He prefers French wine."

"Of course he does."

She untangled herself from his gaze and concentrated on the food.

The sun began to burn her bare arms, reminding her she'd forgotten to put on sunscreen. No matter. Some color might do her good. "This is delicious. Is the cheese local?"

Tanner cut from the wedge of blue cheese and nodded. "There's a farm a few miles down the road. Pretty much everything we serve here is either grown on the property or within the area. Hal refuses to use anything imported if we don't have to."

"Makes sense." Natalie savored the delightful cornucopia of tastes. "So, how is the vineyard doing? I mean, really. My father seems to be under the impression that Hal is running it into the ground, but . . ." She glanced across the picture-perfect view and offered a smile. "I have a feeling that may not be the case."

"Wow. You don't waste time, do you?" Tanner swished his wine and gave her a hard stare. "You don't seriously expect me to sit here and discuss business with you."

"Ah." Natalie stifled a laugh. "There you are."

"What?"

"Nothing." She popped a green olive in her mouth. "My grandfather tells me you're the head honcho around here. The vintner. Yes?" She sliced some cheese and reached for a cracker.

"That would be correct."

"But you don't work on Saturdays?"

His eyes narrowed. "I work every day. I'm only up here because Hal asked me to be hospitable. To make sure you were all right." Tanner's chair scraped over the terrace as he stood. "And since clearly you are—"

"Oh, sit down." Natalie gave up and raised her eyes to the sky. She didn't remember him being so touchy. "I can't possibly eat all this myself. Please."

"I'm not hungry." He sat anyway and stared at the stains on his hands.

Natalie took the opportunity to study him.

Beneath the strong jaw, wayward dimple, and disarming smile when he chose to proffer it hid a haunted expression. Dark shadows under those luminous eyes warned that all was not well in Tanner Collins's world. She wondered what his story was. What he'd been doing over the years since she'd seen him last—what had him so riled up now, and why he seemed to find her so threatening. Well, that wasn't hard to figure out.

She ignored guilt and gave a shrug. "Go on, please eat. I promise not to pull up the numbers until your food is well digested."

He reached for the butter and spread a slab over a piece of bread, stuffed the slice in his mouth, and chewed, his eyes never leaving hers. "Like I said, I know why you're really here." He drank water, an early frost falling over his face.

"Care to enlighten me?"

He held her gaze, unflinching. "Your father told me you'd need full access to all the files and fiscal data for the last five years. You've come here to shut us down."

"I see." She figured he'd already jumped to that conclusion. "And here I thought I was on vacation." There was no telling what else her father might have said to the man. She would have her work cut out for her if she hoped to undo the damage. "All right." There was no sense in denying it. "I'm here to visit my grandfather, but we're also concerned about the winery." Natalie put her wine aside, needing more food in her stomach.

"So I'm right?" His glare challenged the heat of the sun and won. "You want to shut the place down?"

"Do you think Maoilios should be shut down?"

He fairly spat a mouthful in her direction, choked it down, and coughed. "What kind of stupid question is that?" Tanner sat back, his expression grim. "Of course I don't. That would put me out of a job, wouldn't it?"

True enough. "Can you explain the losses over the last few years?"

A flash of anger ambushed his eyes. "Bad weather. A blight. And Hal—" He clamped his mouth shut and looked away.

Natalie squinted in the bright sun and wished she'd brought her shades out with her. "And Hal what?"

Tanner looked about ready to puke up all the food he'd just eaten. Resignation curled his mouth upward. "Hal doesn't realize we're not living in the '70s anymore. Times have changed. The consumer has changed. We can't get by on selling local, supplying a few restaurants and hotels. There are so many things we could do. When I suggest doing anything remotely different, he pitches a fit." His squared shoulders and a tight jaw told his true feelings.

Natalie nodded. "Just so we're clear, what exactly is your role here, Tanner?"

"My role?" The question seemed to surprise him. "Oh, I see. You want to know what my qualifications are."

"If you don't mind."

His expression turned cold enough to chill the Chardonnay in the oak barrels down the hill. "As you know, I've lived here since I was ten. I can walk every inch of this place blindfolded. I know exactly how many employees we have on staff, how many children they have, all their names, and when their birthdays are. I can tell you which vines are planted on each acre of this land, when they're picked, how long it takes to harvest, how many gallons a year we produce down to the last barrel, and how much money we make or don't make, on average. But I suppose none of that impresses you."

"Tanner, I—"

He barreled on, ignoring her. "I graduated from UCLA with full honors, my degree is in horticulture, viticulture, with a minor in business management. I pay my taxes, give to charities, go to church most Sundays, I've never been arrested. Oh, and I'm allergic to cats. Anything else?"

"That'll do." Natalie squelched her smile. "Shame you didn't minor in hospitality too."

The dark look sent her way almost made her laugh. Clearly, he knew the business. And that pleased her. His passion shone through, whether he meant it to or not. In the space of a half hour, she'd come to one conclusion. Her grandfather had the right man in charge.

What if her father *was* wrong about this?

She might be able to convince her grandfather to at least look into making some changes. But she'd have to persuade Dad that Maoilios was not the write-off he'd proclaimed it. Even though she held the power, he would never expect her to wield it.

Could she take on that fight? The fact that she was even considering it proved her upcoming appointment with Dr. Sherman was imperative.

"I'm sure you're already aware," she began, watching Tanner's jaw twitch, slightly aware of taking her life into her own hands, "but in today's market, you need to be flexible. Open the place up. Do tours. Have a tasting room. Private parties. Internet connection at the very least."

He met her eyes in a startled moment that kicked aside the guarded expression. His familiar grin flashed for an instant. "I have Internet in my office. High-speed."

"Lucky you. This house is a dead zone. Which is going to be a problem when I need to check in with the office."

"I thought you were on vacation." His eyes narrowed again.

"I've never been terribly good at relaxing."

"I remember. You were the only kid I knew who could read an entire book in one day and immediately start another."

Natalie warmed to that grin a little too quickly for her liking. "Well. I looked up Maoilios before I left, hoping to find a website. All that came up were directions and a phone number in the yellow pages. I don't suppose you've had any luck convincing my grandfather to step into the new millennium?"

"He says things are fine the way they are."

"If things were fine, my father wouldn't be itching to close the gates and put you out of a job."

"All right, you've made your point." His sigh sagged with regret. "I'm not giving up without a fight. Hal might be stubborn, but he's not stupid. If I have to toss him in the silo to get him to see reason, I'll do it."

"I doubt it'll come to that."

"So you're willing to give us a chance?"

"I'll be fair. That's all I can promise for now." Natalie sipped ice water and caught sight of a couple of kids weaving their way through the vines. Gwin barked and raced down the hill. Hal's two dogs appeared out of nowhere to join in. The kids chased the dogs in circles as their giggles floated toward Natalie.

Memories of a carefree life surfaced, reminded her that no matter how much she wanted to, she couldn't go back in time. Couldn't fix the things that were broken. Couldn't repair the irreparable.

"Did you hear me?" Tanner leaned across the table, his eyes glinting in the afternoon sun.

"Sorry, no."

His scowl told her she hadn't missed much. "I said, I will do whatever it takes to keep the winery open. I'm not going to let you convince Hal to close, not that I think you could, and I'm not about to let you—"

"Tanner." Natalie pushed out a sigh. "I realize we don't know each other anymore, but—"

"I know that your father is a powerful businessman. And you work for him. He will have the final say, won't he?"

Tanner had hated the way she bowed to her father's demands. He always chided her, told her she didn't have to try so hard to please him, didn't have to try to compete with Nicole.

"Tanner, listen . . ."

"Save it." He scraped his chair back and stood. Raised an arm in greeting as the two kids ran up the hill onto the patio. The little girl launched herself at Tanner and he swept her up in strong arms, planting a kiss on her nose. An older boy hovered near the table, eyeing the food.

Tanner shook his head. "Nan's got pizza for you." The boy did a little fist pump and tried to make a dash for the door but Tanner shot out an arm and grabbed him by the shoulder. "Hold up. We have a guest."

Natalie raised a brow. *We.* Like he owned the place.

"This is Jason, and this is Jeni. Guys, this is Miss Mitchell. Mr. Hal's granddaughter."

Natalie smiled and hoped she looked friendly. She'd never been all that good with children. "You can call me Natalie."

"*Miss* Natalie," Tanner interjected. He turned back to the boy. "How was your game?"

"Fine. You didn't come."

"I'll be there next week."

"Sure you will." The boy's dark eyes hinted at trouble. He was on the tall side and she'd put him in fifth or sixth grade maybe.

Were they Tanner's kids? She tried to do the math in her head and quickly gave up, her brain still not fully functioning.

Natalie wasn't sure of the little girl's age, but the big blue eyes and wide smile captured her at once. She couldn't find much resemblance to Tanner. Maybe they took after their mother. Who had to be around here somewhere.

Natalie was suddenly curious to meet the woman who'd managed to melt Tanner Collins's freezer-burned heart.

"Hey." Tanner swatted at the boy's hand as he swiped a piece of cheese. The kids ran off into the house and Tanner sat down again. When he offered to refill her glass she held up a hand.

"That was lovely, but I'm good. Thanks." She noticed he hadn't touched the little he'd poured into his own glass when they'd first sat down. "How old are they? The kids."

"Jason is eleven, almost. Jeni just turned seven." He picked up the bottle on the table and studied the label. Put it down. Checked his watch. Cleared his throat.

"If you have somewhere to be, by all means, don't let me keep you," Natalie said.

He was on his feet in a flash. "I do need to get back to work."

She nodded. "If it's all right with you, I'll come down to your office on Monday morning. Perhaps you could show me your files, let me glance at the numbers. Say around ten?"

Tanner swung her a glare. "Do I have a choice?"

"Not really. I mean, I could ask my grandfather, but why bother him? It will be easier if you'd just work with me."

"I'll do what you ask out of respect for Hal. And because I actually do like my job and I'd prefer to keep it. I suppose, circumstances being what they are, I probably do work for you, but I really don't want to work *with* you. In fact, it'll be a cold day in hell before that happens." He strode across the patio and slammed the French doors behind him.

Natalie eased back into her chair and closed her eyes.

Fantastic.

There was no way to twist the truth or cover it up.

She knew why her father wanted her here, and so did Tanner.

The heaviness she'd believed had gone this morning descended like San Francisco smog, stifling, singeing, and searing her with the severity of the situation.

If she took on this challenge, she might send her already fragile sanity packing. If she didn't, she'd send her grandfather to an early grave and send Tanner Collins and everyone who worked this land straight to the unemployment line.

Six

Tanner poured another cup of coffee that Monday morning and checked his watch again—10:45. Of course Natalie Mitchell would keep him waiting. He thumped against his chair and glowered at a horsefly hovering around the rim of his mug.

His conversation with Natalie on Saturday still rang in his ears. He'd lost his temper. Something he seemed to be doing a lot of lately. When he tripped over Jason's soccer cleats. When Jeni forgot to shut the freezer drawer and he found himself butt first in a puddle of chocolate ice cream the next morning. When Natalie sat across the table from him and somehow managed to look guilty and gorgeous at the same time.

Tanner cringed at the memory of his harsh words. He'd even resorted to using the H-word—the one that made Jeni's eyes bug out of her head whenever he slipped up around the kids—*that's a bad word*, she'd scold, and wag a finger at him.

Who was he kidding? He wasn't cut out to be a dad. With his father such a stellar example, it was insane to even consider it. But letting Rance Harper simply stroll in and swoop the kids away? The man would have to get through him first.

"Tanner?" Leo Kastner stuck his head around the doorframe. "You busy?"

Tanner's stomach twisted tighter. "Always busy, Leo." Busy sitting in his office on a Monday morning when he had a thousand other things to do on the property. He glanced up as Leo strode in, the dogs trailing him. Tanner shot up a brief prayer for patience, as was his practice around Kastner. It was done before he remembered that he and God weren't exactly talking these days.

"Should have all the grapes in by Friday." Kastner strutted around the office like it was his. "Another successful harvest, if I do say so myself."

Tanner gritted his teeth. "The wine will tell us whether it was successful or not." You moron.

Kastner shrugged, lips curled in that smarmy smile. "Just hope we won't have any incidents like that fight last year. You know how some of those migrants can be."

"No. I don't know." Contempt created a few choice words in his throat but Tanner choked them back. Arguing with Leo would only aggravate his heartburn. "Everyone's papers in order this year?"

"Had to send two on their way, the rest look good. Most of 'em have worked here before, know what they're doing." The ranch manager whipped off his hat, rubbed a hand over stringy blond hair, and swept a scrutinizing gaze over the huge pile of manila files Tanner had heaped on his desk that morning. "Are we being audited?"

"You could say that." That would be the better news.

Leo helped himself to coffee and sat, fanning himself with the broad brimmed straw hat. "Doing a little housekeeping or what?"

Tanner pressed air through his lips and placed his palms on one of the piles. "Hal's granddaughter is here. Got in a few days ago. Her daddy sent her out here to do some snooping. I think we're about to be shut down."

Leo's eyes got rounder, his mouth forming a thin line. "No way."

For once they agreed on something.

"Who is this chick?" Leo's crooked grin reminded Tanner of a bad guy cartoon character. "Want me to handle her?"

It was easy to imagine that scenario. He and Leo were probably around the same age, but that was all they had in common. Leo had a reputation with the ladies. Nobody seemed to like him.

Tanner clenched his fingers around his mug. "I can manage Miss Mitchell." Manage not to throttle her for keeping him waiting almost an hour. "Did you need something, Leo?"

Kastner yawned and tossed his hat to his lap. "Those barrels we ordered from Maxiner. When are they coming in? I'm taking a run over there and didn't know which truck to take."

"I don't think they're ready yet."

"You call and find out?" Leo drained his mug and ran his finger around the rim of it. "You know how Max is about returning calls."

"Trying to tell me how to do my job, Leo?"

"Not at all."

"Tanner?" Natalie's voice floated into the office.

Leo got to his feet as Natalie pushed through the door. Tanner widened his eyes as she came into view.

If he had to hazard a guess, he'd say she'd just rolled out of bed. Her hair was loose, just touching her shoulders, light brown curls tossed every which way by the wind. In a pair of skinny jeans and a baggy sweatshirt, she looked more like a college kid than a businesswoman. And he definitely didn't appreciate the way his heart skipped a beat when she met his scrutinizing gaze.

"Sorry to keep you waiting." She pulled an elastic band off her wrist and tied up her hair. Unzipped her purple hoodie, pushed up the sleeves, flicked a glance at her watch, and shook her head. "I'm usually punctual."

Tanner tried not to get sucked in by those blue eyes. "I'll bet you are. But, no worries. I have nothing better to do on a Monday morning than sit around my office twiddling my thumbs. Do come in."

She fumbled through a gigantic green purse and came up with a pair of silver-rimmed glasses. Put them on and blinked at him. Then she turned toward Leo, who watched her with palpable interest.

"The lovely Miss Mitchell, I presume?" Kastner's leer made Tanner feel a little sick. He wasn't about to sit here and watch the slime ball put the moves on Natalie.

Natalie politely took the hand Leo offered. "And you are?"

"Leo Kastner. I run the place."

Tanner cleared his throat, tempted to kick them both out.

"Is that so?" Natalie glanced at Tanner. "I thought Mr. Collins was the one in charge."

"Well, he is, I suppose." Leo positioned his hat on his head and looped his thumbs around his thick leather belt. "But I run the vineyard. He couldn't do all of that fancy chemical stuff without me. I have the more important job."

"You don't say?" She appeared as impressed as she might have been if he'd told her he pumped gas at the Shell station in town. That put Tanner's opinion of her up a notch.

Tanner studied "the lovely Miss Mitchell" with muted curiosity. In his estimation she looked a little sick, seemed to be having trouble focusing.

Time to send Leo on his way.

"I'll get ahold of Max before you take off, Kastner. Thanks for checking in." Tanner wrote a reminder to make sure Hal had set aside the money to pay for the barrels this time.

Kastner got the point. "No problem. A pleasure to meet you, Miss Mitchell. I hope we see more of each other while you're here."

Natalie's expression said she hoped otherwise. "Nice meeting you."

Kastner strolled out. The dogs stayed, sniffing around Natalie. Tanner took a better look at her. Small beads of sweat glistened around her hairline. He shooed the dogs off, shut the door, and turned on the air-conditioning while she shrugged off the thick hoodie, revealing a Harvard T-shirt underneath.

"He seems like an interesting character." She was already seated, palms braced on her knees, head down.

"Yeah. He's interesting all right." He inched closer. "Are you okay?"

"I'll be fine." Her wobbly reply didn't sound fine. She sure didn't look fine.

Tanner got her some water. "Heat still getting to you?" Maybe she was dehydrated or diabetic or something.

"I guess." Her hand shook as she took the glass from him. "I really am sorry I was late. I didn't sleep well last night, and when I finally nodded off, I slept through my alarm."

"Oh." Tanner scratched his jaw and tipped his head toward his desk. "We can do this another time." Or never.

"I'll be all right in a minute." She didn't meet his eyes. "Is this everything? I'll just get started then." Natalie stood, moved toward the desk, and reached for a file. She glanced over her shoulder. "You don't need to stay. I know you're busy. I saw a lot of trucks rolling in on my way down here."

He hesitated. Not that he wanted to babysit her while she made short work of putting him in the unemployment line, but she really didn't look good. "The files are sort of in order. I started with this year and worked down, but they might be mixed up."

She nodded toward his computer. "This is all on there, right?"

"Uh . . ." He'd begun inputting figures a while back, but lately things had gotten so crazy. "I had an accountant come in part-time but . . . she didn't stay long."

"So the answer is no." If he wasn't mistaken, a tiny smile toyed with her lips.

"That's correct." And I'm an idiot. Thank you for not saying so.

"I don't mind inputting the figures for you as I go. If you'll let me log onto your database, that is."

Right. Tanner pushed his tongue into his cheek, moved around her, and booted up his old PC. "Always figured you'd turn into one of those math geniuses, Mouse." He clicked a few buttons, backed up, and pulled out his chair for her. "Be my guest."

She made herself at home behind his desk. "I'm no accountant, and I wouldn't say I'm a genius, but I'll take a stab at it." Her face contorted, reminding him of how Jeni looked right before she was about to hurl.

He narrowed his eyes, half tempted to put a hand to her forehead. "No offense, but you really don't look so hot. Are you sure I can't get you anything?"

Soft laughter petered out as she leaned back in his chair and set her steady gaze on him. Dogged determination played across her face. "Thank you, no."

Tanner drummed his fingers on his forearm, his conscience being a pain the rear. "I'm sorry for being abrupt with you the other day."

"Which day would that be?" Her direct reply hit him square in the chest and made a response impossible.

"Apology accepted." She took off her glasses and wiped them with a Kleenex pulled from the pocket of her jeans. "I'll just get to work, and you can be on your way."

Dismissed.

"Okay, then." He backed out of the office, whistled for the dogs, and strode across the courtyard. So much for trying to be nice. Natalie Mitchell was encased in a glacier-sized ice block. And he had no desire to chip his way through it.

⌒

Natalie managed to stay seated until she was sure Tanner was well on his way to whatever fire he was about to put out, searched the small office, found the bathroom, and sprinted for it.

She'd been warned the meds might cause some nausea. That had been an understatement. But not taking them . . . well, she didn't want to go back there.

"Come on, Nat. Pull it together." She washed up and caught her reflection in the mirror. Tanner's "you don't look so hot" was being kind. She looked like she'd just spent a week clawing her way through the Amazon.

Natalie got more water, sat down, and tried to focus on the task at hand. Being able to focus on anything for any length of time was a big improvement. Actually, getting out of bed was the bigger accomplishment.

An hour later her cell phone rang. She scanned it and rolled her eyes. Almost turned it off, but her conscience wouldn't let her. "Hi, Dad."

"Natalie. I thought you would have checked in by now, your mother is worried. How's it going over there?"

"It's going great." She put some pep in her voice. "I left voice mails and sent you both texts after I arrived. Didn't you get them? Weather is fantastic. The food is amazing and the wine is just heavenly. Oh and by the way, Grandpa Hal is just fine."

"Good, good." He was walking. She heard horns honking and background noise. "Have you got access to their files yet? That boy isn't giving you trouble, is he?"

"If you're referring to Tanner Collins, no, he's not giving me trouble." Giving her the cold shoulder and a monster headache, but other than that . . . "I'm going through things as we speak. It's a bit of a mess."

"Just as I suspected." He barked something to somebody. "On my way to a meeting. Now, how are you feeling? Your mother thinks being out there will be too much for you."

"It's not." Not yet, anyway. Natalie closed her eyes and breathed deep.

"Well, if you have any trouble at all, just come home. We can shut the place down and not give it a second thought."

Natalie frowned. "I'd like to determine if the winery is salvageable first. I'm not anywhere near ready to make that call. Let's see what we've got first, all right?"

He muttered something she didn't catch. "Let me know when you have some clear statistics to report, then we'll talk. Your mother sends her love."

"Okay. Tell her—" Natalie stared at her phone. Dad never said good-bye, just clicked off when he was done. "I'll be sure and say hello to your father for you." She sighed. Why did he want Maoilios shut down now after not bothering with it for so long?

She stifled a yawn and stared at the work ahead of her. Her brain was threatening mutiny and her stomach simply would not settle.

All right. Concentrate.

The sooner this got done, the quicker she could figure out her next move. Natalie squinted at the numbers for a while, until her cell buzzed again. Laura. This call she didn't mind taking.

"Hey, Lars."

"Natalie! Are you okay? How is everything there? How . . ."

She was off and running. Natalie sat back and listened, imagining her friend in her kitchen, chasing kids and the dog, picking up toys and clothes and books as she went.

"Everything is fine. No need to panic." She studied a blot of mold on one of the photographs on the wall. A stench like sour milk crept around the aroma of coffee and Natalie prowled the office while Laura talked.

"I wasn't panicking. It's just that your e-mail didn't say much, and you didn't answer the Facebook message I sent."

"Laura, you know I hate Facebook." Natalie screwed up her nose and found the culprit. A half-empty container of congealed cream hid behind a dirty UCLA mug on top of a rusty bar fridge. Which she would not be opening without a gas mask. "Text me. You know I don't use all that other stuff." Social media was a complete waste of time. Telling everyone in the world your business so they could comment on it? No, thank you.

"Well. You did promise to set up a Skype account."

"I know. I will." Natalie eyed Tanner's dinosaur-of-a-computer a little dubiously. There had to be an Apple store in town.

"Are you really okay out there?"

"I'm okay. I have my appointment tomorrow. I think they need to change my meds. I can't stop barfing."

"Oh no. Are you feeling any . . . um . . . better?"

"You mean normal?" Natalie laughed. "Not quite. Good days, bad days. But I'm out of bed at least."

"Good. How's your grandfather?"

Natalie looked at the old photographs on the wall. Grandpa Hal with his arms around his two sons. A very young Bill, perhaps twenty or so, and Jeffrey, just a couple years younger. "Doing well. It's Tanner who's giving me the real trouble."

"Tanner?" Laura paused. Natalie heard dishes moving, water running. "Oh, is that the guy you used to hang around with in the summer?"

"That's the guy." An odd smile slid out of her, creating warmth she did not want to contemplate. "He's running the place apparently. And none too happy about my being here."

"What's his last name? I'll look him up on Facebook. Is he cute?"

"Laura." She couldn't envision Tanner Collins checking into Facebook every night. But then, stranger things happened.

Like him apologizing.

That had come out of left field.

"Nat? Answer the question." Laura was still talking. "What does he look like now?"

Natalie rolled her eyes. "Let's just say he's not ugly. But he's hardly amenable. And I doubt you'll find him on Facebook."

Laura laughed. "Maybe you can work on that. The amenable part."

"Laura . . ." Nausea shook her again and she blew air through her lips. "I think he's married anyway, hard as that is to fathom. Got a couple of kids or stepkids, I don't know."

"Oh, boo." Her friend's giggle floated down the line. "Well. You sure you're fine? How is it, being there?"

"I'll get through it. Stop worrying."

"I won't. Call me soon?"

"Will do." Much as she wanted to keep talking, find out how Laura's kids were, Natalie had to go. "Lars, I need to run. Thanks for calling. 'Bye." She clicked off, sucked air into her lungs, waited to see if the feeling would pass, then bolted for the bathroom again.

Seven

Tanner left the truck running and ran into the office. He hoped his cell was on his desk where he assumed he'd left it that morning. Hadn't had time to come back for it until now. It was his turn to pick the kids up from school. He and Mom alternated, depending on their schedules. At least once a week he'd take them to their favorite burger or pizza joint, the park, a movie on Fridays if anything kid-friendly was playing. Hanging out with Jason and Jeni was the one thing that kept him going. Today he'd been so busy he'd almost forgotten. After he took them home, he'd head back to the vineyard to supervise the picking. It was going to be a long night.

He stopped halfway in and stared.

Was this the same place he'd left only hours ago?

A minuscule pile of folders sat on his desk. His clean desk. The shelves on the far side of the room were all in order, books and folders placed in perfect position. A large gray filing cabinet he didn't remember being there before sat against the wall. He trailed a finger across the surface of his desk. No dust. He could probably eat off the floor.

Tanner wrinkled his nose at the vanilla scent in the air. He scanned the shelves on the wall. They'd been sorted and tidied, too, and a glass-ensconced candle sat burning on one of them. He rolled his eyes. What would he find tomorrow, potted plants and elevator music?

He scanned the room again and did a double take.

What. Was. That?

A brand-new computer sat where his old one had been. The one he'd used through college and had placed on this desk so proudly the day Hal handed him the keys to the office. The one that was now nowhere in sight.

He strode toward the shiny new machine and stared at the black apple beneath the screen. Tidying shelves was one thing, but tossing his treasured Toshiba for this . . . imposter . . . Natalie Mitchell had gone too far.

He turned at the sound of a toilet flushing.

Natalie stepped out of the bathroom and gave a little jump. "Tanner."

"Sorry." He cleared his throat, anger fading at the sight of her flared eyes. "I didn't know you were still here." Hadn't expected her to last the morning, actually, the way she was looking. He peered at her, searching for signs of illness. She didn't look as green, but her skin definitely had an odd pallor to it.

"I'm just about to leave. I made good progress today. I've put the files in chronological order, which will make the inputting much easier. I'll get started on that next." She offered a weak smile, clearly pleased with herself.

Tanner scowled. "I see you won't be doing that inputting on my old computer. Mind telling me where it is?"

"In that box over there." The box beside the overflowing trash can. "Don't look so horrified. I had the tech transfer all your data over. Nothing was lost. He was here almost all afternoon." She marched toward his desk as though it was hers, picked up her purse, and reached for what looked suspiciously like his cell phone. "You left it this morning. I figured you'd come back for it, but you didn't. I wasn't sure how to reach you."

"Thanks." Tanner took his cell and scanned it. Nothing urgent, thank goodness. "So, this . . ." Is ridiculous. He made a wide sweep with his arm. "Looks different. I didn't realize your skills included interior decorating."

She crossed her arms, a groove appearing between her eyes. "The place looked like something out of *Storage Wars*. I needed some order. How did you possibly function in such a mess?"

"I functioned just fine." Tanner tripped over her revelation, scratched his head. "You watch *Storage Wars*?" Reality TV didn't seem to suit her. "You seem like more of a Bloomberg channel kind of gal."

A semblance of a smile teetered on her lips. "*Duck Dynasty* is my weakness."

Shoot. Really? "I love *Duck Dynasty*."

"Oh, did you see the one—"

"Look . . . Natalie," he charged on before they got totally side-tracked. "I knew where everything was in here. Now how am I supposed to find anything? Replacing my computer? Nuh-uh. I did not give you permission to do this." Anger burned the back of his neck again and he placed a hand there, counted to ten forward and backward.

"No, I don't suppose you did." Natalie shuffled over to the new filing cabinet and pulled open the doors, revealing rows of files. "Assuming you know how to count, I doubt you'll have too much trouble. If it's really a challenge, I could always color-code them."

Hilarious. "How did you get that thing in here?" He couldn't imagine her lugging the huge cabinet across the courtyard from wherever she found it.

"Miguel put it on a dolly and he and another guy set it up for me. My grandfather suggested it, actually. Thought it might make things easier for you."

"Miguel, huh?" How many more of his employees would she enchant before her time here was up? Had her eyes always been that blue? "Well. I guess the place looks better." Dang it, what was she doing to him?

"I believe the phrase you're searching for is *thank you.*" She drained what was left in a plastic water bottle and pitched it into an almost overflowing blue recycling bin that hadn't been there this morning. It bounced off the heap of balled up paper and who knew what else, and fell into the box that housed his homeless computer.

"Oh, I created a new password for the computer. You know how to use a Mac, right? If you don't, I'll show you. It's easy. But the password you had on that old thing was terrible. *Maoilios?*" She laughed. "Who wouldn't try that first?" She moved past him to the door. "Well, I'm all set. I presume you'll want to lock up."

"And I *presume* you'll tell me what that password is?" Tanner slammed the door, fumbled with the lock, and jogged after her.

"It's in an envelope in your top drawer. I suggest you memorize it and throw that piece of paper away."

"I hope it's something I can understand. I don't read so good." Tanner enjoyed the eye roll she gave him.

"You'll be able to memorize it with minimal difficulty, I'm sure."

Much as he wanted to run back in there and check out the mysterious password, he was already running late. The kids would be getting antsy. They tended to freak when somebody didn't show up on time. "Hop in the truck, I'll drive you up to the house."

"Don't be silly. It's only a short walk." She exchanged her spectacles for sunglasses and tipped her face toward the late afternoon sun. "I'm sure you have somewhere you need to be."

Tanner gave up. He did have somewhere to be. And standing here arguing with Natalie wouldn't get him there any quicker. "Suit yourself. Have a good night."

"You too, Mr. Collins." She hoisted that monstrous purse on one shoulder and headed up the hill like her feet were encased in concrete.

Tanner shifted, an uneasy feeling nagging him. He sent Jason a quick text telling him he was on the way. Then he got in his truck, pulled up beside her, rolled down the window, and leaned across the seat. "Get in."

She stopped walking and stared in surprise. "I can get there on my own."

What was left of his patience flew out the truck window. He knew a lot of stubborn women, but this one shot to the top of the list. "Natalie. Get in."

Defeat dulled her eyes as she made her way over, opened the door, and climbed into the seat next to him. She clutched her purse to her chest, leaned back, and sighed. "Thanks. I'm not feeling quite myself at the moment."

"No kidding." He pressed the gas and they moved up the hill. Tanner was careful to avoid the potholes and rough patches. "Why'd you stay down there all day? You're not on the clock. If you felt sick—"

"Could we just not talk?"

He gripped the steering wheel and glared at the road. For the three minutes it took for him to get up to the house, the truck's interior was thick with awkward silence.

He parked by the front steps. She didn't make any sudden moves and he wondered what she was waiting for. If she expected him to be a gentleman and help her down, she could sit there all night.

"Um." She shot him a glance. "I won't be around tomorrow. I have an appointment in San Francisco. Business."

"Okay." What was he supposed to say to that? Have fun?

"Well." Natalie finally gathered her things, took off her shades, and turned to face him. "I know you don't want to do me any favors, but I'd appreciate it if you didn't tell my grandfather that I wasn't feeling well. I don't want him to worry."

"No problem." Hal would worry anyway. One look at her and he'd know something was up. "Hope you get over whatever it is you've got soon. Flu's going around. Jeni had it a couple weeks back."

"It's not the flu." She opened the passenger door, slipped off the seat, and somehow made it to the ground without falling. Tanner watched until she made it safely into the house.

If it wasn't the flu, then he didn't know what had her looking like she'd contracted the next great mystery disease. Didn't care.

Much.

Okay, so maybe he did care. A bit.

What bothered him was why.

Eight

Somehow Natalie survived her first full week in California. Her appointment in San Francisco went well. She liked Dr. Sherman, and he'd prescribed something different for her. Her stomach revolted for the first couple of days, but Sunday morning finally brought some relief.

Her grandfather informed her the previous evening that he'd be off to church, she was welcome to accompany him, but Natalie declined. Sleeping in sounded like the better option. She woke feeling a little more human. With any luck, when she saw the doctor this week, she'd be able to report that the new meds didn't make her feel like she'd spent four hours at an AC/DC concert.

Natalie spent the morning on the patio reading while Sarah bustled around the kitchen and chatted with her when she came in for more coffee. In no time at all, Natalie knew every restaurant in town, the best place to see the sunsets or shop for antiques, and Sarah had a roast in the oven and bread cooling on the counter. She told Natalie she attended evening services so she could be home to prepare Sunday luncheon.

They all ate together, apparently, every Sunday.

The Collins family seemed to have a special place in her grandfather's life. She was glad he had company, but wasn't so sure she liked Tanner Collins and his brood being it. But Natalie appreciated the concern Sarah had shown her the last few days. Grandpa Hal kept his thoughts to himself, but he watched her carefully.

Natalie took refuge in the cool sunny living room at the front of the house. She checked out the various houseplants, studied the artwork on the walls, and finally surrendered to the pull of the array of photographs on the shelves of the built-in bookcases.

So many memories . . .

She smiled as she picked up a picture of her uncle. He couldn't have been more than eighteen at the time. Handsome. Natalie hadn't seen him in years. He and Dad shared certain similarities. The same blue eyes, although Jeffrey's seemed to sparkle more, the same crook of the mouth when they smiled. Her uncle was laughing in this picture and she wondered who'd taken it. And where in the world Jeffrey Mitchell was today. She made a mental note to ask her grandfather later.

Her hands shook as she reached for another silver-framed image that turned back time.

Nicole sat on a swing, smiling. Perfect in every way.

Almost like a magazine ad for a kid's clothing store.

Natalie sank into a soft recliner and stared at her twin.

Mom loved to dress them alike. Nicole didn't put up with that for long. From the time they were eight, her sister insisted they pick out their own clothes. Well, Nicole picked the clothes. Natalie wore them.

They would have been about five or six when this picture was taken. She wondered where she'd been. Probably standing off to one side out of the way, at Nicole's instruction.

Those early years passed quickly. Kindergarten was a blur except for that first day. The day Natalie dreaded all summer. Their nanny drove them to the red brick building, delivered them safely into the waiting teacher's care, and drove away. Natalie didn't want to cry. But there were so many other children and they were all staring at them.

"Come on, Nat. No scaredy-cat stuff today. It'll be fun, you'll see.

Let's go." Nicole took her by the hand and dragged her through the doors.

Her sister had been right, as usual. It had been fun. Lots of fun.

Natalie was good at almost everything and enjoyed learning, especially in later years, when she and her twin weren't in the same class. But Nicole found her on the playground and in the lunchroom, and Natalie still had to play second fiddle.

After that final summer, when Natalie returned alone to face the stares and whispers and unspoken questions of her classmates, school was no longer fun.

She returned to the bookshelf to put the picture back in place.

"Watcha doin'?" A small voice startled her and Natalie jerked her head up. The little girl she'd met last weekend stood beside her. Dressed in a navy corduroy skirt and white blouse with a chocolate stain on it, she flashed blue eyes and a big grin.

"Ah. Hello. Jeni, right?" The little girl nodded and Natalie smiled. "I was just looking at the pictures."

Jeni stared at the bookcase a minute, then turned her big eyes toward Natalie. "Wanna know a secret?"

"Uh, sure."

Jeni puffed out her chest and pointed. "There's steps behind that. It goes up to the tur . . . turpit . . . whatever it's called."

"The turret." Natalie nodded. "I know."

"Jason told me. But we're not 'llowed up there. It's dangerous."

"Right." Natalie wondered when her grandfather had closed off the door.

Jeni tugged on her arm. "But look, that part is on wheels. So you could move it."

"Oh." She hadn't noticed. Natalie frowned at Jeni. "You guys haven't been up there, have you?"

Jeni gave an impressive eye roll and a giggle. "I just said we're not 'llowed."

Oh, well then. Natalie grinned and watched her peruse the photographs.

"Is that you in the picture?"

"No. That's Nicole. My sister."

"Oh. She looks like you."

"Yes." Natalie glanced down at the photograph, her eyes stinging. "We were twins."

"Aren't you twins anymore?" Jeni scrunched her nose and twirled her hair.

"Well, Jeni, it's kind of a sad story." She crossed her arms and wondered how much to say. "Nicole died, you see."

"Oh. How come?" Jeni trailed her around the room, skipping hopscotch in her black Mary Janes.

"There was an accident." Sirens blared within the recesses of her memory. Natalie pushed hair out of her eyes and paused at the piano. Lifted the lid. Ran a trembling finger across the ivory keys and waited for her heart to stop pounding.

"That is sad." Jeni sidled up beside her and touched a few keys. "My mommy plays piano real good. Can you play the piano, Miss Natalie?"

Her stomach clenched. When had she last played? Had to be months. "I used to."

"Don't you like it anymore?"

"I like it fine." She allowed her fingers to fiddle, a few chords forming on their own. "I just haven't had the chance to play much lately." Or the desire.

"Oh." That seemed to satisfy the child. Jeni tapped out the first few notes of *Chopsticks.* "I forget how it goes."

"Like this." They shared the bench and Natalie showed her the notes, waited to see if she would catch on, then joined in until they played it through together twice. "One more time? Let's see how fast we can go."

The little girl's fingers were deft and Natalie laughed as they raced through the tune at top speed. She and Nic could play *Chopsticks* together for hours until their mother begged them to stop.

"I like that song. Mommy used to play it with me." Jeni's smile faded. "My mommy had an accident, too, like your sister. But the doctors are going to make her better. Uncle Tanner promised."

"Uncle Tanner promised what?" A voice drew their attention to the door.

Tanner strode toward them, arms crossed, a hint of amusement on his face.

Natalie stared, then looked at Jeni. *Uncle Tanner?*

Tanner leaned on the top of the piano. "Natalie. I take it you didn't succumb to whatever was ailing you."

"No." She mustered a smile. Today was a good day and she wasn't about to let him ruin it. "I'm feeling better. Were you at church too?" She tried not to sound surprised, but the grin that slid across his mouth said she hadn't managed it.

"Don't sound so shocked." He stifled a yawn, shadows under his eyes again.

They harvested the grapes at night, when it was cooler. Natalie had seen them out there on nights she couldn't sleep.

"He slept through the sermon," Jeni whispered to her. "Jason told me."

"Hey, now." An unexpected chuckle filled the room and coaxed Natalie's real smile out of hiding. She snuck a glance his way.

His usual work attire—dirty jeans and stained shirt—had been replaced by a pair of smart khakis, a green and black plaid button-down, and almost shiny brown oxfords. His hair was neat, save a few strands that fell across his forehead, tickling one dark eyebrow.

The man cleaned up well.

Natalie looked away, ignoring the fluttering in her stomach. He wasn't the first handsome man she'd ever laid eyes on. And she was in no position to be considering him attractive. For a lot of reasons. The first being if her father had his way, she would probably put him out of a job.

"Jeni, Nan says time to wash up," Tanner instructed. "Go fetch Jason, he's out back with the dogs."

"Okay." The little girl scrambled off the bench, threw her arms around his legs before she ran off, yelling for her brother.

Tanner stood at the glass doors, his stance stiff. Natalie played a few chords, trying to figure out what to say without sounding stupid.

"So, you're their uncle?"

"What?" He made a slow turn, light hitting the gold flecks in his eyes.

"Jeni called you 'Uncle Tanner,' so you're their uncle? Not their father?" Natalie tried to get a look at his left hand. She hadn't noticed a ring before, but that didn't mean he wasn't married.

"Say what?" He looked at her like she was a lunatic.

"I'm sorry. I just . . . I didn't know. I thought maybe the kids were yours."

"Mine?" His brows shot upward.

"Well. Yes. I assumed you were married with a family by now." She folded her arms and met his look of astonishment.

"You assume a lot." Tanner gave a snort and crossed the room. "They're Marnie's kids. My sister."

"Marnie?" Natalie swiveled, watching as he studied the photographs she'd been looking at earlier. "I don't remember her."

"You never met her." He sighed and massaged the back of his neck. When he faced her again, his eyes had turned stormy. "She's a couple years older than me. She lived with my dad." He shifted from one brown loafer to the other. "Lunch is almost ready."

Natalie got to her feet. "So . . . you're not married?" Okay, that just jumped out all on its own.

Tanner waggled his ringless fingers in front of her. "Not married. Now if you're done with the cross-examination, can we go eat?"

They enjoyed their meal outside under clear skies and a warm sun that almost made Natalie forget that back home winter was on its way. She didn't even miss the changing leaves. Maybe she'd stay in California a bit longer.

"Natalie Grace, you don't eat much more than a bird." Grandpa Hal raised bushy eyebrows.

"Sorry, Grandpa. It's all delicious, but I'm afraid my stomach is still giving me trouble." Natalie shot Sarah an apologetic smile. She managed to eat all of the vegetable soup and tried a few bites of the beef, but ended up pushing the rest of her food around her plate.

"You've been working too hard at that job of yours, haven't you?" Grandpa teased. "Good thing your father sent you out here. We'll force you to relax a bit. Maybe even have a little fun. Tanner can join you. He hasn't taken a day off in years."

"Tanner has too much work to do," Tanner muttered, "and I don't think Natalie came out here to have fun." He picked up his wine glass, tipped it toward the sun. "What did you think of the Cab, Hal?"

"Can we be excused?" Jason asked, sounding bored. They were released, and he and Jeni raced down the hill, the dogs tearing after them. Natalie noticed a new swing set down there and wondered when that had been built.

"Smooth. Bold. I think it's ready to go. More, Natalie?" Grandpa offered to refill her glass but she shook her head. Tanner put a hand over his glass, so Sarah got the remainder.

"I'd like to meet with Mike Spencer next week, Hal," Tanner said. "He's offered a fair price for the two fields beyond the bridge.

I think you should consider it." He pushed his chair back and stretched out long legs.

Her grandfather's eyes narrowed as he straightened his shoulders. A lock of white hair curled over his furrowed brow. "That man has being trying to buy my land since 1975. I'll never sell to him. We might need those fields someday, my boy."

"We haven't needed them in two years. We have ample supply for our demand at the moment. If you sell, we can pay off—"

"We're getting by, Tanner." Hal reached for a bottle of slightly chilled Pinot, poured the light red liquid into his glass, swirled it around, and lifted the rim for a sniff. "Very nice nose on this one."

Natalie considered their interaction in silence. From the numbers she'd studied so far, she suspected things were worse than Tanner would admit to. If Grandpa wasn't willing to make some changes, her father might just get his way.

Something in her shifted.

She'd always been drawn to a challenge. Always rooted for the underdog, perhaps because she identified with them. Since this bout of depression started, she hadn't felt like rooting for anything or anyone. Hadn't wanted to get involved in everyday living. Deep down she was terrified of getting sucked under again. But maybe . . . maybe this time it would be different.

Maybe she was stronger than she believed.

Or more insane than she wanted to be.

She leaned forward and touched her grandfather's rough hand. "Grandpa, *getting by* isn't good enough in this economic climate. You need to make a profit. You can't continue to ignore that times have changed."

"Ah, yes. Times have changed. Where've I heard that before?" Hal took a sip and wagged a finger at them. "Are the two of you in cahoots now? Want to get me to change the way I do business or you'll shut the gates on Maoilios?"

"No." Tanner and Natalie spoke in unison. She ignored Tanner's eye roll.

"Nobody's shutting anything down," Tanner added, giving her a pointed stare. "Not if I can help it."

"Grandpa." Natalie focused on her grandfather instead of Mr. Grump across the table. "It's about protecting your investment. You've spent years of your life on this land. You've worked hard to make Maoilios the wonderful winery it is today. But you have to continue to invest. I don't know much about wine making, but I do know that it takes time. I know that there is a process to it, formulas that you follow. When things don't work, say you get a bad batch, you try to figure out what went wrong, and you make the necessary corrections and try again. Am I right?"

"Yes, but . . ."

"It's the same way with a business." Natalie smiled at his look of chagrin. "If it doesn't work, change it. Throw different ideas around until you find something that does work. All we're saying is that you should consider something different. We don't have to overhaul everything overnight, but you must give some thought to new ideas."

"Such as?"

She had his interest now. Tanner's, too, although his expression was more one of disdain, but he was listening. Natalie summoned courage and continued. "I know you have a tasting room in town, but why not have one here? A nice, bright space where people can come and enjoy the land, learn about the wine, and really get a feel for the vineyard."

"Things like that cost money." He pulled at his earlobe and looked at Tanner. "Aren't you telling me that we're losing money?"

"Yeah," Tanner admitted warily, drumming his fingers on the table. "But if you're willing to put out some cash for a few improvements, I think we can turn things around."

"You've got to spend money to make money." It was her favorite saying. "I noticed an old barn off to the side of the offices down the hill. What's that used for?"

"Nothing." Tanner glanced at his mother, who stood and began to clear their plates. "Sometimes we'll use it for employee events, like the harvest celebration, but usually it just sits there. Right, Hal?"

"Maybe you could show it to me, Grandpa." Natalie gave him a smile she hoped he would succumb to. "And I could show you a few websites of wineries where things like we're suggesting are working. Would you think about it?"

"If it will make you happy, my dear, I will take your suggestions under consideration." Hal finished his wine, stood, and pecked her on the cheek. "I'm off for a wee nap. Perhaps we'll amble down the hill later this afternoon."

"I'll look forward to it." Natalie watched him head inside, released a sigh, and wondered if the air out here was making her crazy. From what she'd seen so far from their financials, her father was right. Maoilios was in trouble, and it was clear her grandfather didn't realize it. If she really wanted to jump on board here and help turn things around, she'd have her work cut out for her.

She pushed her chair back and reached for a couple of empty plates.

"Not so fast." Tanner crossed his arms and regarded her coolly from across the table.

So much for a hasty retreat. "What did I do now?"

"Oh, come on."

"Give me a break." She was so not in the mood for an argument.

Natalie walked across the patio to the bench that overlooked the stunning vista. The vines had been stripped bare over the last few nights. Yesterday had been cooler, and they'd worked most of the day. Hoping some fresh air would help, she'd taken a walk and watched the activity in the vineyards. Watched the way the workers interacted with one another, Tanner moving in and out of the rows, stopping to chat and share a laugh every now and then. It was clear he had the respect of the men and women who worked for him, but it was obvious they liked him too.

She wondered whether the man might ever give her a reason to like him again. Because, right now, all he seemed capable of was igniting her temper.

"So, I'm confused." He strolled up beside her and cleared his throat. "What's the point of trying to convince Hal to make changes when you're only going to turn around and shut the place down on him in a few weeks?"

Natalie rounded the bench and sank onto it. "You really don't trust me, do you, Tanner?"

"Pretty sure we've established that." Tanner perched on the arm of the weathered bench and studied her with a quizzical expression.

She sighed and took off her sunglasses. "You know, since we do seem to be in a position where we're going to have to cross paths, a little civility would be welcomed."

"I have been civil."

"That's what you call it?" She lifted a brow. "Sometimes I find it hard to believe we used to be friends."

"Ditto." He marched off toward the row of rosebushes that lined the border of the patio and then stood, silent.

Natalie gave up. She didn't know what to say to this surly man who seemed threatened by her every move.

"I'm not sure you see what's at stake here, Natalie."

Apparently he wasn't done.

"You're talking about putting people out of work, uprooting families who have lived here for years, mine included. I understand your father's reasoning and the need for a business to be profitable, but it doesn't seem like he's willing to give us a chance. You rich people don't think twice before signing on the dotted line. Don't care who you're hurting in the process. Well, you can tell your old man that we're not done here. I want six months. If things haven't improved by then—"

"Okay, already." Natalie held up a hand. He loomed over her, waiting. "I do see what's at stake, Tanner. The truth is, my father can talk all he likes, but he doesn't have the power to shut this place down. Do you know who owns the majority of shares in Maoilios?"

"That would be you." His skewed look screamed *I'm not stupid*.

"Exactly. So if the winery is losing money, so am I. Wouldn't it be prudent of me to investigate things first? See whether we can find a way to increase profits?"

"You haven't shown any interest up to now. Why bother?"

"I don't know yet. And I don't know why my father wants to shut the place down so badly, other than the financial losses." She watched the way his jaw pulsed as he pondered her reply. "My uncle and my father are the other shareholders, as you probably know. We'd all have to be in agreement to close. I have no idea where my uncle is, and I don't think my father has tried to contact him. If you're really that concerned about your position, why don't you just offer to buy my father out?"

Tanner's mouth fell open. "You're kidding, right?" He gave a harsh laugh. "I don't have that kind of money. Even if I did, I doubt your father would sell me the time of day let alone his part of the vineyard. But I don't discount your influence over Hal. He listens to you. I saw that just now."

"So why is that a bad thing?"

"It's not. But you're going to have to be a little more persuasive if you want me to believe you really want to help."

Uncomfortable silence fell heavy around them, made it hard to breathe. "I'm not sure how I can do that when you've made it perfectly clear you won't work with me."

Eventually she heard him give a ragged sigh. "Yeah. About that."

Tanner shrugged, still wary, but a new light sparkled in his eyes. "If you're really serious, I'll give you a chance. We can work on some ideas together if you want. Getting Hal to understand the gravity of the situation, that'll be the first hurdle. Are you up for that?"

"I think so." Natalie's heart rate jacked. What exactly was she agreeing to here?

"Will you ask your father to cut us some slack? Talk to Hal. Get him to see reason. Give me six months to make some changes and I promise you, you'll be looking at a very different set of numbers."

Natalie nodded. "From what I've seen so far, it's not going to be easy. But I think things can improve. My father won't like it though."

"What's his beef with this place anyway?" Tanner shoved his hands in his pockets.

"I'm not sure." Natalie rubbed her nose. "He doesn't like losing money, that's for sure. I know that he and my grandfather don't have the best relationship. But I guess all families have problems, right?"

"Yeah. They do." His eyes clouded in an expression that was unreadable. Then he brightened, dimple flashing. "You actually thought I was married, huh? Who would put up with a jerk like me, really?"

"Nobody in their right mind, that's for sure." She was only half kidding.

"That's what I keep telling myself." A spark of humor flashed across his face. "Look, I can't promise to stop being a complete moron, but I'll make a more concerted effort to improve my civility."

She waved off the remark with a laugh. "That's not necessary. I'll just put an extra jacket on when I see you coming."

His smile created a flush that raced upward and caused her cheeks to tingle.

"So that password you picked took me back a few years."

Natalie nodded. "Yes. *GodsWinepressRev141920*. I thought you might remember." Whether it still meant anything to him, Natalie couldn't tell.

Tanner's expression softened. "'And in the eyes of the hungry there is a growing wrath. In the souls of the people the grapes of wrath are filling and growing heavy for the vintage.' *The Grapes of Wrath*. I remember."

Steinbeck was not an author your average junior high school student would gravitate toward, but her grandmother had owned his entire collection. That last summer, Natalie had been curious, started reading, and dared Tanner to join her. To her surprise, he had. They'd spent a lot of time together discussing the novel, arguing over it, and eventually talking about other things as well. Things she'd never shared, not even with Nic.

"We talked about that book for hours," he said, cutting into her thoughts. "I think I read it three times after that summer."

"I never read it again."

The past skulked around again, unwanted. Natalie wished it would disappear for good and let her start over.

"Why did you stop e-mailing me, Mouse?"

"What?" The question startled her.

Tanner shrugged and pulled at his collar. "After you left that summer. I wanted to keep in touch. But then you stopped writing back." That surly look returned. "Guess you figured I wasn't going to end up with a six-figure salary like your rich country-club pals so I just wasn't worth your time anymore, right?"

Natalie stared. His efforts to redeem himself were short-lived. "Right. That's exactly what I was thinking." A sad sigh slid out of her. "Tanner, what is your problem?"

"Sorry." He kicked at a small rock and sent it flying down the hill. Amber eyes blazed under the afternoon sun, his lips pressed together in a thin line. Everything about him said *back off*. "But ever since you showed up, all I can think about is that in a few weeks, I could be out of a job. And that's not exactly a comforting thought."

"Oh. Well, I'm sorry." Natalie shook her head, realizing how her presence here might make the other employees feel. "I don't want anyone to worry about the future of Maoilios. You haven't mentioned the possibility of closure to anyone else, have you?"

"Only Leo. Not that he does much to help us along anyway."

She sat back and crossed her legs. "Like I said, if things are salvageable, I'll go that route first."

"And your father?"

"I'll have to convince him. Call it a personal challenge." One she was starting to think might tip her over the edge.

That seemed to pique his interest. "You think you can prove him wrong?"

"At the moment I have no idea. But I'd like to try." God help her.

"Really. I never pegged you for someone willing to go against their old man."

She gave a brief shrug. "I don't see it as going against him if we can turn a profit. It's more a matter of me having something to prove." She'd leave it there. "Anyway, that's where things stand. Believe what you want about me. I'm not here to impress you or make nice. That was Nic's domain."

A low whistle came from his direction. "You're really going there?"

Nine

OH, GOOD GLORY. SHE REALLY DIDN'T WANT TO GO THERE.

Natalie hoped she didn't look as flustered as she felt. "You seem to call it like you see it. So do I."

"Fair enough." Tanner nodded. "Nicole knew how to get what she wanted; I won't deny that. That doesn't mean she always succeeded."

"Whatever. She would have. If . . ."

"Natalie." Tanner leaned forward, his eyes piercing. "We were kids. And no disrespect, but your sister wouldn't have had much use for me in later years. We come from different worlds. She knew that even then."

Nicole's obsession with Tanner Collins had been the biggest wedge between them. Natalie could put up with her sister's bossiness, snide remarks, the calculated schemes that left Natalie holding the bag every time, but the final insult was the look on Nic's face when she'd snuck in late one night, her face flushed, eyes lit with excitement while she eagerly relayed the events of the past few hours.

He's such a good kisser, Nat. Oh my gosh. I'm so in love . . ."

"Oh, please. You're thirteen. What do you know about love?" Natalie rolled over in bed, squeezed her eyes shut. Why had she been so stupid to confide in her sister? To think she could actually trust her. Hot tears trickled down her cheeks.

Two days ago, after Natalie and Tanner spent the afternoon together, reading and swapping stories, Tanner had done the unexpected. Leaned in, looked her in the eye for a long moment, then kissed her. Short, but oh so sweet. It had taken her breath away. And she'd come home and confessed her undying love for Tanner to her sister.

"Natty? I know you said you liked him, but . . . you're okay with this, right?" Nic crawled onto the bed and rubbed Natalie's back. "Tanner said he likes you, but only as a friend. He wanted to make sure you wouldn't be upset."

"You told him how I felt?" Natalie sat up and stared at her sister in horror. "Nic! You promised."

"Aw, come on, Nat." Nic laughed and patted Natalie's wet cheek. "Everyone knows you've had a crush on Tanner for like, forever. But unfortunately, he only likes one of us."

Natalie shook her head at the memory. "I guess you feel things more intensely at thirteen."

"What does that mean?" Tanner squinted down at her.

Natalie stiffened and realized she'd said that out loud. Why did the man turn her into an absentminded dolt? "Nothing. Forget it."

He moved off, stood in silence for a while, then gave a low chuckle. "I still can't believe you thought the kids were mine."

She silently thanked him for changing the subject. "Well, it did cross my mind. But given that Jason's almost eleven . . ."

"That would have made me a teenage dad. No thanks." Tanner practically shuddered. "I've got nothing against marriage and family, but it's not for me."

"Then we have one thing in common." She rubbed the bare spot on her left hand. "My friend Laura has two kids and she's constantly exhausted. She loves being a mom and wife, but I don't think I'd want that life."

He pulled up a chair and sat, contemplating her like she was some strange new strain of bacteria. "Interesting."

"What is?"

"Your grandfather mentioned you got engaged a while back."

Of course he had.

"I'm not anymore."

"Okay." Tanner fiddled with his watch, guarded interest in his eyes. "What happened?"

How to answer that? Natalie decided on the short version. "We realized it wasn't the right decision, so we ended it." Something like that.

"No regrets?"

"Only that I said yes in the first place." She shifted on the bench. "Does your sister work here at Maoilios as well?"

Tanner's lips twitched in what could have almost been a smile, but the light in his eyes faded. "No. She doesn't. She used to teach music, piano. But she . . . well, she was in a wreck back in August and she's uh . . . not doing so well."

Natalie suddenly remembered Jeni's words. "Oh, gosh. Jeni did say her mother was in some kind of accident, I completely forgot. I'm sorry."

"Yeah." He leaned forward, exhaled in a way that tugged at her heart, and then sat up again. His eyes glistened and Natalie swallowed regret. His chest rose and fell, his eyes never leaving her. "So, anyway. How long until you know where we stand with the winery?"

Clearly he didn't want to talk about his sister.

"It shouldn't take much longer. But I have to go back to the city on Wednesday. That might put me back a day or two."

"Another appointment?" He raised an eyebrow. "We have hair salons and spas out here, you know."

"Very funny."

Interest gleamed in his eyes. "What are you up to?"

"Nothing. And what I do with my time is none of your

business." The retort popped out before she could stop it. But she had her own topics she didn't want to discuss.

"Okay, then." Tanner stood and put his chair back at the table. "Nice talking to you, Natalie. I'm going to check on the kids."

He strode off, kicked up dust along the path, and Natalie shook her head. Whatever. Tanner Collins could stew in his own juices all he liked. She had more important things to worry about. Like holding on to her sanity for the rest of her time here.

Natalie brought the remaining dishes into the kitchen and set them beside the sink. Tanner's mother was still cleaning up. "This is the last of them. Thanks for lunch, Mrs. Collins. It was great."

"You're quite welcome. And please call me Sarah."

"Sarah, then." Natalie hesitated, not sure what to say. "I, um, I'm sorry to hear about your daughter. Tanner said she was in an accident."

Sarah shot her a look, followed by a brief smile. "Thank you. We'll get through. Has Tanner gone home?"

"He said he was going to check on the kids."

Sarah stretched to put plates away. "We live on the property, you might remember, just on the other side of the hill. There's a path through the vineyard. I can be here in five minutes if I need to be."

"That's good." How many times had she needed to be? Natalie ran a dish towel over a wine glass. "Do you think my grandfather is really all right?"

"He seems to be doing just fine." Sarah scrubbed a large pot a little too vigorously. "I think the question is, are *you* really all right?" She dried her hands and smiled. "You probably don't know this, but I actually trained as a nurse. I worked hospice care for the last few years I practiced. I've learned to read people pretty well."

"What made you quit?" Natalie picked up a plate to dry and veered her gaze from the kind eyes that seemed determined to unlock her secrets.

CATHERINE WEST

"Oh, life." Sarah laughed and shook her head. "When I was married to Tanner's dad, I worked. We lived in Seattle then. When Tanner and I moved back here, I could only find shift work at the hospital. Your grandparents offered me the position here at the house, and it made more sense with Tanner having a hard time adjusting as it was. So we moved onto the property and I never looked back."

Natalie pinched her lips and put the plate up in the cupboard, flinching as another round of nausea snuck up.

"Natalie." Sarah put a hand on her shoulder. "Come and sit down."

Exhaustion propelled her to sit next to Sarah on the couch in the family room.

"I'm fine, really," Natalie insisted, even as tears pricked her eyes. "It's just . . ."

"Natalie," Sarah said softly, "whatever it is, you can trust me. I hope you know that."

Natalie nodded, met Sarah's kind smile and knew she spoke truth. "All right. Well. A few months back, after I found my fiancé cheating on me, I had a bit of a breakdown."

She told Sarah the rest, the return of her panic attacks, that she was seeing a doctor in the city, and felt strangely relieved when the truth was out.

"Please don't tell anyone." Natalie wiped her eyes and drew in a shaky breath. "If I can just get through the next couple months, I'll go home. Maybe Thanksgiving. Things should be much better by then."

"I hope they will be." Sarah squeezed her hand. "I'm glad you're getting help, but don't you think you should tell your parents? You can't use coming here as an escape. You need support, sweetheart. And Hal—"

"No! I don't want to worry him. And I really can't tell my

parents." She couldn't handle the fallout from that conversation. "Things were such a nightmare after Nic died. I can't put them through that again."

Sarah nodded, moisture shimmering in her eyes. "You always were the stubborn one, Natalie Grace. Your sister knew how to fly off the handle, but she got over things and moved on. You, on the other hand, never gave in. Not if you knew you were right."

"It didn't matter much." Natalie gave a halfhearted laugh. "Nic always seemed to get her way whether it was right or not. I learned to give in eventually."

"I'm so sorry about Nicole, sweetheart," Sarah said. "We never got the chance to talk afterward. Once you were released from the hospital here, your parents took you straight home."

"Yes." Natalie pressed her fingers into her thigh and blinked back tears. Tears wouldn't help. Wouldn't bring Nicole back.

"Well. I'm glad you told me what's going on." Sarah stood, put a few pictures to rights on the mantel. "I'll give you my cell number. I want you to call me if you need anything, day or night. All right?"

"Thank you, Sarah." Natalie felt a strange relief, sharing her burden with somebody. "Please don't mention this to Tanner. I don't want him feeling sorry for me. He's having too much fun hating me at the moment."

"Oh, my dear." Good-natured laughter bounced across the room. "Tanner doesn't hate you, Natalie. He just . . . well, he's concerned. We're all concerned. This place is our life. I can't imagine not being here. And your grandfather—"

"I know, I know." She clutched a colorful cushion to her chest. Did everyone think she was on some personal vendetta to destroy their lives? "My dad only cares whether or not the place is making money. If I can convince him Maoilios is still a good investment, if indeed it is, then you don't have anything to worry about."

"And if you don't think it is still a good investment?"

Natalie shrugged and pushed to her feet. "Sarah, honestly, the best I can do right now is try to make it through one day without puking. I came out here because Grandpa Hal wanted me, but I also came here to get away. I never intended to come back, to face the past. But here I am. And maybe it is time I dealt with it. All I can tell you is that I'm taking it one day at a time."

"I didn't mean to sound harsh." Sarah took her by the hands. "Of course you must focus on getting well. Don't worry about Tanner. He'll come around."

"I'm not worried about Tanner," Natalie said. "I can hold my own where he's concerned. And I hope he'll soon realize that I really do want what's best for everyone."

Sarah nodded but didn't look convinced.

Natalie refused to concern herself with it.

Tanner Collins broke her heart a long time ago. She wasn't about to let him do it twice.

Ten

Tuesday morning was turning into a nightmare.

"How did this happen?" Tanner spat sour wine from his mouth and stared at Hal. He'd been so careful this time. Thorough. Even more than usual. Since Natalie's arrival and the implications of her visit, he was second-guessing his every move. No room for mistakes. "Is it the only tank?"

"Just two from what I can tell so far." Hal shook his head and muttered under his breath.

"Two?" Tanner leaned against the cold stainless steel and waited for the room to stop spinning. Please God, let that be all. "That's two too many."

Hal shrugged. "It happens, Tanner. It could be worse."

"The tanks were clean. I double-checked everything myself, Hal. I don't get it."

"We'll run some tests. See if we can figure out where this came from. Don't worry."

Tanner closed his eyes. This was not what he needed. Not on top of everything else.

He grabbed a glass from a nearby shelf and strode to the next tank. Tasted. Coughed and spat the rancid stuff onto the cement floor.

"I told you." Hal shoved his hands in his pockets, his expression grim. "It's just the Meritage. Everything else up here and down below should be fine."

"*Should be* isn't good enough." Tanner kicked the air as a cat strolled by. "I want everybody on-site tomorrow morning. I want to know who touched what. I want to know exactly who has been here and who hasn't and I want—"

"Tanner." Hal's steady gaze cut off Tanner's tirade. "You can interrogate everyone down to those darn cats for all I care, but the damage is done. Accept it, son."

"Hal . . . I'm sorry." Tanner wished for a thousand miracles right about now. Wished to wake up and be at home in his bed, ready to start this day over. Except he'd been wishing that same wish for three months and it hadn't come true yet.

"We'll survive. We'll drain those two and clean them out and start over. It'll be fine."

Tanner sighed and wished for some of the older man's optimism. They crossed the courtyard to Tanner's office.

Hal glanced around the room and whistled his approval. "This looks different."

Tanner grunted and refused to go there.

Tanner poured two cups of lukewarm coffee and they sat in silence. After a while, Hal put his mug down, hooked his thumbs into his belt loops, and stared at his boots. "What do you know about depression?" He lifted his head, his eyes full of questions.

"Depression? Not a whole lot. Why?" Tanner leaned back in his chair and regarded the old man carefully. Surely if Hal had been exhibiting signs of depression, he'd have picked up on it. His friend seemed just fine to him, but Tanner was no doctor.

"Don't look at me like that." Hal glared. "Not me. Natalie. I think she's depressed."

"Natalie?" Tanner choked back laughter. Everything he'd seen about the strong-willed woman vetoed that theory. Sure, she might have been a little under the weather, but depressed? That seemed unlikely.

"You knew her pretty well at one time, Tanner. Does she seem like herself to you? Does she seem happy?"

"Happy?" They were heading toward territory Tanner had no desire to explore. "Hal. Your granddaughter and I were friends a lifetime ago. I don't know her anymore and wouldn't have a clue whether she's happy or not." And didn't care. At least that's what he'd told himself the other day as his heart snagged on her anguished look when they'd talked about Nicole.

"She seems awful quiet," Hal persisted. "I know she's still checking in at the office even though she's meant to be taking a break. Doesn't eat much. She's tired a lot, not real talkative, although she never was. I think being here is bringing back memories she doesn't want to deal with."

"Then she shouldn't have come." Tanner regretted the sharp words as soon as they were spoken.

"You still think she's going to sell us out." The quiet proclamation rang around the office, settling on Tanner like a wasp about to sink its stinger into flesh.

"A logical conclusion under the circumstances."

"You have trust issues, son." Hal got that look in his eye. The look that said *I know you, what you're hiding from, and how you really feel.* The look Tanner, even at ten years old, could never duck out from under.

When his mother announced they were moving to Sonoma, back to the place she'd grown up, Tanner had been furious. Bad enough to have his family ripped apart, but now he had to start over someplace new. He revolted. Refused to say much to anyone here for about three weeks. Until Hal found him wandering amongst the vines, took him aside, and talked sense to him.

Tanner couldn't remember what he'd said now, but he remembered being sort of terrified of the older man. Two days later, Hal took him fishing and Tanner had a new best friend.

One who was now getting on his last nerve.

"We both know her father sent her here, Hal. He wants the place shut down."

"That's not entirely true." Hal twirled his thumbs around each other. "Bill may have a bee in his bonnet about the winery, but I asked for Natalie."

"You what?" Tanner sat forward, confused. Hal's smile wasn't doing much to stave off the feeling that he'd just tumbled down a rabbit hole. "You asked her to come here?"

"I did. Natalie is my trump card, son. The only way this place is closing is if she does it herself."

Awesome. "Then we're done."

"Not so fast." Hal smiled. "I'm not convinced Natalie is going to side with her father."

The man was deluded. Tanner squelched the thought. He didn't like the tension between them. "I disagree."

"Oh, I can see that." Hal rubbed his chin, pensive. "But I have a feeling. Grace and I prayed long and hard about giving Natalie those shares, and—"

"Not this again." Tanner groaned, leaned back in his chair, and slung one arm across his eyes. "Are you seriously going to sit there and tell me that Natalie Mitchell owns half of Maoilios because God told you and Grace to give it to her?"

Silence told him what he already knew.

Tanner pulled his arm down and opened one eye.

"Your skepticism will get you nowhere." Hal wagged a finger. "That's exactly what I'm telling you. I also know that Natalie is here for reasons that have nothing to do with Maoilios."

"Well, if she wants a vacation, I suggest Hawaii."

"Tanner . . ." Hal's warning tone made him sit a little straighter. "She's going to need your help, son."

Tanner sucked his teeth. The old man was losing it.

Hal stared him down.

"Enlighten me." Tanner raised his hands in mock surrender. "How do you see me being the slightest bit helpful to someone like Natalie?"

Hal's eyes narrowed. "That's my granddaughter you're talking about. I suggest you take it down a notch."

"Fine." Tanner crossed his arms and swallowed his anger. "Can we get back to the subject of the winery?"

"I thought that's what we were discussing." Hal's innocent expression did little to diffuse Tanner's temper. If Bill Mitchell succeeded in shutting them down, Hal had brought it on himself.

"All right." Tanner sighed. "I think we might stand a chance if we can show her the potential of the place. She claims to want to help, thinks things can improve. But on the surface it doesn't look good. The numbers speak for themselves."

"Do you think we can turn things around? Natalie seems to think so, but she claims I'm holding you back. Am I?"

Finally they were getting somewhere. So she had kept her word and talked to Hal. Tanner's pulse jacked a bit.

"Yes." He kept a handle on his emotions and nodded. "There are things we can do. Changes we can make. But you have to let go, Hal. You have to trust me enough to let me do the things that need to be done. I can't help you with both hands tied behind my back."

"I have never not trusted you." A pink hue flared in the man's weathered cheeks. "You're like a son to me. Always have been. You know this place better than my two boys put together. It's just . . . ." Hal released a reticent sigh and shot Tanner a watery smile. "It's hard not to wish for the old days, you know? Things were easier then. We never had to worry whether we'd make ends meet. We had our regulars, the suppliers, the restaurants."

"Times change, Hal. The economy has changed. People are

more discerning. They're not interested in the mom-and-pop businesses of days gone by. They want new, exciting, different."

"And you think you can make Maoilios into something new, exciting, and different?" Hal's doubtful look displayed his true feelings.

"I think we can mix the old with the new." Tanner tried to be gentle. "It's not about reinventing the wheel. It's about improving what we have. Building on it and making it better, more appealing. I have some new wines coming out this year that I believe can hold their own against the competition. But we're not going to sell much if nobody outside of Sonoma knows we exist."

"Okay." Hal's wan smile gifted Tanner a glimmer of hope. "You do what you need to. But make sure you bring Natalie on board. Whatever you think of her, she's a smart cookie. Knows business. And maybe if she's got something more constructive to do, she'll get over whatever it is that's bothering her."

"I really have to work with Natalie?"

And here things were going so well.

"I would strongly advise it." Hal gave a sly smile. "Unless, of course, you don't think you can handle my granddaughter."

"Oh, I can handle her all right," Tanner scoffed. "I'm not so sure she can handle me."

"I wouldn't bet on that, son. I think Natalie can handle you just fine." Hal guffawed as he got to his feet. "Keep an eye on her for me. If you think she seems unwell, you come talk to me. And try to be nice. It won't kill you."

"It might."

"I very much doubt that. But she might kill you if your attitude doesn't improve. Now, run me up the hill. I need to take my pills."

A few minutes later, Tanner left Hal heading upstairs, his smile broad. He never could win an argument against the man. Like it or not, he was going to have to get over himself.

He wandered through the house to see if his mother was around. Finding the kitchen empty, he remembered her saying something about the kids having dentist appointments after school. Which explained the Crock-Pot on the counter and her handwritten note to Hal on when to lower the heat. Which had been a half hour ago. Tanner flicked the dial to Warm.

He grabbed a glass of water and gathered his grim thoughts. If things didn't improve, he could give up now and let Natalie give her father what he wanted. Maoilios was all but ancient history.

And Rance Harper had called twice last week.

He'd wanted to speak with the kids, but so far Tanner and Mom had persuaded him to take things slow. They needed to tell the kids about Marnie at the right time, and then reintroduce them to their father.

There was no right time for either event.

Rance's claims of being a changed man sounded suspicious. Tanner wasn't about to pull the rug out from under Jason and Jeni simply because their father demanded he do so. And if he found out Harper wasn't telling the truth, he'd see him in court before giving up the kids.

Tanner's cell buzzed and he checked his voice mail.

He scanned the list and almost dropped the phone when his father's number came up. Tanner listened to Brian Collins's voice, his heart thudding. Wanting to see how he was. Hoping they could talk.

Nothing he hadn't heard before.

Too little, too late.

And knowing the close relationship his father had with Rance, at least according to Marnie, he was probably calling to plead Harper's case.

The shrill ring of the house phone made him jump.

Seriously? Tanner waited to see if Hal would pick up, but it kept ringing. Surely his father wouldn't try to reach him here. He glanced at the clock on the wall. Four thirty. A little early for telemarketers, but you never knew. He needed somebody to yell at.

"Mitchell residence."

Silence. He tapped his boot on the tile and glared at the colorful paintings on the wall. "Okay, look, we're not interested in whatever it is you're selling, so just—"

"Tanner?"

"Yeah?" Sounded like Natalie. But she was in San Francisco. For whatever she was doing there that was none of his business. "Who is this?" A grin slid across his mouth.

"Is your mother there?" She sounded far away and not up to dealing with him.

Too bad.

"My mother? No. Who is this and what do you want?"

"Tanner . . ." She let go a long sigh. "It's Natalie. But you know that. Are you sure your mother isn't there?"

"She's not. Took the kids to the dentist. Where are you?"

"I'm . . . never mind." Her voice dropped. "Is . . . my grandfather around?"

"Hal's upstairs." Tanner foraged in the fridge for leftovers but came up wanting. He'd skipped lunch and now his body was paying him back with a headache. "I can go get him if you need him."

Silence. Maybe she hung up. Good. He had things to do. Namely get something in his stomach before heading back to the fields tonight. Whatever was in that Crock-Pot would do nicely. He went to the cupboard to fetch a plate. "Natalie? You need him?"

"No. I need you."

"Excuse me?"

He fumbled with the china plate, put it down, and tried not to laugh.

"Please. I'm not kidding. I'm stuck. My car . . . I've pulled off the highway and I need you to come get me."

"You what?" He lifted the lid of the pot and sniffed. Chili. Awesome. Tanner shook his head. "Do I look like I work for Triple A?" His sarcasm was met with more silence. He knew she hadn't hung up because he could hear her breathing. Shallow breaths that pushed his pulse up and kicked him on the backside at the same time. Proceed with Caution flashed in neon lights across his brain. "Natalie? Are you all right?"

"If I was all right we wouldn't be having this conversation." She muttered something that sounded like a word he couldn't imagine her using. "Forget it. Sorry to bother you. I'll try to flag down a cab. Call a tow truck tomorrow."

She's going to need your help, son.

Tanner tripped over the dogs' water dish and sent it flying across the floor. They scrambled over and came to his aid, lapping the spilled water. "Wait! Don't hang up. Tell me where you are." He stepped around the animals on his way to the counter and found a notepad and pen.

"GPS says I'm in San Rafael. In the parking lot at the Marin Center."

"What are you doing there?"

"I took an exit off 101, thought if I drove around a bit, slowly, it'd . . . look, I can't explain now. My phone's battery is running low."

"I'll be there in about forty-five minutes, give or take. Don't move."

Faint laughter floated through the phone. "That won't be a problem. Thanks, Tanner."

He placed the phone back in the holder, pitched a spoon into the Crock-Pot, and stole a few mouthfuls. Then he grabbed his keys and whistled for Gwin. "Yeah, I know," he said to the dog as they headed for his truck. "I'm a sucker for punishment."

Eleven

IT WAS DARK BY THE TIME TANNER REACHED THE MARIN Center. Natalie's car wasn't hard to spot. It was only one of about three vehicles left in the lot, and the others were trucks. The place appeared to be deserted. The thought of Natalie sitting out here alone didn't give him a warm fuzzy feeling. Tanner pulled up beside the silver Jag, shut off his engine, and glanced downward. Natalie wasn't in the driver's seat.

His throat constricted as he scanned the area.

Surely she wouldn't have abandoned her vehicle. Unless she figured he wasn't coming and decided to call a cab after all. But he'd told her not to move.

Confound the woman. If he'd driven all the way here for nothing, he'd wring her neck.

"Stay." Gwin whined as Tanner jumped down and peered into the darkened car. Sweat started at his hairline as a thousand scenarios, none of them good, raced through his mind. He pulled out his phone, switched on the light app, shone it around, and let out his breath. Natalie was stretched out on the backseat, asleep by all appearances.

This was getting weirder by the second.

He tried the door, but it was locked. At least she was smart enough to lock herself in. He rapped on the window and waited. Nothing. His pulse picked up.

"Natalie!" Either she was a really sound sleeper or . . . no, he wasn't going there. Panic thrummed through him and Tanner banged on the roof of the car. "Natalie, wake up!"

He tried not to laugh as she jerked her head up, caught sight of him, and scrambled to sit. It took her a moment to get the door open, but she didn't make any effort to get out. She sank against the leather seat instead and let out her breath. "Thank goodness you're here."

He did laugh then. Never thought he'd hear those words come out of Natalie Mitchell's mouth. Tanner stared at her over the vehicle's open door. "If you wanted to tie one on, you could have just stayed at a hotel."

"I'm not drunk, you idiot," she mumbled.

"Oh, I'm an idiot now, am I? Can I just remind you I dropped everything and drove all the way out here at your request? What's going on, Natalie?"

She grabbed her purse and lunged forward. "Can you tow this thing or will we have to come back tomorrow?"

Tanner took a step back. She stumbled toward his truck and leaned against it, like she was about to pass out. If she wasn't drunk, she was sure doing a good impression.

"Why didn't you call the rental company?"

"Because there's nothing wrong with the car. I just can't drive it."

O-kay . . . Tanner stared and scratched his head. "Natalie, I'm a little confused."

Tears welled in her eyes. Tanner sighed, moved her out of the way, opened the truck's door, and stood back. "Get in. It'll take me a few minutes to hook up the winch."

"Thanks." She dropped her purse onto the floor of the truck and put both hands on the seat, then stepped back again. "There's a dog in there."

Gwin's tail thumped wildly and he knew the minute Natalie

got in, she'd be getting a face wash. "Yeah. Gwin. You're okay with dogs, right?" She'd seemed at ease with them until now.

"I love dogs."

Then get in the truck already.

She stared at his 4x4 like it was some monstrous beast about to swallow her up. Her legs didn't seem to want to cooperate with her. She mumbled another word that surprised him, but he didn't dare comment on it.

To his annoyance, her obvious discomfort and embarrassment wasn't enjoyable to watch.

"Mouse?"

"What?"

"Need a hand?"

"No."

"You sure?"

"Just . . . give me a second." She lifted her leg, placed her foot on the running board, then gave up and put it down again. "I can't."

His patience vamoosed as she made one more valiant attempt to climb into the truck. He so did not have time for this. "Right." Tanner closed the gap between them and snaked an arm around her waist. Her squawk of protest pulled a thin smile from him and a bark from Gwin. "Assuming you want to get home tonight, let's do this my way."

"Tanner, don't. Really. I can't—"

In another minute she lay across his arms as easily as Jeni might. He'd wager she weighed less than an empty oak barrel. A faint hint of her perfume lingered and heightened his awareness of her femininity. Not going there.

"Bet Triple A wouldn't provide this kind of service." His attempt at humor seemed to have the opposite effect. Her face crumpled.

Tanner silently agreed with her earlier proclamation. He *was* an idiot.

"I can't get in the truck, Tanner. I'm afraid." Big tear-filled eyes stared up at him through the semidarkness.

Reality hit him square in the jaw as he registered the terror on her face.

She wasn't here with him at all. She was on the back roads of Maoilios, in an out-of-control Jeep she was powerless to stop.

Air hissed from his lungs and he tightened his hold around her. "It's okay. I've got you. We'll get you in, and then I'm going to drive you home, okay? Natalie? Take a breath."

She did. A soft shuddering sigh that woke her from the trance, but sliced him through.

Her eyes flashed wide. "I'm sorry. I don't mean to be so much trouble."

Oh, she had no idea. Because, God help him, even with the fear in her eyes, the way he felt right now was definitely trouble. Big trouble. The kind he did not need. He should throw her in the truck and floor it home.

Instead, he let himself look at her for a long moment. Saw her for who she was and what she'd once meant to him, young as they had been. Part of him even succumbed to the sensation of having a gorgeous woman in his arms.

"If you're contemplating carrying me back to Sonoma, it's going to be a long night." A shy smile lifted her lips and sent his pulse racing again.

"Cute." Tanner swallowed traitorous emotion and cleared his throat. "Unfortunately, I still have work to do tonight, so I think we'll have to drive." He lifted her in and onto the seat in one swift move and stepped back. Gwin nuzzled up to her and Natalie turned her attention to the dog.

Once he'd secured her car, he got in the truck and glanced her way. Her eyes were closed, Gwin's head in her lap.

She turned her head toward him. "All set?"

"Yeah."

"So we can go, then?"

"Not yet." He swiveled to face her and ignored the pounding in his temples that told him this was probably the worst idea in the world. "We're not going anywhere until you tell me what's going on."

"No." She stared out the window.

"Were you always this stubborn?"

"Were you always this nosy and bossy? Just drive, Tanner."

He glared at the back of her head. Watched her shoulders rise and fall as she reached for her purse. She foraged around, came up with a prescription bottle, popped the lid, and threw a small pill in her mouth. Tanner flinched as she swallowed. "What are you taking?"

"I don't want to talk about it."

The ensuing silence both unnerved him and accelerated his aggravation. "Well, that's too bad. After the day I've had, I'm not in the mood to play guessing games. Right now I'm working on about six hours sleep over the last four days, so I suggest you start talking or I'll dump you on the pavement and let you fend for yourself."

Gwin's whine accused him of the lie.

As if.

"I can't tell you."

"Can't or won't?"

"Tanner . . ." The way she said his name—like Jeni calling out after a bad dream, a desperate plea—slammed him against his seat.

Something was very wrong.

She buried her face against Gwin and Tanner's anger slipped into the shadows.

Finally she faced him, slowly, painfully. Tears trickled down her cheeks.

The hostility he'd harbored toward her since she'd stepped foot on Maoilios faded into the black night around them. A crushing weight pressed on his heart and forced him to face the truth. Told him he was still capable of feeling. Still capable of raw emotion that scared him silly and made him do stupid things. Like reach out a hand and wipe that tear away with the tip of his finger.

"Talk to me, Mouse."

She grabbed his hand and held on, as though he possessed some supernatural strength she didn't. And then, she spoke. "Three months ago I had a nervous breakdown."

"You what?" Tanner's chest tightened.

"Yeah." She screwed up her nose at the confession. "There. Now you know. Can you handle crazy?"

If she only knew . . .

"You're not crazy."

"I've heard that a few times."

Tanner watched more tears slide down her cheeks. "What happened?"

"Life happened." Natalie pulled at the pendant around her neck, twirling a finger around the silver chain.

His eyes rested on the charm. Looked like some kind of zodiac sign, which surprised him. She didn't seem the type to put stock in horoscopes.

"You don't have to tell me." He'd pressured her enough. On all fronts. Guilt slammed him sideways as he let out a breath.

"It's okay. I brought you all the way out here. You should know why." She studied him. "A few months after the accident, after Nic died, things got pretty bad for me. It took years of therapy and a lot of different meds for me to function normally. As I got older, it got better. Then this year, at the start of summer, I began having nightmares again. Seeing Nic. Reliving the accident . . . panic attacks like the one you just rescued me from."

"Like PTSD?" Tanner frowned.

"Exactly PTSD. That's what they tell me." She gave a feeble laugh and flipped Gwin's soft ears. "It may never fully go away. I've been seeing a shrink in San Francisco. Last week I drove, and I was fine. This week, between the stupid meds that make me feel like crap, and the flashbacks, today I knew I wasn't going to make it, so I called the house."

"You didn't want to talk to your grandfather, did you?"

"No." Fear flickered again. "Please, Tanner, you can't say anything. Your mom knows, but I don't want to tell Hal." She lowered her head.

His mom? Well, that figured. Mom was intuitive, always looking out for others. Tanner was too preoccupied with pushing people away to pick up on their problems.

Natalie stifled a sob and he slid an arm around her and pulled her against him. Crying women were his weakness. "I don't think not telling him is an option, Mouse. He's going to know something's up at some point." Hal already did, but Tanner wouldn't tell her that.

Her defeated sigh blew across his chest. "I thought coming here might help. I thought if I faced things, I'd finally get over it. Sounds good in theory, but now that I'm here . . . I'm scared I'll get worse. But I didn't want to deal with telling my parents and I—"

"Your parents don't know about this?"

"No." She lifted her head, her face ashen in the light of the truck's cab. "You don't know them. Don't judge me."

Don't judge me.

That's exactly what he had been doing since she arrived.

Assuming she was some stuck-up society snob who cared only about herself. He never imagined that she might have issues, might be dealing with her own wounds, same as the rest of the world.

Same as him.

Guilt pinned Tanner again and told him he needed to ask her forgiveness.

One day.

Natalie moved back to her side of the seat. From what he remembered of her parents, and his brief conversations with Bill Mitchell about Hal and the winery, Tanner could hardly blame her for keeping secrets.

"I'm not in any position to judge you, Natalie." He reached back and lifted the lid of the cooler he always carried with him. The water bottles wouldn't be cold at this hour, but they'd be wet. He cracked the lid and handed one to her. "Should you call your doctor or something?" He wouldn't be responsible for anything happening to Natalie Mitchell. Hal would string him up from the nearest tree.

"I did. He said I'm fine to go home, not to drive, of course. And to take it easy the next few days."

"You know how to do that?" Tanner lifted a brow and tried out a grin.

"Not really." Her soft laughter made him relax a tad.

"Didn't think so." Tanner ran his tongue across his bottom lip and started the engine. "Looks like it's lockdown for you, Miss Mitchell." His mind scrambled over pieces of her puzzle, tried to put it together. "Why did you really come here, Natalie—to Maoilios?"

She hesitated, nailed him with those sad eyes, and shrugged. "To prove myself to my father."

Twelve

SHE'D FINALLY SAID IT.

The answer she knew Tanner had not been expecting.

Natalie could see confusion written all over his face.

"Explain."

She sighed, stared at him through the semidarkness, and tried to voice her thoughts. "My whole life, I've never felt good enough in my father's eyes. Nicole was the smart one, the pretty one. The perfect one. I was always running to catch up. Of course everything was a competition with her. Since her death, I've felt that pressure even more. To be everything my parents expect me to be. Not the miserable failure I actually am."

"You're not a failure." Tanner scowled. "What does this have to do with Maoilios?"

"Well, my father has pretty much written the place off. You know that." She brightened a bit, still bolstered by the challenge. "And I've always gone along with everything he does. You probably know that too. But this time . . ." A smile shook off the dark thoughts. "I don't know, Tanner, something about saving Maoilios, bringing it back to life . . . I feel like it's my redemption."

"Do you really believe that saving Maoilios will get rid of the past?" he asked quietly.

The pointed question surprised her. Everything about their conversation tonight surprised her. Made her say things she hadn't intended. Made her feel . . .

"I don't know. I'd just like to do something right for a change."

He tapped his fingers on the steering wheel. "And your father doesn't think you can do it."

"No, he doesn't," she whispered. "He's never had faith in me. You don't know what it's like to look at your father and wonder . . . wonder if he will ever love you again. Wonder if he ever really did."

Tanner slid his window down and turned his head. He sat like that for a moment, not moving. Not speaking. Finally he faced her. His eyes hinted at a haunting memory. "You're wrong, Mouse. I know exactly what that feels like." He pulled out of the parking lot and didn't press further about her father. Probably just as well. She'd bared enough of her soul for one night.

She ran a finger over the photograph of Jason and Jeni taped to the dash. "They're good kids."

"Yeah, they are." Tanner tightened his grip on the wheel.

"Do they ever see their dad?"

"Nope."

"Where is he?"

Tanner's reticent sigh said he didn't want to talk, but he shot her a sidelong glance. "Seattle. He's a drug addict."

"Oh. That's awful." She couldn't imagine living with that kind of legacy.

He let go a muted groan. "To be fair, he's been clean a few years, or so he says. Been in rehab, got his life together apparently. He lives near my dad and I gather they're close. All I know is, my sister wouldn't let him near the kids. Far as I know he hasn't seen them since she left him to come here."

"And now?" Natalie didn't know whether to bring it up or not. "Your sister's condition, is she . . ." Somehow she couldn't bring herself to ask.

"Yes, it's that bad and no, he's not getting them," Tanner snapped. "Not if I can help it."

Natalie let the subject drop. She drank water and watched the lights from oncoming cars until she couldn't stand the silence. "What happened today?"

"What?"

"Earlier, you said, *after the day I've had* . . . What kind of day did you have?"

"Oh." He stared at the dark road ahead. "We lost a couple of tanks. The wine went bad."

"Why?"

"I'm not sure."

Natalie rested her head against the seat and registered the way his jaw tightened. Like he was giving her further proof that the winery should be shut down. "I'm sorry. Is it a significant loss?"

"Nothing we can't survive. It happens, but it sucks. Could be bacteria. Something got in there somehow. I supervised the cleaning of those tanks myself. And the formula wasn't new. I was thorough with my calculations. It's frustrating."

She stretched out her arms and yawned. "I'll try to get through the rest of your files this week. We need to get some of your ideas put in place. You know, a tasting room on-site, tours. I didn't get down to see that barn the other day."

His skewed look surprised her. "Maybe you should worry about yourself first. Those facts and figures aren't going to improve no matter how long you stare at them. Given your current state, are you sure going against what your father wants is wise?"

Natalie laughed. "Oh, I'm sure it's absolute insanity. But it's given me a purpose, Tanner. Worrying about the winery gives me something to do." Worrying about herself wouldn't change a thing. "I know you're skeptical, but I really don't want to see this place close. I'll do whatever I can to stop that from happening. But it will be easier with your help. You're going to have to start trusting me."

"Ha." Tanner scowled as he changed lanes. "According to your grandfather, I have trust issues."

Natalie gasped in mock surprise and they shared a smile. "I did pick up on that."

A smile settled on his lips. "All right. Let me get through harvest first. I'm not great at multitasking."

"How long does harvest last?"

"All depends on the season and the crop yield. Could be a month or more, give or take. We've got a smaller yield this year and we were a couple weeks in when you arrived. This is the last week of picking. And I can't wait for a full night's sleep."

"I hear that. Maybe I should get out there and help you." The thought of taking a selfie picking grapes in the middle of the night and sending it to her father made her giggle.

"What's so funny?" Tanner shot her an amused look.

"Nothing." She'd keep that one to herself.

When they hit a stoplight, he foraged in the back again, yanked on a Mexican blanket, and sent Gwin to the backseat. "Here. Wrap up in that. You can sleep if you want."

She pulled the heavy blanket over her legs. "Do I detect a hint of concern?"

"No concern. Just don't want to have to dig a hole for you out back anytime soon. I'm a busy man." His smile was positively wicked and far too devastating.

"I'll do my best not to keel over during the next while then."

Tanner's laughter filled the space between them, filled a bit of the empty spot in her heart. "At least you haven't lost your sense of humor, Mouse."

"Warped as it is. It's about the only thing keeping me going."

"You'll get through this."

Some days she doubted it. "Thanks for coming to get me."

"That's what friends are for."

Natalie stared at his sincere expression. For a moment, she forgot that thirteen years stretched out a childhood friendship that had no business being resurrected.

"What?" A smile crested his handsome face.

Natalie smiled back. "You do the knight-in-shining-armor thing quite well, Mr. Collins."

His laugh sent small flames shooting through her veins. But she couldn't tear her eyes from him.

"Don't look too closely." Tanner's smile slipped. "There are major chinks in the armor, Mouse. Major chinks."

Thirteen

FBI Legat, Prague

Jeffrey Mitchell splashed through puddles as he headed toward the American Embassy, his heart thumping in time with his heavy steps. He'd expected the call days ago. Expected the summons that came first thing this morning. Part of him wanted to take those written words back, say he'd made a mistake, had a chance to think, reconsider.

He flexed his fingers underneath the white plaster cast he'd been wearing for weeks, due to come off tomorrow. A broken arm, four cracked ribs, and a couple of chipped teeth. A fair price to pay considering he figured he wouldn't be coming out of that last operation alive.

He'd been the lucky one.

The loss of three men on his team kept him up nights and haunted his days. For all his training, when it came down to it, he had no idea how to get through the aftermath. But his mind was made up. He wouldn't put anyone at risk again.

He was done.

But after waiting outside the legat for fifteen minutes, he reconciled with the truth. He was about to walk away from the only life he'd known for the past thirty years.

"He'll see you now, sir."

Jeffrey followed Colin Brant's secretary into his boss's office. She ushered him to a chair, offered coffee—which he declined—shimmied out, and closed the door behind her.

Brant was hanging up the phone. "How're you doing, Mitchell?"

"I'm alive." Some days he didn't want to be.

"You've been cleared medically." Brant leaned over his desk, bushy black brows knit together. "So let's talk about this letter." He tapped the thin envelope against his desk.

"My resignation. What's to talk about?" Jeffrey swallowed the self-inflicted sentence like castor oil, stared out the window watching storm clouds creep across the skyline.

"Why not a leave of absence? Paid, of course. You'd continue with counseling—"

"No amount of counseling will change my mind, Brant," Jeffrey growled. "Those men died because of me. I panicked. Let me save you the trouble of firing me, let me walk."

Brant gave a low chuckle. "You're fifty-six years old. What do you plan to do with your days? Sit around playing Tiddly Winks?"

Jeffrey shrugged. "Will there be an investigation?"

"No. I've read the report. I believe you did everything possible to salvage that mission. Bit of bad luck, bad timing. You're one of the best men I've got over here, Mitchell. Don't throw away a stellar career over one mistake. What you've been through—"

"I let you down, sir. Let everyone down."

Failure.

His old friend had come to stay again.

This time, Jeffrey would let him move in.

"Don't make any rash decisions. It's too soon. Why not take a few months off?" He smiled amenably. "Take a break. Go on a holiday. Doesn't your family have a vineyard out in California?"

"Yeah." The last place he'd be welcomed.

"Get yourself a plane ticket. On us."

"You're serious?" There had to be a catch. He didn't deserve a second chance. And the FBI was not known for giving them.

"Jeffrey, you've always been too hard on yourself. I'm not accepting your resignation and that's the end of it. What are we now, October first? Take three months. We'll talk in the new year. If, at that point, you still don't feel you can handle another assignment, we'll reassess. All right?"

Only because he hadn't yet managed to come up with a long-term plan that didn't involve tying cement blocks to his feet and plunging into the murky waters of the Vltava, did he agree with Brant's suggestion. He stood on shaky legs, managed to choke out a few parting words.

He couldn't stay in the Czech Republic. Couldn't return to his flat in London. Too many memories there. Pretty much all of Europe was out of the question. Which meant he might actually have to consider California.

Later that evening, after a couple of beers and more than several second thoughts, he picked up the phone and dialed a number he hadn't used in years.

The housekeeper answered and took his request. Eventually the line crackled. "Bill Mitchell." His brother's voice boomed down the line and Jeffrey almost hung up.

Jeffrey had always prided himself in being even-tempered. Few people had the ability to make him want to slam them against the nearest wall. His brother sat at the top of the short list.

"Hey. It's Jeff." A long silence made him wish he'd listened to his gut and not called.

"So you're not dead."

"Nope, not dead." He attempted a laugh. "How are you?"

"Busy. We're entertaining."

"Well, I won't keep you then. I called because I've got some vacation time coming and—"

"Have a good trip."

"Bill, wait. Don't hang up." Jeffrey gripped the receiver and sucked in a breath. "I was thinking of going to see Dad. Do you think . . . well, how would he take that?"

"It will probably give him another heart attack."

"Dad had a heart attack?" Fear chilled him.

"Happened over a month ago. Didn't keep him down for long apparently."

"You should have called me."

"Oh, yes, I probably should have. Except nobody knows where the devil you are and you haven't bothered to check in with me but once or twice since Mom's funeral."

Can't imagine why.

Jeffrey squeezed his eyes shut and took measured breaths. "How is he, really?"

Bill snorted. "Fine, from what I can tell. They kept him in the hospital a few days, but according to Natalie, he's in better shape than most teenagers."

"Natalie? Is she out there?"

"Yes. She needed a vacation, so I sent her on a little fact-finding mission." Bill's disgruntlement floated down the line. "The old man seems to be running Maoilios into the ground."

Jeffrey studied the scar on his right forearm. "I find that hard to believe. Dad loves that place. It's always done well." Bill had a tendency to exaggerate. Things couldn't possibly be that bad.

"Not anymore. They're barely getting by. Of course Natalie has gone all sentimental on me and insists the place can turn around."

Jeffrey raised a brow. Good for Natalie.

His brother muttered something to someone, probably one of his lackeys, although Jeff supposed "staff" was the politically correct way to address the hired help these days. "Look," Bill continued. "Since I have you on the phone . . . Dad isn't getting any younger, and frankly, I don't have the time or the inclination to clean up his mess. Despite what Natalie thinks, I'm recommending we shut down the winery. Sign your shares over to me, I'll have the money wired to you by the end of the week, once the paperwork is processed. I think this is the best option for all of us."

Jeffrey sat in silence. "Are you for real?" Some things never change. His brother's gall was one of them.

"What?" Bill chuckled. "The feds pay you that well, little brother?"

"What about Natalie? She's the majority shareholder."

"Natalie will see reason."

Something in his brother's tone raised the hairs on the back of his neck. And cautiously confirmed that California was exactly where he needed to be. "I'm not selling you anything, Bill. Enjoy the rest of your evening; sorry I disturbed you." Jeffrey clicked off and headed for the minibar.

The wine selection was pitiful, but then again, this wasn't the Ritz. He stretched out on the bed with a coke and stared up at the ceiling, thinking of the place he'd once called home.

If he believed in having a "happy place," Maoilios would definitely be it. He'd worked hard, spent summers alongside college kids and migrant workers picking grapes, hauling crates, eventually learning the process his father had honed to a natural science. Jeffrey knew his way around the property blindfolded.

Used to.

Bill had hightailed it east for bigger and better opportunities in his early twenties. Broken Dad's heart in the process. Jeffrey was willing and able, and he looked forward to filling his brother's shoes, working alongside his father, one day taking over the business. He'd settle down and start a family of his own.

But things changed.

The wedge between him and Dad had still been just as apparent when he'd flown home for Mom's funeral. And they'd left things unsaid. Dad and Bill's issues were none of his business, but he did regret not trying to make amends with the old man himself.

Maybe now he could deal with that.

Deal with Sarah too.

He'd caught a glimpse of her at his mother's funeral. He'd missed his connection from Tel Aviv, and by the time he arrived, the service was half over. Afterward they'd gone to the graveside and he'd lingered, wanting to be alone. To say his good-byes, his apologies, in private. Later, she'd been busy serving guests and tending to Hal, and there hadn't been an opportunity to talk. Not that they would have. Jeffrey was so blindsided by grief and guilt that he hadn't been able to say much of anything to anyone. She'd spent the evening avoiding him anyway. And he was gone before dawn the next day.

How many years had it been since he'd parked outside the white stone church in Sonoma, heart pounding, vision blurring? He'd stared at the blazing pink bougainvillea, viewed the arriving guests, realized that soon he'd speak words that would forever change his life, and suddenly he knew he just couldn't do it.

He hadn't been a total cad. He'd driven over to Sarah's in a cold sweat, convinced her family to let him in, and then tried to convince her they were making the biggest mistake of their lives. He'd already convinced himself. Surely she'd understand and agree . . .

She hadn't.

He left her then, standing in her bedroom of her parents' home wearing the wedding dress nobody would now see, knowing what it felt like to be truly despised. Knowing that whatever came next, wherever he went, no matter how many years separated them, he would never be forgiven.

And didn't deserve to be.

Fourteen

Good morning, my girl."

Natalie stirred, sat up in bed on Saturday morning, and watched Grandpa Hal push back the drapes and open a window. Fresh air flooded the room. "Morning, Grandpa."

"There you are, lassie." He set a cup of steaming coffee on her bedside table. When they were younger, he'd bring them hot chocolate. "It's going to be a lovely day. Shall we have breakfast outside?"

"I'll let you know when I'm awake." She snuggled back under the covers. After Tanner dropped her off on Tuesday night, she'd found her grandfather waiting up for her. He'd been so concerned, that she'd given in and told him about her PTSD. The past few days, as she recovered from the episode, they'd really talked. He was a good listener. Only gave advice when asked, didn't judge. She'd even heard him fielding a couple of calls from her father. Grandpa was quite the storyteller when he wanted to be.

He sat on the edge of her bed and studied her through worried eyes. "I wish you'd told me what was going on when you first arrived. I would never have let you get started on those files. I would have given your father what for and—"

"Grandpa." Natalie shot him a look of chastisement and took his hand. "I've told you now. And look where it got me. You've barely left me alone. Honestly, you need to take care of yourself, too, you know."

"Don't you worry about me, young lady. It's you we need to mind. How are you feeling this morning?"

"Better." Nights were still hard, sleep interrupted by visions she couldn't control. Today might be a good day, but she still lived in fear of tomorrow. Her stomach growled, the sound almost producing a smile. "I wonder if Sarah would make me her famous French toast. I think I could actually eat." The idea brought silly excitement.

"Of course she could." Grandpa's brow furrowed. "Is it my imagination or is your hair . . . a bit lopsided?"

"Not your imagination." She remembered the sorry state of her appearance. Last night, after waking drenched and drained from another nightmare, she'd caught her reflection in the mirror and balked. She looked too thin. And her hair looked like a family of rats had made their home in it.

Angry with herself, she'd grabbed a pair of scissors without thinking. Next thing she knew, she'd made a royal mess and almost resembled Anne Hathaway's look as Fantine in *Les Mis*. She'd leaned back against the tiles, closed her eyes, and let the tears come. Crawled back to bed and promised to fix it in the morning.

Natalie shook her head at the memory. "You wouldn't by chance have one of those home hair-cutting kits, would you?"

"There's something like that in the kitchen somewhere. Sarah gives me a trim now and then. Best let her sort you out. Or find someplace in town if you like." He gave her a wink and stood. "We'll get you through this, Natalie Grace. A year from now you'll barely remember any of it."

"That or I'll be in the loony bin." She ducked out from under the hand he tried to swat her with, and he left the room grumbling. Natalie wiggled her toes as warm fingers of sunlight crept over the covers to tickle her face. She could hear the kids and dogs outside.

Perhaps there was hope to be had after all. Perhaps God hadn't seen fit to punish her. Perhaps He'd answered her halfhearted pleas for mercy.

Natalie still wasn't sure.

Who was she to ask anything of a God she barely knew? And why would He answer her prayers? Religion was just something people made up to make themselves feel better. At least that's what she'd spent most of her life believing. Lately, she was having doubts about that, wondering if there was more out there than she knew or had ever been willing to explore. She found herself skimming through the Bible that Laura had given her. Pondering over words like *faith*. *Grace*.

Mercy.

That was all well and good for people like Laura, people who had nothing to hide.

Natalie didn't need it.

Except, maybe she did.

But she certainly didn't deserve it.

⌒

Tanner sat at their kitchen table and glowered at the fly buzzing around his coffee. His first Saturday off in weeks. The crew would take a well-deserved break today. Harvest was over at last. Tonight they would celebrate, and then it was up to the wine. With any luck, this year would be the one to pull them out of the red.

Aside from losing those tanks, and the incident with Natalie on Tuesday—having to explain to Hal why her rental was hooked up to the back of his truck and why she sat in the front seat looking like death warmed over—last week had been manageable.

He'd negotiated a sweet deal with two new restaurants in town and they'd agreed to feature Maoilios's wine on the menu. One was even planning a wine-tasting night to introduce Maoilios to the restaurant's patrons. Tanner loathed those events as much as Hal, but he'd agreed to attend. He'd persuade Hal to come along. The old guy was practically a legend in his own right. Not that he'd ever admit it. And maybe—Tanner almost grinned at the thought— maybe he'd even ask Natalie.

"Everything squared away out there?" His mother came into the room carrying several large photo albums.

"Finally." Tanner leaned back in his chair, bone weary but still wired from running on adrenaline and caffeine. "Cleaning up now. Getting ready for the party tonight. I still wish I could figure out how that wine went bad, though. But, nothing to do about it, I guess."

"Nope. No use crying in your coffee." She placed the books on the table with a thump. "I'm heading to the hospital. Jason and Jeni are up at Hal's, on the swing set."

Tanner groaned at the mention of his nephew. "How mad is he?"

"That you missed another game? What do you think?"

He'd hoped to get out to the soccer field by nine this morning, but he'd still been in the sorting room supervising the last of the bins. "I know. It was crazy busy this morning and I couldn't leave in time."

"Don't tell me. Tell him. And make sure you're there next week."

"How'd they do?"

"Lost. But Jase scored two goals. I got video."

Tanner produced a tired smile. "Don't tell me you finally figured out how to use that camera I gave you last Christmas."

"No, I used my iPhone."

"Really. I suppose you do Instagram too?"

"Of course. What, you think I'm old or something?" She refilled his coffee and tapped the back of his head as she headed toward the door. "Go check on the kids when you're done, and take these to Natalie for me. I found them in my cedar chest, thought she might enjoy having a look."

Tanner reached for the first album, thumbed a few pages, and rolled his eyes. "Mom. Seriously? I'm not taking these to her." Skipping down memory lane with Natalie was the last thing he wanted to do. *Yeesh*. What in the world had he been thinking with that long hair? And what was that fur above his lip?

"Tanner." She walked back to the table, placed her palms down while piercing him with that I-know-you-better-than-you-know-yourself look.

"What?"

"Deal with it."

He pushed the books away as coffee churned in his stomach. "Those pictures are downright embarrassing. I'm not going to stand there and let Natalie laugh her guts out over me."

"This has absolutely nothing to do with those photographs, and you know it. Natalie has PTSD, Tanner. It's not a communicable disease. I know you. There's nothing you can do to fix it and you hate that. You're avoiding her the same way you've been avoiding Marnie."

"Don't." He held up a hand, the sudden sting in his eyes making him blink.

"Tanner, let me say this; you need to hear it." Her tone warned of what was coming. "Marnie isn't going to get better. We know that. Those machines are keeping her alive. Dr. Blair says it will only take a little while before she passes. She's not in pain. We need to let her go. It's the right thing to do." She pulled a Kleenex from the pocket of her slacks and wiped her eyes.

"Is it?" Words he would regret scratched his throat and tried to claw their way out. He smashed his hand onto the table, then stood and marched across the room. His chest heaved and his throat burned so badly he thought he might puke right there. "Is that what you're going to tell Jason and Jeni? That it's 'the right thing to do'?"

"Tanner . . ." Mom raised a hand to her mouth, her tear-filled eyes wide. "We have to. Soon. And I want you to go see her before it happens. Make your peace."

"You don't ask for much, do you?"

"You can blame yourself as long as you live, but that won't change a thing. The only thing it will do is hurt you in the long run. If you push away everyone who cares about you, you'll end up a lonely man."

"I enjoy being alone." Out the window, a pair of birds landed nearby, picking at crumbs on the ground. The blue sky and bright sunshine mocked him, said all was well in the world, when clearly it wasn't.

Hadn't been for a long time.

"When did you last talk to David?"

Mom so needed to learn when to back off. She was a fine one to talk about letting go.

"I'll drop these off." He picked up the books, grabbed his jacket, and sent his mother a sidelong glance. "Talking to a priest or pastor or whatever David's calling himself these days won't help. Won't change a thing."

"He's your friend, Tanner. He wants to help."

"Well, he can't help. Nobody can help."

Fifteen

NATALIE SCOURED THE KITCHEN FOR THE KIT GRANDPA HAD referred to. She finally found it in one of the cupboards, an inch of dust on it. She didn't want to shave her head or anything. It at least contained scissors that looked in better condition than the ones she'd used last night. She just had to figure out how to fix the mess. Or find a salon in town that would do a better job. But the thought of going out in public was too mortifying and she'd convinced herself she could do it.

The kettle boiled and she pulled down her favorite mug—the one with the sunflowers on it—scooped some orange pekoe tea leaves from the canister into the small sieve, and poured water over them. While she waited for the tea to steep, she spied Tanner's niece and nephew heading up the hill toward the house, the dogs at their heels.

She hadn't seen Tanner since Tuesday, and part of her was relieved. As awful as she'd felt that night, being with him, confiding in him, stirred something in her she wasn't prepared to consider. Had no business even contemplating.

Chances weren't in her favor, but if she did manage to steer clear of crazy, if she ever allowed herself to fall for anyone again, a guy like Tanner Collins would be first on her list. And that scared her more than the thought of not getting well.

Jason barreled through the back door, took one look at her, and stopped in his tracks. "Whoa." He stared down at his soccer cleats and muttered something about coming in for a drink of water.

Jeni was less subtle. "What happened to your hair?"

"Well." Natalie smiled, took her tea to the table. She pulled out a chair and motioned for the little girl to sit next to her. Jason grabbed two bottles of water, gave one to his sister, and perched at the far end of the oak table, veiled curiosity in his eyes. "I thought I needed a new look," Natalie explained. "Had a little run-in with the scissors and it didn't turn out so well."

"Why'd you do it yourself?" Jason wanted to know.

"I figured I could. A bad decision."

"I'll say." The kid was as blunt as his uncle.

"You're still pretty, Miss Natalie." Jeni put a hand on Natalie's arm, her big eyes filled with worry. "Don't be sad."

Natalie nodded, her throat tight. "Thank you, Jeni."

"At least you're not bald. My friend's mom had cancer," Jason said, taking a long swig of water. "She lost all her hair. Bald as a baby. Then she died."

"I'm sorry for your friend." Natalie sipped her tea. Anger marked the boy's features, but she had a feeling it wasn't brought on by the thought of his friend's mother.

"Nan says we shouldn't question when people die before we think they're supposed to." Jeni lifted the lid of the cookie jar and took one out. "Sometimes God has other plans for them."

"Like rotting in the ground? Please. That's a bunch of baloney." Jason grabbed a cookie and shot his sister a glare. She glared right back.

"No, they go to heaven, dummy."

"Yeah, right."

"Do too. Right, Natalie?" Jeni turned to her. Natalie groaned inwardly. She was the last person to be answering these kinds of questions. Where was Laura when she needed her?

"Well, I suppose . . ." The imploring look on the little girl's face did her in. "Of course they do. And I think heaven must be a very peaceful, beautiful place." That sounded convincing.

"If Mommy doesn't get better, she'll go to heaven." Jeni's lower lip began to tremble.

"Shut up, stupid." Jason spewed cookie crumbs and smacked her arm.

"Ow!"

"Hey, what's going on in here?" Tanner strode through the door, eyebrows knit together. He carried a pile of what looked like photo albums.

"Perfect timing," Natalie whispered.

Tanner raised a brow and focused on the kids. "Did I hear you yell at your sister?"

"No, sir." Jason grabbed his water bottle and headed for the back door.

"Don't move, we're not done talking," Tanner growled.

"Uncle Tanner!" Jeni ran to Tanner, tears flowing. "He said Mommy's not going to heaven."

"I did not!"

Tanner put the albums down, picked up his niece, and held her against him. His eyes widened at Jason. "Why would you say something like that?"

"I didn't say that. Not exactly."

"Did too!" Jeni pouted. "And he hit me!"

"Jason?" Tanner's expression darkened and tears welled in the boy's eyes. Natalie suddenly felt sorry for him. For all of them.

"I didn't mean to, I just . . ." Jason's lower lip began to tremble.

"Never mind." Tanner shook his head. "You and I will discuss this later."

"Oh, like you'll actually have time to talk to me? Yeah, right." The dark look he sent Tanner made Natalie cringe.

"Jase, chill out." Tanner waited a moment. Probably counting to ten. Or a hundred. "I know you're miffed because I missed your game."

"We lost anyway."

"Nan said you scored two goals."

"Big whoop." Jason attempted to leave again.

"Hold up." Tanner grabbed the boy's shoulder. "I don't like what just happened in here. And I don't like your tone."

Jason shrugged him off but stayed put, his face thunderous.

Tanner put Jeni down and crouched before her. "I want the two of you to go down to the barn and see what you can do to help Miguel and Iliana get ready for the party tonight." He wiped the little girl's tears.

Jeni sniffed, her smile coming out to play. "Last year I got to help with the flowers. Do you think she'll let me do that again, Uncle Tanner?"

"I think she might." He kissed her on the cheek and straightened. "If you ask nicely and do what she says." Tanner cast a wary glance at his nephew. "You need to help too. I'll be checking up on you."

"Whatever. You're not my father."

Jeni clapped a hand over her mouth and inched toward Natalie.

"What'd you say, Jase?" Tanner rose to full height and loomed over the boy.

"I said you're not my father! He wouldn't tell me what to do!"

Tanner ran a hand down his face, backing up like he'd been slapped. "I'm as close as you're going to get to a father right now, Jason. So don't sass me again."

"That's not true. My dad is coming here to get me. He told me."

"He told you?" Tanner's jaw began to pulse.

Jason nodded, defiance curling his mouth downward.

Natalie sucked in a breath. She took Jeni by the hand and led her to the cupboard where Grandpa hid his secret stash of candy.

"When, exactly, did he tell you that?" Tanner's voice trembled with an edge Natalie hoped the kid would respect.

"Last night. Nan was outside and you were working. I answered the phone."

Natalie slipped a handful of M&M's to Jeni, hoping she hadn't heard.

"Can we go to the barn now?" Jeni skipped over to Tanner and pulled on his hand. He stood ramrod straight, tension oozing from him. "Uncle Tanner?"

"Yeah." He seemed to wake at the sound of her voice, stroked her head, and turned her toward the door. "Off you go."

Jason waited with folded arms.

Tanner nodded, his mouth a grim line. "Go with your sister. We'll talk later." His nephew stomped out the door, calling for the dogs.

Natalie winced at Tanner's heavy sigh. The way he clenched his hands at the base of his neck, his body stiff . . . her heart broke for him.

"For what it's worth, I think you're doing a great job with them."

Tanner turned her way. "Did you hear what he said? He talked to Rance. How dare that man call the house and talk to Jason without my permission!"

Natalie poured coffee into a mug and handed it to him. "Apparently he doesn't think he needs your permission."

"I'll set him straight on that."

"Tanner." She dropped into a chair, measuring his anger. "Do you or your mother have legal custody of the kids?"

He sipped and stared out the back door. "No. We don't." His voice caught and he cleared his throat. He joined her at the table and put his head in his hands. "You know, I'm pretty sure there's a verse in the Bible that talks about God not giving us more than we can handle."

"I just said that to my friend Laura yesterday." Natalie smiled at the coincidence. "But she claims it really means He doesn't give us any more than *He* can handle."

A trace of a smile tilted Tanner's lips. "Maybe we should introduce Laura to my friend David."

"David?" Natalie frowned. "The same David you hung out with when I used to visit?"

"The very one. Except he's a pastor now. Puts me to sleep practically every Sunday."

"You're kidding." That was surprising. "He was shyer than I was."

"Not anymore. Just mention Jesus and he'll yak your ears right off." A grin whipped across his face. "But he's still pretty cool."

"I'm sure. Well, Laura is married. She does have a younger sister, Stacey, who is equally enthusiastic about all things Jesus."

"Let's do it." Tanner's eyes sparked. "Maybe it'll get his nose out of my love life."

Natalie flushed under his stare.

"Not that I have one. Anyway." Tanner nodded toward the books. "I brought those old albums for you. My mother thought you might want to have a look."

Natalie didn't. But Sarah wouldn't know that. "Thanks." Tanner was staring again, trying hard not to, and she remembered her hair. Their eyes played tag a minute before she decided to put him out of his misery. "Attractive, I know." She ran a hand over her head. "I'm debating a buzz cut. I'm not sure it's salvageable." She tapped her fingers on the box of the kit she'd placed on the table earlier.

His eyes widened but no words came. Great. She'd rendered the man speechless.

"You did that to yourself?"

"A lapse in good judgment. Any idea how this thing works?"

Tanner reached for the kit and lifted the lid. "You weren't serious about the buzz cut."

Natalie shrugged. "How hard can it be? Buzz, buzz, buzz. All done."

He quirked a brow and pushed up the sleeves of his blue Henley. She watched him exhale a long breath, then he picked up the black cape she'd pulled from the cupboard as well. "In good conscience, I'm afraid I can't let you do that. Come with me."

"What?" Natalie wanted to laugh, but his expression was so serious she didn't dare. He was already heading for the door with the scissors. "Where are you going?"

"Outside. Barstools. Let's go, I don't have all day."

"You think I'm going to let you cut my hair?" Laughter shot from her mouth as she shook her head. "Absolutely not."

"Because you did such a good job?" A smile simmered and lit his eyes. "I cut Jason's hair all the time. I know what I'm doing. Trust me."

Jason's hair hadn't been cut for a while. And as far as trusting him . . .

"If this is your warped way of trying to get back at me for my father's threat to put you out of a job . . ."

"Seriously? That's about the stupidest thing I've ever heard you say. Well, apart from that time you told me I looked like some dude from the Backstreet Boys."

"I don't think that was me." Natalie walked on wobbly legs behind him to the patio. "Nic was always saying dumb stuff like that."

"Yeah. Pretty sure it was you though." His chuckle floated around her as she positioned herself on a stool at the stone bar and he fastened the cape around her neck. "I remember it quite well, you see, because it was right after I kissed you."

A squeak of protest stuck in her throat. Okay, this was not happening. "You say trust me, then bring that up? Forget it." She attempted to get down, but he was too quick for her.

Tanner rounded the stool, held her arms, and took her eyes prisoner. "Do you want to know what really happened that summer?"

"No." Natalie swallowed as Tanner rolled his eyes. "Okay, fine."

A half smile played on his lips. "Whatever your sister may have told you, she was the one coming after me. I told her I wasn't interested. I kissed you because I wanted to, Natalie. I liked you. A lot. Now you know."

Heat raced through her veins and lit fire to her face. "She said you kissed her."

"Never happened."

"But you wrote me that note. You said you were sorry."

Tanner let out a groan. "I said I was sorry because I thought maybe I'd been out of line for kissing you. You looked so . . . shocked. Whatever, Natalie. We were kids. It was years ago. So can we just put it to rest?"

"Absolutely." She'd like nothing better. "You brought it up."

"I did." His smile brought a bit of humor to his eyes. "But your response intimated that we should clear the air."

"Intimated. Now that's a big word."

"I have a plethora of them in my back pocket." Tanner examined the scissors, snapped them open and closed a couple times. "These look sharp enough. Are we done with this conversation?"

"Definitely done." Natalie nodded. "And just so you know, I haven't spent all these years pining for you."

"Well, that's a relief." Tanner stood behind her, then cupped his hands around the back of her head and gave a gentle push. "Sit like that and don't move until I tell you."

"You really liked me?"

Muted laughter came from behind. "I thought we were done. Keep still."

"You're not just saying it to make me feel better?"

His hand stilled. "I think that razor probably still works pretty well. How do you feel about a Mohawk, Mouse?"

Natalie grinned and kept quiet. And very still.

Fifteen minutes later, she stared into the handheld mirror he'd brought her.

Somehow, Tanner had worked a miracle. She'd resigned herself to being bald by the time he was done cutting and snipping. Instead, he'd given her an almost attractive, albeit fairly short, hairstyle. She'd always had shoulder-length hair, but she kind of liked the shorter look. Might even get used to it.

"How did you do that?"

"Dumb luck, I guess." He pulled the cape from her and shook it, sending bits of hair flying across the bushes. "You'll look just fine for the harvest celebration tonight."

"Oh. That." She'd never been here for the big party, but her grandparents always ranked it right up there with Christmas. Grandpa Hal had invited her to come tonight, but let her know it was okay if she wasn't feeling up to it. "I wasn't planning on going."

"You weren't?" Either her imagination was playing tricks or he sounded slightly disappointed. "Are you still feeling lousy?"

"Just not all that fond of parties." Natalie watched him pack up the box and fold the cape. She stretched her arms above her head and worked the kinks out of her neck. "You know if this wine-making thing doesn't work out, you could open your own salon in town. What could we call it? Oh, I know: Tanner's Tresses. I'm sure you'd do a booming business."

Tanner stared like she'd lost her mind, then his face cracked into a smile.

A real, honest-to-goodness, gorgeous smile that warmed her all the way through and made her stomach flip.

"Tanner's Tresses, huh? I'll keep it in mind." He brushed a hand across her shoulder. "Just a few stray hairs." His hand moved to rest under her chin. Natalie was helpless to do more than stare at him as he turned her head to one side, then the other. "Not bad if I do say so myself."

"Thank you." Stupid tears pricked and she blinked them away.

"It was just a haircut." His cheeks darkened.

She sniffed and nodded. It was so much more. But she couldn't tell him that. Couldn't tell him that something had awakened her sleeping soul and brought a breath of fresh air to her mundane existence. And she couldn't tell him that for the first time in what felt like forever, she wanted to live.

"What time is this hoedown tonight?"

His dimple flashed as he stepped away from her. "It's not a hoedown. David kicks things off around five with the blessing."

"Okay. We'll see." She maneuvered her way off the wooden stool.

"Hey. Wait a sec." He caught her hand in his.

Natalie blinked in surprise, taking in Tanner's solemn look. "What's wrong? Did you cut my ear off?"

"No. Your ears are intact. But . . ." His smile faded. "I owe you an apology." Tanner let her go and folded his arms. "I'm sorry for acting like a jerk when you got here. I'm pretty stressed with things right now, with the winery, the kids, but that's no excuse for bad manners."

"Apology accepted." She smiled at the relief that crept into his eyes. A fierce desire to help him de-stress came over her. And that was so not a good idea. In fact, as she weighed her options, it would be so much better if he'd continue being that jerk.

"So you'll come tonight?" he asked. "To the party?"

No jerk in sight. She was dealing with Tanner the Nice Guy now.

Natalie retreated to the kitchen and poured herself a glass of water. His heavy steps followed her. "If you promise me I look presentable enough to appear in public, I'll come to the party." She turned to find him a few feet behind her.

"Good. It will mean a lot to Hal. And you do. Look presentable." His grin wasn't totally comforting. "You know sometimes you sound like a walking dictionary, right?"

"I definitively do not." She prepared to protest, but gave up and laughed at herself. "Well, perhaps I do, at times." She put her hands on her hips and tipped her head. "I might could throw a little slang in now an' again, whachoosay?"

His grin widened and gave way to laughter. "Maybe you should stick with the familiar. Wouldn't want people thinking you're over-fermented or anything."

"Goodness, no." She drained the glass and set it in the sink. "I suppose I should take advantage of the fact that I actually feel normal today." She opened the dishwasher and put a few clean dishes away. Tanner stepped over to help and they soon completed the task.

"Okay, I gotta get going." He picked up his keys from the kitchen table. "When is your next appointment in San Francisco?"

"This Wednesday. I go every week." Natalie tried to keep surprise out of her voice. "Why?"

He shrugged and pulled at his jaw. "I have some things I need to do in the city. I'll drive you."

"You'll drive me? Tanner, that's really not necessary."

"Because driving yourself worked out so well the last time?"

What was he up to? "Okay, you've apologized. You can stop being nice. If you didn't know about my problems, you'd still be throwing darts at my photograph."

"Probably." He pulled on a pair of shades and jangled his keys as he headed for the door. "But I'm really not being nice." He glanced over his shoulder, inched his shades down to reveal eyes spiked with mischief. "I've just always wanted to drive a Jag."

Sixteen

It was just after noon by the time Tanner summoned the nerve to actually get out of his truck and walk across the parking lot of the acute care facility.

He hated this place. Hated coming here. Hated the smell. Hated the looks of pity on the faces he passed at the nurses' station. Hated that Marnie was in here.

Most of all he hated that she wouldn't be leaving.

"Tanner. Whoa. Where's the fire?"

He jerked his head up as he banged shoulders with the guy whose voice he so did not want to hear right now. Typical.

"Did my mother tell you where to find me?"

"What?" David Grearson took two steps back and tipped his head. "I haven't talked to your mother since last Sunday, Tanner. I was visiting a member of my congregation."

"And Marnie?"

David shrugged and pitched a smile. "I always pop in to pray with her when I'm here."

"Why?" Tanner shoved his hands into his pockets. "She's brain-dead. It's not like she'll hear you."

"Maybe not, but God can hear me just fine."

"Then He's not listening. Because for all the prayers going up around here, my sister should have jumped out of that bed and walked out the doors of this place weeks ago."

"Tanner." David's expression softened. "Why don't I wait for you? We can grab lunch afterward."

"So you can drone on about how this is all God's will, whether we like it or not, and we have to accept it because He knows best and, what else, oh yeah, not my fault. You all like that one too."

David pulled up the zipper of his beige Windbreaker and looked toward the parking lot. "Actually, I was kind of hoping we could talk chicks and basketball."

"Right." Tanner almost smiled. "Kinda busy, though. Harvest celebration tonight."

"Uh-huh. And I know they don't let you do much down there until it starts, Hal's orders. So what's your next excuse?"

Tanner looked away. Sorrow clogged his throat, made him want to gag. Coming here somehow dislodged the cork he'd wedged so firmly into the bottle that housed his emotions. He fought it for a minute, then gave up. "Dude . . ."

David had been his best friend since fourth grade. They'd played on almost every team together. Gone to camp together. Worked the vines together. Found their faith together.

David's faith stuck. Tanner's . . . well, his was on hiatus. But David never wavered in their friendship. He'd been right there since Marnie's accident, whether Tanner wanted him to be or not.

Tanner swallowed the burn in his throat, ignored the wet in his eyes. "I don't think I can do this."

His friend nodded. "I know you don't. But you can." David flung an arm around his shoulder and positioned him toward the front doors. "We'll do it together."

⌒

After a while, David left Tanner alone with Marnie.

Tanner barely noticed his friend slipping out the door. The moment he walked into Marnie's room, it got hard to breathe. Hard to see.

The pale blue walls of the small, comfortable but sterile room closed in on him. A shelf opposite her bed held teddy bears and countless cards, letters from the kids, and Jeni's carefully colored creations tacked to a bulletin board.

The first couple weeks, the flowers kept coming. After a month, they stopped. A couple weeks later, no more cards. No more calls from well-intentioned individuals wondering if there was anything at all they could do.

There wasn't.

Tanner stood at the foot of the bed and stared at his sister, hoping somehow she'd wake up and tell him to quit giving her the stink eye the way she used to when they were kids.

The day after the accident, their father showed up. Full of excuses for Rance of course, why he couldn't get here, would they be okay with the kids? Tanner almost lost it at that point. Who exactly did his dad think had been looking after the kids the past few years when Marnie went off her meds, disappeared for days?

She looked exactly the same as when he'd last seen her. That visit had taken so much out of him he swore he'd never come back. The doctor had talked to them that day, showed them the latest round of tests, told them the brutal truth, and asked if they were any closer to making a decision.

They hadn't been. Now it had been two months with Marnie like this. Tanner wondered if he'd pressured Mom too much, dragging this out. But he'd held on to hope, wishing for what he knew now was the impossible.

And once Marnie was gone, they'd have to deal with Rance. Loser, poor excuse for a man, and a bunch of other descriptives Tanner attached to his sister's ex. If that louse thought for one minute he'd show up now and take Jason and Jeni away, he had another thing coming. Tanner was ready for that fight.

"Hey, you." He stood at the end of Marnie's bed and curled his fingers around the blanket covering the top of her foot. Squeezed. No reaction. He rounded the bed, pulled up a chair, and took his sister's limp hand in his. "Whatever happens, I'll take care of the kids, Marn. I promise."

The steady beeps of the life support machine and the slow sucking sound of the intubation tube filled the room, pressed down hard, closed around his throat as though to take his life in exchange for hers. Tanner worked at regulating his own breathing and noticed a few gray strands in Marnie's dark hair.

She would be thirty this year. Early December. When he was younger, he'd always hated her birthday because he was never allowed to stay for the parties. Not that he would ever admit wanting to. Of course, he got to hang out with Dad, which was cool. They'd go to a ball game or go fishing, sometimes go-karting. And pizza. Always pizza. When they got home, Marnie presented him with a slice of whichever flavor cake she'd picked that year on a paper plate that matched the theme of the party. Usually it was stupid flower power stuff or Barbie. But cake was cake, and she always saved the biggest piece for him.

And then, the year she turned twelve, their world turned upside down.

Dad left without warning. And took Marnie with him.

We have to go, bud," his dad said, his eyes bleary, like he'd been up all night. There were suitcases by the front door.

"Why? Why can't I come too? Why aren't we all going?" They'd awakened him early, he was tired, and he didn't understand. But his dad kept insisting it was for the best, that he had to get Marnie to a special doctor. And it had to be now.

Tanner, still in his pajamas, raced down the driveway in bare feet, screaming at the car to stop. It didn't. Eventually he sank to *his knees, tears coming harder and faster than his breath. "Come back!" It was a final attempt and it didn't work.*

"Tanner, stop. She's gone, sweetheart." Mom sneaked up from behind, wrapped him up tight, and hugged hard. "They're both gone."

His mother's explanation later that morning didn't make sense to him at ten years old, but who was he to argue?

He fell asleep that night, bereft, bewildered, and broken, calling Marnie's name.

And woke up screaming it.

"I don't want to lose you again, sis," he rasped, hot tears pooling. "It was hard enough the first time."

"You never lost me."

It was one of the first real conversations they'd had since Marnie showed up in Sonoma, two kids in tow, the year he came on board at Maoilios.

Mom had been a little wary, happy to see the kids of course. Tanner watched their interactions with muted curiosity. He wasn't quite sure how to react. What to say to this sister he hadn't had much contact with for the last thirteen years of his life.

She cornered him one evening, dragged him out onto Mom's back patio, opened a bottle of wine, and they'd finally talked.

"You never lost me, Tanner," Marnie said again, probably because he wasn't looking at her so she didn't know if he was paying attention. "It was for the best. I needed help. Dad knew that."

"What kind of help?"

"It doesn't matter now," Marnie told him. "What matters is how we go on from here." He remembered her out-of-control tantrums. Remembered her expulsion from school. Remembered

Mom and Dad fighting over her escalating bizarre behavior. Then they were gone.

His dad kept calling, kept asking Tanner to visit them in Seattle once he and his mom moved back to California. He never went. Never understood why things happened the way they had.

And somehow, over the years, Tanner placed the blame for their severed relationship squarely on his father's shoulders.

Had it really been five years since his sister breezed back into his life? When she'd shown up in Sonoma, he saw the extent of her problems resulting from her bipolar. Saw how his mother still couldn't deal with Marnie, seemed almost afraid of her.

When she accepted the help they offered, kept her doctor's appointments, and took her medication, Marnie functioned well. She was great with the kids, got a job teaching piano to a handful of students, and the last couple years Tanner was hopeful that his sister had a shot at normalcy.

But then something shifted, set her off on a course of self-destruction, and the last year before her accident, they lived with an out-of-control and often absent Marnie. He still thanked God she never took off with the kids. Somehow he and his mom had managed to give his niece and nephew the stability they needed. But now their world would be upended again.

David returned, squeezed his shoulder. Tanner dried his eyes. Didn't move while David prayed, just stared at the figure in the bed, still beautiful, still breathing, but gone.

Once again without his permission.

Later, they sat in one of Tanner's favorite burger joints. Eventually he and David edged toward normal conversation. He filled his friend in about Natalie Mitchell's unexpected arrival, and the revelations the last few weeks had brought.

"Wow, I haven't seen Natalie since that summer. You must have been surprised to see her." David poked a fry in a pile of ketchup and studied Tanner with that bland expression he was so good at producing when need be.

Tanner sipped his Coke and studied a poster of Elvis. "You could say that."

"I'd like to come by and say hello. Do you think she'd be okay with that?"

Tanner shoved the last of his cheeseburger in his mouth. "I have no idea what Natalie is okay with. She's a little hard to read."

David tossed a pile of paper napkins his way. "I'm sure your mother taught you not to talk with your mouth full. Hard to read like how?"

"I don't know, she's just like . . . quiet, I guess."

"And you've been your usual charming self?"

Tanner scowled, "I don't do charming."

David simply smiled. "From what you've told me, it sounds to me like Miss Natalie might need a friend."

"Be my guest." Tanner swiped a handful of fries off David's plate.

"You live closer." David pulled his plate back. "I wasn't done with those."

"Natalie and I can't be friends. Her father wants to put me out of a job," Tanner reminded David . . . and himself. "Huge conflict of interest there."

"She must be pretty."

"What?" After he'd finished decimating her hair this morning, Tanner figured she'd never speak to him again. But she'd liked it. And it hadn't looked that bad. He'd shocked himself. Been even more shocked by the way her smile made him want to stare at her all day. "She's all right."

"And smart."

"Harvard Business School." Tanner was slowly beginning to realize she wasn't the elitist snob he'd pegged her for.

"And good with the kids, right?"

"She hasn't spent much time with them. She could hate kids for all I know." He remembered Natalie sitting at the piano with Jeni. The way she'd taken her aside this morning when he and Jase got into it . . .

"We done here, David?" He reached for a paper napkin and wiped his mouth.

"Ah-ha."

Tanner wagged his fork at his friend. "No."

"Pretty, smart, and loves kids. And you're running as fast as you can in the opposite direction."

"I'm not running anywhere," Tanner growled, fully aware that David knew his MO too well. "Stop looking for things that aren't there. You're worse than my mother."

"Sure there aren't any leftover sparks?" David waggled his brows. "You were pretty interested in her the last summer she was here."

"I was fifteen, dude. I grew up. You should give it a try."

"When's the last time you went out on a date?"

"I saw Theresa last week." Tanner fiddled with his watch.

"Theresa, your dental hygienist?"

"We had a date. I showed up, she cleaned my teeth. Boom."

"Collins, you're a lost cause."

Tanner slurped the rest of his shake. "Want me to take Candy out again?"

"Please, no." David choked on his Coke. "That is not the woman for you, my friend, much as she'd like to be. Surely there are more suitable candidates in the vicinity?"

"Want to take a look at my schedule? I don't exactly sit around twiddling my thumbs all day. What little time I have to myself I usually spend paying bills or attempting sleep. I have no time for a relationship, even if I wanted one."

"And what about your relationship with God?" David sat back. "Got time for that lately?"

"Ah, here I was, actually enjoying your company." Tanner shook his head.

"Just asking. It is what I do, after all."

"What happened to talking chicks and basketball?"

"We've exhausted both subjects." David's keen gaze seared him. "Which brings us around to God. But maybe we've done enough talking for one day."

"Yeah. You know where I stand with God right now. Nothing has changed." Especially not with the threat of Rance Harper hanging over his head. But he didn't want to discuss that either.

David's look of pity made Tanner want to slide under the table.

Tanner refused to feel guilty. He went to church. For all intents and purposes, he was an upstanding Christian who could amen along with the best of them.

But David knew the real story.

Knew Tanner had put God up on a shelf.

Left Him there the night of Marnie's accident.

"This was great, but I need to get going." Tanner pushed his chair back.

David glanced at his cell. "Is Natalie coming to the harvest celebration tonight?"

"Says she is. Oh, Hal wants you there early. Like you really need a sound check. You're praying, not giving a rock concert."

"I'll be there on time." David stood and grabbed his jacket. "You coming to church tomorrow?"

"Don't I always come?"

David's smile said more than he probably meant it to. "You

come for the kids. If you actually stayed awake during one of my sermons you might get a bit more out of it."

"If you actually gave a sermon worth listening to, I might not fall asleep so easy."

"Ouch." David put a hand to his heart. "I was about to offer to pay for lunch."

"All right, all right." Tanner laughed and waved a hand. "Save your money. This is on me. Let me spend my hard-earned cash while I'm still making it."

Seventeen

NATALIE SMOOTHED HER BANGS AND BRUSHED HER SHINING short hair one more time, added a bit more blush to her cheeks, and scowled at her reflection in the mirror. She was no runway model, never had been, but she'd never worried about scaring old people and small children when she walked down the street.

She'd picked a white cotton sundress with a Kelly-green cardigan, Grandpa Hal's favorite color. She'd debated on the dress, not really sure what people wore to this thing, but in the end she figured it was fine.

"Natalie, you ready, honey?" Grandpa's yell startled her and she blew out a breath. Ready or not.

"Well, don't you look lovely," he said as she came downstairs. She followed him out the front door and stopped short.

"Grandpa!" A bubble of glee burst from her and she clapped a hand to her mouth. "We're taking the wagon?" She was slightly aware that she sounded like a kid on Christmas morning.

The old wagon was parked at the foot of the steps, two black Morgan horses impatiently pawing the ground. Sarah, Jeni, and Jason waved to her from the back. Tanner sat up front, reins in hand.

"C'mon, Miss Natalie, we're waiting!" Jeni called.

"Surprise, darlin'." Grandpa laughed, pushing her forward.

In the past, Grandpa used the wagon a lot. He'd taken them for long rides, driven them and however many kids could fit, into town or just meandered down the country roads, leading them all in songs he'd sing at the top of his lungs. Back home, Grandma waited with ice-cold lemonade and cookies fresh out of the oven.

When was the last time she rode in the wagon? Probably when she was about thirteen. But . . . she remembered now . . . she hadn't.

"I want to drive! Grandpa, let me have the reins." Nicole was already marching to the front of the wagon, her jaw set. Natalie shot Tanner a despairing look. He shrugged and watched her sister hop up next to their grandfather.

"Let's go." Tanner nudged Natalie's shoulder with his and started walking down the road.

"Tanner! Where are you going?" Nicole's petulant cry punched through the air like a hawk about to pounce on its prey.

"Walking. I don't trust you in charge of those horses. You'll tip the whole thing over."

"'Bye, Nic!" Natalie grinned, stuck her tongue out at her sister, and ran to catch up with Tanner.

Natalie left the memory behind as her grandfather helped her maneuver the step, and Sarah assisted her to a seat near the front. "There you go, honey. Take that blanket in case you get cold." Sarah settled back down. Jeni scooched next to Natalie.

"D'ya like my new dress? I got it special for tonight. Nan let me pick it." Her grin was wide as she pulled at the blue and orange polka-dotted cotton material to show it off.

"It's beautiful, Jeni." Natalie smiled back. She was too cute. "This is fun, huh? When I was your age, we used to do it a lot."

The scent of straw tickled her nose, conjuring up more childhood memories. The afternoon sun crested the hills around the house and a gentle breeze kissed her warm cheeks.

Tanner glanced back at them. Natalie noted his neatly combed hair, pressed white button-down untucked over his jeans, and almost clean-shaven jaw, and felt her stomach do a little twirl.

For crying out loud.

Her cheeks heated and she figured he'd bust out laughing any second. But he didn't. He held her gaze, his eyes hinting at interest she didn't dare contemplate. It was more probable that he was wondering if riding in the wagon might bring on another flashback.

"You can quit staring. I'm not going to jump out and run away screaming. Although you are driving, so you never can tell."

He shot her a wink and faced front again. "Watch out for corners."

Hal hoisted himself up beside Tanner. "Concentrate on the road, son. Least until we get there." He chuckled and gave Tanner a nudge.

Natalie rolled her eyes and stared at her painted toenails sticking out the top of her white sandals. If this was her grandfather's way of pushing her and Tanner together, it was going to be a long night.

⌒

The thought of Tanner's eyes on her wouldn't leave her alone. Perhaps her pitiful attempt at looking presentable hadn't worked. She couldn't hide the sallow cheeks and shadows beneath her eyes. She'd only pretended it was possible.

But what did it matter? Tanner Collins wasn't interested in her.

Natalie laughed at herself. Maybe the fact that she just might want him to be meant she was getting better.

Or crazier.

The area outside the barn was crowded with workers and friends, and the inside was beautifully decorated. She walked the perimeter, taking note of the fairy lights that tiptoed down the beams. Flowers in mason jars hung from various positions along the wood walls. Sunflowers, dried lavender, and daisies—all her grandmother's favorites. Straw lay strewn across the floor and food tables were set up around large oak barrels with the Maoilios emblem burned across them. On top of the barrels sat this year's offerings.

Natalie picked up the bottles in turn and studied them. A Chardonnay, a Malbec, a rich looking Cab, and a Syrah. That was new. From her study of Maoilios's previous years, they did well with their Chardonnays each year, but the recent best seller was the Cabernet.

Outside, people milled around, chatting. A band was setting up on the lawn near a makeshift dance floor. She watched her grandfather shaking hands and talking with a few guests. His health improved daily and Natalie hoped he wouldn't have any more issues. She had enough for both of them.

"David's about ready to start." Tanner's voice startled her.

"Oh. The blessing of the grapes thing?" Natalie popped a piece of cheese in her mouth and moved away from the food.

"No." He smiled and wrapped a warm hand around her wrist. "The blessing of the wine. And you need to come up front. I'll be calling on you in a minute."

"You'll what?" Natalie squeaked. He maneuvered her through the crowd until they stood in front of the bandstand.

"Stay there." Tanner jumped onto the bandstand and stood between her grandfather and a man she recognized as David Grearson.

"Evening, everyone." Tanner's deep tenor cut through the noise and silenced the crowd. He cleared his throat and rubbed the back of his neck, a nervous habit she remembered him doing years ago. He clutched the mic in his other hand. "Hard to believe another year has passed, huh? We . . . uh . . ." He seemed to be struggling for words and cleared his throat again. "We have a lot to be thankful for tonight." He gave a hoarse laugh. "You all know I hate doing this, I don't know why he makes me." He sent Hal a sheepish smile.

"Well, this year hasn't been easy, for a lot of reasons. But I think it might turn out to be one of our better years, despite the odds." The crowd murmured their agreement. Tanner waited a moment.

"After David prays, we're going to have a special guest come up and do the honors of the first taste. Some of you might remember Hal's granddaughter, Natalie Mitchell. It's been a long time since she's visited Maoilios. I don't think she's ever been here for harvest, but hey, first time for everything, right? Come join us, Natalie." Tanner handed the microphone to David, his eyes locked on her.

Natalie made her feet move forward. She found herself positioned between Tanner and Grandpa Hal while David began the blessing.

She pushed down an unexpected lump in her throat as David prayed, looked up, and found Tanner watching her. "Remind me to kill you later," she whispered.

The corners of his eyes crinkled. "Hal's idea. I tried to talk him out of it."

"Not hard enough, obviously."

"Sorry. Hope you have your dancing shoes on because that's next."

Natalie shot him a look. "You better be kidding."

"As Tanner said"—David's voice rose a little—"we have much to be thankful for tonight." He put great emphasis on Tanner's name and Natalie squashed a giggle.

"Not kidding." Tanner waggled his brows.

"Stop. You're joking right?" she whispered back.

Tanner bowed his head and crossed his arms. "You know we're supposed to be praying, right Mouse?"

"Yeah, you better pray." Natalie scowled and shut her eyes.

When David finished, he marched up to them like they were in high school, about to get detention for disrupting the class.

"Sorry." Natalie offered an apologetic smile. She remembered him to be kind, quiet, with a dry sense of humor that caught you off guard.

And now he was a pastor, apparently.

"I think you're up." David walked behind her as Hal moved to the table where the wine sat and indicated she join him.

Natalie performed the obligatory tasting, said a few words that she couldn't remember later, and tried to make good her escape while the band set up.

"Oh no you don't." Tanner blocked her path. "You're the guest of honor. You'll dance with your grandfather, then you'll dance with me. Then you can go."

If he was kidding, it wasn't funny. "I don't dance."

Tanner frowned. "A debutante that doesn't dance? I find that hard to believe."

"Okay, fine, but I don't enjoy it." This was ridiculous. "Why must I dance with you?"

"Because I'm the vintner. It's tradition." Tanner mirrored her scowl. "You don't have to make it sound like a punishment. I promise not to step on your toes."

Natalie blew a frustrated breath and marched off to wait with her grandfather. Sure enough, once the band began to play, Grandpa grabbed her hand and whisked her onto the dance floor.

"I'm so glad you're here for this, Natalie Grace." His eyes sparkled as they moved smoothly across the floor to a slow country tune.

"Me too." She remembered him dancing with her grandmother one night when they'd gone to a fancy hotel for dinner, recalled the way everyone had stood back to watch and then clapped when they were finished.

"Outside of Christmas, this was your grandmother's favorite night of the year."

"It's wonderful." Natalie's heart jumped as she caught sight of

Tanner waiting nearby. "I'm glad I could be here." If they could just skip the next part, that would be even better.

But there was no escape. As soon as the next song started, Grandpa handed her over to Tanner with a broad smile.

"Haven't seen the old guy this happy in a stretch." Tanner held her hand in his, the other around her waist. "He's really enjoying having you around."

"I guess so." She gripped his shoulder and followed his steps. This couldn't get any more awkward. To her surprise, Tanner knew what he was doing on the dance floor. "You've done this before."

"A few times. Your grandmother taught me. Relax and at least pretend you're enjoying yourself, would you?" Tanner attempted a crooked smile. "You're stiff as a board."

"Sorry, I haven't danced in a while." Not since her engagement party. But that didn't bear thinking about. She forced herself to loosen up a bit in his arms and allowed him to lead.

"Better." He pulled her a little closer. "But that fake smile you're wearing makes you look like you just had a round of Botox."

"Really?" Natalie positioned the kitten heel of her sandal above the toe of his deck shoe and brought it down hard.

"Ow! Crap, Natalie." His eyes widened, but a grin got away.

"Told you, I'm out of practice." She set a sweet smile on him. "And you should be more careful with your compliments."

After a few more awkward minutes, the dance was over and he let her go. "Now that wasn't too terrible, was it?"

"I suppose not." Truthfully, she rather enjoyed it. But she wasn't about to tell him that. She headed for the barn.

Food. She needed food. Maybe some wine too.

"Are you going to eat?" Tanner sidled up beside her, hands deep in the pockets of his blue jeans.

"I'm thinking about it." Natalie released a shaky breath. Why was he following her? "It smells good, but I'm not sure what I can handle." She surveyed the long picnic tables almost buckling under a foray of culinary delights. Mounds of ribs and chicken, huge bowls of coleslaw, potato salad, mixed greens, bean salad, even shrimp, oysters, and mussels. No clams. "Maybe I'll wait a bit." People moved past them, eager to begin the meal.

Tanner grabbed a plate and she watched him make a few selections from the feast. When he returned, he presented the plate to her. "Here. The chicken isn't spicy. The rice and beans have a bite but they're good, coleslaw is amazing, and if all else fails, that green Jell-O should go down pretty easy."

Natalie met his anxious eyes and smiled. "Thanks." She was suddenly hungry. "That's suspiciously thoughtful of you. What do you want?"

He narrowed his eyes. "I thought we were calling a truce."

"Well, that would be fine with me."

"Good. I'll be right back."

After he got his own plate, they found a spot at one of the tables. She washed down her meal with a bottle of water and glanced around while Tanner made short work of the biggest mound of food she'd seen in a while. She didn't doubt he'd go back for seconds.

Natalie looked around again, the twinkling lights in the trees catching her eye. And then the idea popped like the cork from a champagne bottle. "Oh. Tanner. Weddings."

He glanced up, practically choking on his last mouthful of potato salad. "Excuse me?"

Natalie laughed and waved a hand. Everything started to take shape in her mind. "This venue. The barn. It's perfect for weddings. There's a huge market for barn settings. I can't imagine why, but there you go. Brides will be beating down the doors."

Skepticism settled over his face. "Really? A wedding in a barn? Well. That's an idea, I guess. How do you know so much about weddings?" He blanched and looked away. "Sorry. Forgot."

"Oh, please." Natalie feigned nonchalance. "I'm over it, really. Peter wasn't the guy for me. End of story."

"What is the story?" Tanner pushed his empty plate away and propped his elbows, resting his chin on his hands. "If you don't mind me asking." Topaz eyes mesmerized her, made her want to tell him all her secrets.

"Not much of one. He came across a better opportunity."

"Come again?" His brow furrowed.

Natalie shrugged. Her former fiancé hadn't infringed on her thoughts in quite some time. She wasn't sure she wanted him here tonight. Not when she was just starting to have a good time. "He found someone else. While we were still engaged." The daughter of an oil baron. With more money than her father could ever dream of making, and that was saying something.

He leaned back in his chair and gave a long whistle. "And this happened when?"

"Don't miss much, do you?" She studied her fingers a minute, waiting for the tremors. Her hands were steady. No shakes. Natalie let her breath out in a slow exhale. "At the beginning of June. I'd been working long hours. Working on a few projects, starting to make mistakes. I'd been having nightmares again. I suppose I wasn't paying Peter that much attention. One night I came home early from a business trip, thought I'd go over to his apartment and surprise him. He was surprised all right. So was I." Surprised, shocked, dumbfounded. And then decimated. "A couple days afterward, everything crashed. I was in my office working on a presentation, and suddenly I was on the road, staring at a flipped Jeep, Nicole laying facedown in a pool of blood."

"I can't believe your parents didn't see what was going on," Tanner said.

Natalie shrugged. "I think they have their suspicions. I did a good job of avoiding them all summer, covering it up with my dad at the office. They assumed I'd just taken the breakup with Peter rather badly. Truthfully, I'm not sure they'd be terribly helpful if they did know."

How was she so calm? No tears or tremors? Her food wasn't threatening to reappear. Natalie studied Tanner's serious expression and wrestled with the truth.

He gave her strength.

Whether he knew it or not. Whether she liked it or not.

He'd always had that effect on her.

Natalie broke his gaze and stared at her plate. No. She wouldn't fall into that trap again. She didn't need Tanner Collins.

She didn't need anyone.

The touch of a hand over hers made her look up.

Tanner looked at her through serious eyes as he gave her hand a squeeze. "I'm sorry, Mouse."

"Thanks." She gave his hand a pat with her other hand. A friendly, sisterly pat. One that said *thanks for being a good pal.*

"How'd you wind up with someone like that anyway? He sounds like a real piece of work."

Natalie smiled and sipped water. "Peter and I grew up together. Our parents ran in the same circles. My father liked him, my mother thought he could walk on water, and I, well, I guess I thought we were a good match."

"A good match?" Tanner sputtered. "You were willing to spend the rest of your life with someone on the basis of him being 'a good match'?"

Natalie grinned at his astounded expression. "People get married for the wrong reasons all the time. Been doing it for years."

"I wouldn't." He leaned in and captured her with his eyes. "If I ever get married, and that's a big *if*, it will be because I've found the one person in this crazy world who really gets me. The one I'd want to go to bed with at night and wake up for in the morning.

Someone who keeps me sane, makes me laugh, and knows what I'm going to say before I say it. And I'd know, without a doubt, that she felt the same way about me."

Natalie stared at this sweet and surprisingly romantic man who'd taken over Tanner Collins's body when she wasn't looking. "For someone who says they're not interested in marriage, you've given this a lot of thought."

"Those are my terms." His mouth curled attractively before sliding into a frown. "But the older I get, the more convinced I become that I'm better off alone."

"Or maybe you just haven't found the right someone yet."

"Not really looking." He shrugged and sat back, drumming his fingers on the table. "You think it's possible? For two people to live entirely separate lives, suddenly find each other, and realize they haven't been complete until that moment?"

"Kismet."

Tanner's brows nearly touched his hairline. "Did you just say 'kiss me'?"

Unexpected, uncontrollable laughter tumbled from her in waves and there wasn't a thing she could do to stop it. Finally she sobered and gave herself a shake. "No, silly. KIS-MET. What you're talking about. It means fate. Destiny. And no, I don't believe in it."

"Kismet, huh?" He undid his watch and rubbed the top of his wrist. His tanned skin created a perfect outline. Tanner fastened the strap again, shooting her a curious glance. "Do you believe in God, Natalie?"

"Ah." The question didn't surprise her. She could pull conversations from memory where they'd argued over faith and the existence of God—a loving father who watched over them, and guided them through life—Natalie could never get her head around it. Not when her own father held her at arm's length most of the time, dictated and controlled, and didn't seem capable of loving anything other than his bank account.

Tanner never tried to persuade her to share his faith, yet on some level, she always wished she had. "Essentially, I suppose so. But if God is up there plotting out every moment of our lives, He's not doing a great job."

He nodded. "I've done my share of questioning lately. But I have to admit, when it comes down to it, I'd rather have faith than nothing. God doesn't decide for us; He lets us make choices. It's just sometimes we make really bad ones."

"What bad choices have you made, Tanner?"

"Well . . ." His stare was so intense that Natalie was almost afraid to hear the answer.

"Tanner! Yoo-hoo!" A female voice diverted their attention. A willowy blonde headed toward them, followed by a frazzled looking David Grearson.

Tanner got to his feet and met them halfway. Natalie watched the woman pull Tanner into a tight hug that lasted a little too long.

Perhaps Tanner had succumbed to his kismet after all. Strange disappointment pricked her. Natalie brushed the feeling aside along with the crumbs on her dress, stacked their plates, about to head for the trash when David blocked her path.

"How's it going, Natalie? Sorry for the interruption." His sly grin hinted at his opinion of the "interruption."

Natalie forced her eyes away from Tanner and onto the kind face in front of her. "We've finished eating." And maybe it was for the best. Having heart-to-hearts with Tanner wasn't the wisest idea. "You're looking well, David. It's good to see you."

"Likewise. How are you feeling?"

"Getting through, one day at a time. I haven't had an easy time the past few months."

"I'm sorry to hear that. But you look great, really."

She touched the back of her hair. "I thought holy men weren't supposed to lie."

His laughter somehow soothed her rattled nerves. "I'm not all that holy. But I always mean what I say." Brown eyes twinkled at her. Natalie was about to reply when Tanner approached, the blonde still hanging on his arm.

"Natalie, this is Candace Giovanni. She's our sales rep. Works at the office downtown. Candy, meet Natalie Mitchell."

"Hal's granddaughter," the woman gushed. "I've heard so much about you." She extended a hand with bright pink manicured fingernails toward Natalie.

"Nice meeting you." Or not. Bleach-blond hair, way too much makeup, a barely there blouse, and a skin tight black leather skirt stretched across a pair of legs that went on forever until they reached a pair of leopard print heels.

If this was Tanner's taste in women, she'd sorely misjudged the man.

"I just got back from meetings in San Francisco," Candy informed them breathily. "I've managed to get several restaurants to add Maoilios to their list of stocked wines."

"Attagirl." Tanner patted her shoulder.

"Great." Natalie smiled, her stomach rolling. Although she doubted it was from the food.

"Natalie was just saying how this place might be a good venue for weddings," Tanner mused. He surveyed the area, actually appearing to consider her suggestion. "What do you think, Candy?"

"I think it's a marvelous idea." She glowed under her fake tan, white teeth sparkling. "Natalie, we should do lunch. What do you say?"

Shoot me now. "Oh. Sure." Natalie glanced at David and widened her eyes in a *help me* plea. He nodded to where her grandfather was trying to get their attention across the crowd.

"Hey, Tanner." David jogged Tanner's elbow. "Hal wants you."

Tanner turned toward Hal, raised a hand in acknowledgment, and left them, the blonde following him at a clip. If she'd been a dog, her tail would have been wagging.

Natalie scowled. "She really works for us?" She seemed more suited as a cocktail waitress.

"Candy's all right in small doses." David tipped his head. "So what's the deal, Natalie? Are you really here to shut this place down?"

"Don't beat around the bush, do you?" Natalie smiled and started walking away from the crowd. "You've been talking to Tanner."

"He's concerned, yes. Does he have a reason to be?"

She scanned the groups of mingling employees, children running in and out, couples dancing. Hal had called Tanner over to talk to an older couple. A dark-haired child joined them and she watched Tanner scoop him up and place him on his shoulders. He listened intently to something the child whispered in his ear, then laughed, nodded, and placed him on the ground again. The older woman gave Tanner a big hug before they moved off. Her grandfather was pulled aside by another gentleman and Tanner was soon immersed in conversation with a few younger men.

Everyone here seemed to know one another, and Natalie felt like an outsider. The hearty embraces, lighthearted teasing, groups of gossiping girls, and children of varying ages darting in and out of the crowd, all told her what this place was really about.

Maoilios was more than just a business.

It was a family.

And suddenly she wanted more than anything to be a part of it.

"Natalie?" David waited for her answer. "Is your father shutting this place down?"

She turned back to him, her eyes stinging. "Not if I can help it."

Eighteen

TANNER LISTENED WITH HALF AN EAR TO WHAT MIGUEL WAS saying. On the other side of the gathering, Natalie walked around with Hal. When they stopped to speak to someone, she was fully engaged, attentive, and she paid special attention to the children. He'd heard her conversing in Spanish with Iliana. He hadn't been aware she spoke the language. But he was beginning to realize there were lots of things about Natalie he didn't know.

Lots of things he wanted to.

When she'd come down the front steps of the house that afternoon, her face lit as she caught sight of the horses, she'd taken his breath away. She looked perfect in that simple dress and possessed an elegance that surprised him. The strand of pearls around her neck added a touch of class that reminded him of her grandmother Grace, even if that necklace with the strange charm still sat under them. And the way she'd looked at him? Just for a moment, when she smiled, he saw the Natalie he remembered.

He wondered if she'd had any happy years. Any moments since Nicole's death when she felt free to be herself, just have fun. Wondered what she'd say if he offered to help her with that. She probably hadn't walked a beach or seen a sunset in a long time.

What the heck was happening to him?

Since that night on the road when she'd confided in him, allowed him to see the vulnerable side of her, the carefully constructed wall around his heart began to crumble.

If he wasn't careful, this woman could bring it crashing down.

Tanner wasn't sure that was a risk he was willing to take.

He noticed Jeni run over to where Natalie stood. The smile she gave his niece was sincere, like she really wanted her there. Jeni slipped her hand into Natalie's, and Natalie immediately crouched to hear what Jeni had to say. She nodded and pulled the little girl into a brief hug before Jeni ran off again.

Tanner's throat tightened. It was good to see Jeni smiling.

His niece put on a brave front, but inside, Tanner knew she was hurting. She missed Marnie. Missed having her mother tuck her in at night, tell her how special she was. How much she was loved.

And then there was Jase. What if Rance really did come to California? Of course he would. It was inevitable. But this morning's altercation twisted his stomach into a tight ball.

Tanner had to spend more time with Jason. Knew he'd been running short on patience lately. This afternoon, after he'd come home from the hospital, emotionally tapped out, he'd sat out on the back deck for a bit with Gwin, her head in his lap. As he'd played with the dog's soft ears, he found himself praying. Not the heartfelt prayers he used to say, but a general *God, if you're still listening to me after all this, I could really use some help.*

He was getting close to the bottom of the barrel and didn't have a clue how to scrape his way out.

Natalie looked his way, and their eyes met. For a moment she simply stared. And then she smiled. And there it was again. The smile he remembered from his youth, the one that set his heart beating too fast, yet somehow reassured him, calmed his harried thoughts, as though she knew exactly what he was thinking.

Tanner felt his lips lift on their own accord.

He was getting sucked in.

Nope. Not gonna happen.

He spun around and almost knocked David over.

"Okay, that's twice in one day, dude. We have to stop meeting like this." David chuckled, holding up a plastic wine glass in salute. "Excellent Cab this year. I think you've outdone yourself."

"From your lips to God's ears."

"Naturally." David's humor lightened Tanner's mood. "Natalie seems to be enjoying herself."

"That's good." Tanner shoved his hands in his pockets and stared at the ground.

"I saw you watching her."

"So?" *Shoot.* He moved the tip of his deck shoe back and forth across the grass.

"I thought to myself, now there's someone my friend could fall in love with."

Tanner's head shot up. "What?"

David's eyes twinkled with a knowing smile. "I wonder if you're not half in love with her already, Tanner Collins."

"David, you're whacked."

"What? I think she's perfect for you."

Tanner huffed. "She's dealing with some serious stuff. She could be suicidal for all we know." He doubted it, but it might get David to back off.

"And whose future is certain, Tanner? Better to have loved and lost than never to have loved at all."

"Did you just make that up?"

"No." David laughed. "Tennyson did. But food for thought, don't you think?"

"Don't you have a sermon to go write or something?" Tanner started walking.

"Nah, dude. I preach on the fly every Sunday. Just stand there and wait for God to give me the words."

Tanner stopped and stared at his friend. "Serious?"

David pounded him on the shoulder and gave a belly laugh.

"Kidding, man. But come on . . . Natalie seems really nice. Not at all like I pictured her after talking to you."

"David," Tanner growled. "The rest of your congregation might appreciate you sticking your nose in their business, but I don't want you in mine. Back off or I'll find someplace else to go to church. After I rub your face in the dirt."

"Empty threats." David finished his wine and pitched the plastic glass into the trash can they passed. "You're not a violent man, Tanner. Kind of dim at times, though. If you let that girl get away, then I don't see any hope for you."

"Grearson, for the last time, quit. I'm not interested in Natalie Mitchell. Even if I were, she and I aren't exactly on the same playing field. So it's a moot point."

"Don't be so sure about that, my friend. In fact, I'd say if you explored the idea, you might find yourself pleasantly surprised."

Tanner crossed his arms and watched David walk off. The dude might know a thing or two about God, but he wasn't the greatest at reading women. Could be why he was still single. Not that Tanner was doing much better. No, that wasn't true. He was single by choice. That kismet mumbo jumbo wouldn't work for him.

Natalie's laughter rang through the crowd. Made him smile. Made him turn to find out where she was.

Who was he kidding? Natalie would probably even pick Leo Kastner over him. Just because they'd had a couple of conversations that came close to the ones where they'd bantered back and forth all those years ago didn't mean . . .

Speaking of Kastner . . . Tanner's pulse jacked as he caught sight of Leo standing next to Natalie. And Natalie didn't look at all happy about it.

"No, thank you. I really don't want to dance." Natalie wound her hands together and wished the ground would swallow her up. Or a tornado would come along and whisk Leo Kastner away.

"You sure now?" His breath hinted that he'd been imbibing in harder liquor than the wine. "Pretty lady like yourself shouldn't be alone. Have you seen our wine cellars? I can give you the grand tour."

"I've seen them, thanks." Seen them when she was twelve, but there was no way she was entering a dark cavern with this creep. "I'm going to go find my grandfather. Excuse me. Enjoy the party, Leo."

"Hey, now." He snaked a clammy hand around her wrist. "Don't run off so fast. Come on, sweetheart. One dance, huh?"

"No, really." She shook her head, relieved to see Tanner marching toward them.

"Everything okay here?" His voice hummed with warning as he clapped a hand on Leo's shoulder.

Leo let go of her wrist and glared at Tanner. "Everything's fine. I was trying to persuade Miss Mitchell to dance with me."

"Looked to me like you were getting a little too persuasive, Kastner. You okay, Natalie?"

"Fine," Natalie mumbled, her wrist smarting. Leo's leer made her want to run and lock herself in the house. "I believe Mr. Kastner was just leaving."

"Hey, lady,"—Leo's eyes widened, his cheeks getting redder— "you can't kick me out for asking you to dance. I work here! I have every right to be here. You might be the boss's granddaughter, but I don't work for you."

"But you do work for me." Tanner sidestepped him and planted himself in front of Natalie in a protective stance that might have annoyed her had it not been necessary. His pulsing jaw hinted at anger ready to be unleashed. "You're drunk, Leo. Go home and sleep it off. We'll discuss this on Monday."

"Ain't nothing to discuss, Collins. Like I said, I didn't do anything wrong. Just trying to show the lady a good time. Looks like she could use some loosening up. Unless you're already taking care of that." Kastner's eyes glinted dangerously. "Think she won't shut the place down if she's sleeping with you? Smart move, dude."

Tanner's sharp intake of breath made Natalie take a step backward.

"Tanner—" She put a hand on his arm, but pulled it back in the next second, disgust for Leo Kastner overriding common sense. "Never mind."

Tanner's fist hit the man square on the jaw. Kastner reeled back, clearly unprepared for the punch. But then he launched himself at Tanner. A few women screamed and men raced over to where Leo and Tanner were now rolling on the ground, fists flying.

Somebody pulled Natalie out of the way. Sarah appeared, clapped a hand to her mouth, and looked at Natalie through wide eyes. Jason and Jeni ran up with a few other children. Jeni began to cry as soon as she caught sight of her uncle, and Sarah picked her up and hurried away. Jason seemed impressed, a look of disbelief lighting his face as Tanner landed another punch.

"Go, Uncle Tanner! Hoorah!"

Tanner was bigger and stronger and Kastner didn't have a hope. Tanner would probably have pounded the guy into the ground if some men hadn't pulled him off first.

"What's going on here?" Natalie's grandfather shoved his way through the crowd.

The two men struggled up, breathless, still shooting venomous stares at each other. Hal stood between them, arms akimbo. "Well, somebody better explain!"

"Tanner was defending me." Natalie spoke up, hoping her voice didn't sound as shaky as she thought it did.

"Defending you?" Her grandfather's face turned stormy. "What did you say to my granddaughter, Kastner?"

"You don't want to know." Tanner brushed dirt off his shirt and took a cloth that David produced.

"Don't worry about it." Natalie put a hand on Grandpa's arm, meeting his anxious eyes. The last thing they needed was for him to have another heart attack. "No harm done."

"This time," Tanner took a step toward Kastner.

David rolled his eyes and put a hand on his arm. "Enough, cowboy. What I said earlier about you not being a violent man?" He dabbed at a cut above Tanner's eyebrow with a second cloth. "I take it back."

"He deserved it." Tanner flinched and shook David off.

"Hey, I didn't do anything." Kastner spat blood and pinched his dripping nose. His left eye was swelling nicely.

"Yeah, you did. He accused them of—" A younger man glanced at Natalie and switched to Spanish. "I heard the whole thing."

Her grandfather set a steely gaze on Leo Kastner. "Get on home, Leo. Go to bed. Be in my office first thing Monday morning. We'll discuss this then."

After Leo skulked off, the party slipped back into full swing as though nothing had happened. Grandpa Hal hovered, but Natalie convinced him she was fine and urged him to get back to his guests. Longing for a moment alone, she found a secluded spot, spread out the blanket she'd retrieved from the wagon, and stretched out on it.

David approached a little while later, Jeni hanging onto his hand. "Want some company?"

"Sure." Natalie smiled and moved over to give them room.

He lowered himself down with a groan as Jeni hovered between them. "Can I sit with you?" She stifled a yawn and placed a hand on Natalie's arm.

"Of course you can." Natalie patted her lap. Next thing she knew, Jeni was snuggled against her. Her warm little body created a stirring in Natalie that she wasn't prepared for.

Ever since college, her sole focus had been on her career. Even when she and Peter discussed their future, children never came up. As much as she enjoyed being around Laura's kids, she'd never considered having her own.

But this suddenly felt so natural.

"Is Uncle Tanner going to be okay? He was bleeding."

Natalie smoothed down the child's blond hair and kissed the top of her head. "I think he'll be fine." She wouldn't explain that Jeni had seen Leo's blood on Tanner. Tanner had walked away pretty much unscathed. Leo, on the other hand, was probably going to need a few stitches.

Natalie hugged Jeni close. She missed Laura's kids. She made a mental note to call her friend tomorrow. "Tired, sweetie?"

"It's nine o'clock, Uncle David said. Past my bedtime."

"Ah, but staying up late every once in a while is fun, right?" David handed her a water bottle and Jeni took a sip. "You all right, Natalie?"

"Are you kidding? I haven't seen this much excitement in years." She grinned but knew he saw past it. "I'm okay, really. A little rattled and tired." Tired of watching what's-her-face rub her hands up and down Tanner's arms. She was all over him after the fight, making a way bigger deal about everything than was necessary. "Have you seen my grandfather?"

"He's sitting over there." David pointed to a small crowd of older gentleman, playing cards. "They'll be there all night if Hal has any say in the matter."

"He does seem to have an endless supply of energy. Wish I could borrow some of it." She was only half joking.

Understanding crested his smile. "I'm praying for you, Natalie. And my door is always open if you want to talk. Anytime."

"Thank you, David." Natalie was touched by his kindness. "I'm not much of a talker, really."

"No? Seemed like you had a lot to say to Tanner earlier while I was praying." His teasing tone made her cheeks tingle.

"I was caught off guard. I didn't know they were expecting me to go up there. I'm sorry if I was disruptive."

"I'm kidding." His good-natured smile set her at ease. "But if you so much as whisper during one of my sermons, that'll be another story."

"You assume I'll be hearing one of your sermons." Natalie hiked a brow. "Not much of a churchgoer either, I'm afraid."

"How come you don't go to church?" Jeni piped up.

Natalie and David laughed. She'd thought the little girl had fallen asleep. "I go sometimes, Jeni." Christmas. Easter. Weddings. Funerals.

"That's good." Jeni yawned and snuggled closer. "Everyone should go to church."

The music slowed and couples came and went on the dance floor.

"I wanna see the fireworks," Jeni mumbled.

"Fireworks?" Natalie looked at David as he glanced at his watch.

"Any minute now. We've got a prime spot."

"Want Uncle Tanner to watch with us." Jeni smothered another yawn.

Natalie shifted Jeni to her other leg. "I'm not sure where he is, Jeni."

"Heading our way," David informed her, chugging water. "Alone, thank our good Lord."

Natalie hid her smile in Jeni's hair as Tanner reached them.

"So this is where all the pretty girls have been hiding. Keeping them all to yourself, preacher man?" Jeni giggled and Natalie flushed. Tanner seemed to be in a good mood this evening, and she wasn't quite sure how to take it.

"Out of harm's way." David studied him with a frown. "How's the jaw?"

Tanner rubbed the red welt and grimaced. "I'll live."

"Sit with us, Uncle Tanner. Fireworks are gonna start soon."

Tanner crouched before them, moving Jeni's curls away from her sleepy eyes. "Fifteen minutes, princess. I just checked. They had a little hiccup, but we should be ready to rock 'n' roll pretty soon. Think you can stay awake that long?"

"I'll try." Jeni's eyes drooped.

"You and me both, Jeni." Natalie gave her a quick hug, meeting Tanner's gaze. "We can go after that, right?"

"Sure. Whenever you want," he replied. "You all right?"

"Oh, sure. I'm just usually in bed with the *Wall Street Journal* by this time of night."

"Well, then, Miss Mitchell. Maybe it's time you lived a little dangerously." He stood, swooped Jeni up, and promptly deposited her in David's lap. She didn't protest, but snuggled against his chest and closed her eyes. Tanner held his hand out. "Come on, Mouse. Let's do it properly this time."

Natalie blinked. He was asking her to dance. *Oh, for the love . . .*

Nineteen

Tanner. I really don't—"

"Can I just say arguing with Tanner Collins is never a good idea," David put in lazily, sounding half asleep himself.

"He's right. You won't win." Tanner grabbed her hands and pulled her to her feet.

Natalie swallowed her protests. Clearly the better decision was to keep quiet and let him lead her onto the dance floor. The band was playing one of her current favorites, "Dancin' Away with My Heart" by Lady Antebellum.

"You're really willing to take another chance with me, Tanner?" she teased. "Talk about living dangerously."

"My feet are a lot bigger than yours." Tanner's voice was soft in her ear as he pulled her close, one arm around her waist, his other hand cradling hers against his shoulder. "Keep that in mind the next time you're tempted to stomp on them."

"Will do." Years ago, a teenager with stars in her eyes, she'd dreamed about this moment. The moment Tanner Collins would appear out of the crowd, take her in his arms, and sweep her off her feet. She banished the thought and examined his face under the twinkling lights strung around them.

"So, what happened to Candy?" The question escaped before she could stop it.

"I don't know." He got a blank look. "What do you mean what happened to her?"

"I thought . . . well, from what I saw earlier, I thought you two might be an item."

"Candy?" His eyes widened as laughter shook him. "You thought she and I were . . . together?"

"Looked that way to me."

"Wow. Heck, no. Give me some credit. Sheesh."

Natalie refused to acknowledge the relief that raced through her. "Are you sure you're okay? That bruise looks bad."

"Doesn't hurt nearly as much as my foot."

"Stop." She smiled, enjoying the teasing lilt in his voice. "You know, I've never had anyone come to my defense that way before. I'm sure Leo would have left on his own. You didn't have to punch his lights out."

"You're probably right. But I've been waiting for an excuse to deck that man for two years." Humor jumped in his eyes.

"Ah. Then I'm glad I could oblige."

"I'm surprised Hal didn't fire him on the spot." Tanner sounded annoyed he hadn't.

She'd been thinking the same. "Maybe he will on Monday."

"He'd better." Tanner turned her in a circle. "I've been pushing for it the last few months. The guy is a jerk, doesn't do any more than he has to. He's always down at the bar. He's trouble. But you know Hal, always likes to give the benefit of the doubt."

"Well, after tonight, I'd say he's changed his mind." If he hadn't, Natalie would certainly do it for him. They didn't need somebody like Leo Kastner in the mix.

They danced for a bit in silence until Tanner spoke again.

"I had a chat with Hal the other day. He's finally given me carte blanche control on some of my marketing ideas. Probably thanks to you. So, I thought maybe we could go to some wineries on Monday. Check out the competition. If we can gather some data, let Hal know what the other guys are doing, I think we'll be one step closer to getting him to come around to our way of thinking."

"Monday. Uh-huh." Sleepiness descended without warning. She followed his smooth steps with a happy sigh, unable to resist placing her head on his chest.

"You'd be up for that, right?" he asked. "We'll make a day of it. Better than sitting in my office crunching numbers. You might actually have fun."

"I know how to have fun." She was having fun right now. His cologne was intoxicating. Woodsy with a hint of citrus. He felt good. Solid. Protective. She shivered as his thumb pressed against the top of her hand.

"Did you try the new Syrah? Got a lot of compliments on it tonight."

"Uh-huh." She could lose herself in this embrace.

"You're not listening to a word I'm saying, are you, Mouse?"

"Uh-huh."

Laughter rumbled from him and he pulled her a little closer. "We should take the Jag on Monday. I can't wait until Wednesday."

"I'll drive." Natalie lifted her head and managed a smile. "Thought you'd get that past me, did you?"

"I was hoping." His eyes sparked with mischief.

"Well, I do owe you for coming to my rescue, yet again, so I suppose you can drive. But remember, it's a rental. No joyriding or . . ." She sucked back the words and clamped her lips together.

Memories rolled in like a sudden storm, and she shut her eyes against them.

A sigh slid out of Tanner and he tightened his arms around her. "Breathe, Nat."

"I know. I'm trying," she whispered. But the shaking had already started.

They moved in another circle as Natalie fought emotion, concentrating on the rise and fall of his chest, letting his closeness calm her. "Sometimes it seems like it never happened," she confessed. "Like Nic is suddenly going to appear, as though she's always been here." She blinked back tears and met his eyes. "I should have listened to my first instinct, stayed in New York, not gotten on that plane."

He maneuvered her off the dance floor. Next thing she knew they were standing by the stream, away from the party, away from the noise. But not away from the thoughts that screamed in her head and made her wish she'd never voiced them.

"I'm sorry." Natalie sent him a small smile. "I didn't mean to drag you into my morose world. I'll be fine. You go on back to Jeni. I'll be there in a minute." She put her back to him and watched dark water skim over large boulders on its way downstream. If only she could toss the past into that rushing water, watch it slip away, never to return.

"I'm not leaving you."

She turned, saw the stubborn look, recognizing the boy she'd once known. "There's no need to stay. I'll be all right."

"Do you ever let your guard down, Natalie?" He stood beside her, the question humming in the cool night air.

Natalie gripped her elbows and shivered. "I don't know what you're talking about."

"Yeah, you do. Ever since you got here, I've watched you, tried to find the girl I remembered, the one who used to be my friend." Softly spoken words nudged truth into her soul. "Back then, I could talk to you about anything. There was no trying to impress, trying to sound smarter, be better. I could just be me. I was fifteen years old. I didn't know a whole heck of a lot about life, but I knew I liked the way I felt when I was with you. You were sweet, innocent. Sincere. You were the real deal. Where'd you go, Mouse?"

She turned, lifted her chin, not caring about the tears that slid down her cheeks. "I grew up."

Tanner gave a half shrug. "So did I. But growing up doesn't mean forgetting where you came from, forgetting who you were. It doesn't mean you have to forget the past and pretend it never happened."

"Yes, it does." She choked on the words. "The past hurts, Tanner. When Nic died, everything changed. I changed." Natalie drew a shaky breath and fiddled with the pendant around her neck. "Nic was everything I wasn't. She was funny. She was smart. She was beautiful. Everyone loved her. And I was just Natalie."

"Why can't that be enough?"

"It never seemed to be."

Tanner shook his head, thumbed the zodiac sign that sat beneath her pearls. "What is that?"

"It's a zodiac symbol. Leo, our birth month. Ironic, huh?" Natalie lowered her eyes, waiting for the next question.

Tanner snorted. "You believe in that stuff?"

She shook her head. "No. It was Nic's. She bought it at some little shop in town, for her birthday that summer. I've worn it ever since she died."

"You think about her all the time, don't you?"

Natalie nodded, her heart thudding. "I keep hoping it'll get easier. My parents don't like to talk about her, so I pretty much keep my thoughts to myself."

Tanner placed his hands on her shoulders. Moonlight caressed his face, adding extra light to his eyes. After a while, he shook his head. Certain sadness crept over him. His hands moved upward to cradle her face and he wiped her tears with the base of his thumbs. "When are you going to stop trying to please everyone? Make Natalie happy for a change?"

The question smothered her, dragged her down to its depths,

and tried to drown her in truth. Natalie shook off his hands, backed up, and pressed her lips together. "I am happy. I'm exactly where I want to be, doing what I want to do."

"Really?" His eyes challenged her. "The Natalie Mitchell I knew would have hated being stuck in boardrooms with a bunch of stiff-lipped bureaucrats."

Her chest tightened and her throat burned. "Like I said, I grew up. You don't know me anymore, Tanner. You've got no right to tell me I don't make my own choices."

"I'm not sure I believe that." He shoved his hands in his back pockets and rocked on his heels. "And I don't think you do either. In all the time I've known you, you always gave in first. Nicole would argue anything. But you never did. But coming here . . ." He smiled a little, his gaze reaching right through her. "If what you say is true and you want to keep the winery open . . . it's the first step. I'll bet it'll be the first time you've gone against your father's wishes."

"True." Natalie swiped her cheeks.

"I also think you need to deal with the past. Deal with the memories of that summer. Let it go, once and for all. Let Nicole go. It's the only way you'll ever be free to live your own life."

He may as well have taken a sharp blade, cut out her heart, and held it up for the world to scrutinize.

A slow, unexpected anger rose up.

"You're making a lot of assumptions, Tanner. I think you're the one who needs to let go of the past."

"I will if you will."

"Fine." Talking to him was like walking an emotional tight-rope. With no net to catch her if she fell.

"I have my own regrets, Natalie. I should have been there that night," he told her, his voice taut. "That's the thought that's stuck with me all these years. I should have been there."

Natalie brushed a hand across her face, her heart racing. What was he talking about? "Do you think if you had, things would have turned out differently? That you're some savior?"

"Maybe." His honesty hit her with the force of a slap. "Maybe I could have stopped it. Maybe I—"

"Could have saved Nic?" Of course. It was still about Nicole.

"Yes." Tanner placed two fingers beneath her chin, forcing her eyes upward. "If I could have stopped things that night, saved Nic and saved you from the hell you've been through since, I would have."

"Well, you weren't there, were you?" Was she really angry with him because of it? It had hardly been his fault. His mother had grounded him.

No, it wasn't him she was angry with.

What happened that horrible night had nothing to do with him. It was all on her.

Tanner put his hands on her shoulders again. Infringing on her personal space. Making her think about things she didn't want to. "Look at me."

His eyes pulled her in, probed, peeled back layers, and peered into her soul.

Made her feel things she didn't want to feel.

"Don't you ever get angry, Natalie? Don't you ever just want to lose it and scream at someone?"

All the time.

She lifted her chin in resignation. "What would be the point?"

His shoulders rose and fell in conjunction with his smile.

"What do you want from me, Tanner?"

"I want you to stop blaming yourself for things you can't change."

A simple request.

Impossible to grant.

"But I *should* have stopped her, should have done something! How can you say I'm not responsible?" No, she couldn't do this. Couldn't go back there.

Back to where she couldn't think, breathe . . . feel.

Life was so much easier when you didn't feel.

"You were only thirteen years old, Natalie! Your sister decided to take that Jeep, you didn't make her do it. We both know you couldn't have stopped her. Once Nic made up her mind, it was a done deal. It was not your fault. Life is too short to go on blaming yourself for something you had absolutely no control over."

Too short to let one night ruin the rest of your life.

He didn't say the words. Didn't have to.

Natalie gulped air, her emotions raw, laid bare in front of him.

What would he say if he knew the whole story? Knew the truth?

"That day on the patio, you asked me why I stopped writing to you. Remember?"

"Sure." He shrugged.

Natalie steadied her breathing, clutched her elbows, and plowed on before she lost her nerve. "I told you things got bad for a while after the accident. Bad is an understatement. I stopped writing to you because my world imploded. Three months after Nic's funeral, I woke up in the middle of the night screaming, and I couldn't stop." She sank to the grass, drew her knees up, and held tight. Tanner slowly lowered himself beside her.

"My parents didn't know what to do with me. I was hospitalized for three weeks. Well, they called it a hospital. It was more like something out of *One Flew Over the Cuckoo's Nest*. When I went home, my father could barely carry on a conversation with me. Crazy doesn't fit the family image, apparently. Eventually I learned to avoid any discussion of what had happened. I stayed out of school until Christmas. In January they packed me off to boarding school."

"They sent you away?" Tanner's voice trembled, like he, too, was holding tight to emotions about to bolt like a runaway horse.

She didn't dare look at him. Hadn't planned to tell him any of this. She felt exposed again, vulnerable. "My parents don't solve problems, Tanner. They simply get rid of them."

"You were still a kid."

"I know." Natalie pushed to her feet and walked to the bank of the stream. She stood near the water and stared at the shimmering ripples. Cicadas sang in the tall trees above them, passing along secrets as old as time in their lullaby.

Tanner joined her at the water's edge. "You deserved better."

"Did I?" Would he say that if he knew the rest?

His searching eyes plumbed her depths, like he knew there was more.

"Sometimes I think my relapse is some kind of punishment from God. Because of what happened. Maybe it is. Maybe I deserve it."

Tanner blinked under the moon's glow. "I don't think your struggles are a punishment from God, Natalie. Not that I'm any expert, but I think He'd rather help you than hurt you."

"Some help might be nice." She pulled her fingers through her hair, glanced down at her dress, and gave a wan smile. "I like to pretend I've got it all together, but I don't. I've created a simple no-fail existence. Get up, go to work, go home, work some more, and maybe sleep a few hours if I'm lucky. Outside of my one long-term relationship, which ended in catastrophe, I have the social life of a slug."

Tanner flashed a quick grin. "You must have some friends."

"I have Laura." Natalie smiled. "But she has Jim and the kids. I tend to limit the time I spend over there."

"Why?"

"Oh . . ." A frustrated sigh slipped out. "Because their life makes me think about things I'll never have. I think I try so hard to succeed in business because I know that world is all I've got."

"What do you mean?" Confusion settled in the creases around his eyes.

"I'm not going to get married, have a family. No happily ever after. No kismet for me. Not if I can't get better. Who'd want to marry crazy?" She pushed her shoulders back, produced a smile, and summoned the woman who could face down a table of board members, handle million-dollar marketing presentations, and rebuff the strongest of arguments. The woman her father expected her to be. Strong. Dependable. The woman who hid her feelings, put on a brave face, only cried when she was alone.

And fooled everybody.

"Honestly, I don't why I told you all that." Any thoughts of further revelations faded. This was too hard. "I don't know what I was thinking, coming back here. Telling myself I could save Maoilios. Thinking my father might actually listen to me for a change."

Tanner studied her with a pensive look. "Maybe you're here so you can heal. If you give yourself a chance, give it time, you will work through this."

"You really think it's possible to get over the past?"

Tanner hesitated, breaking eye contact. "I don't know. I'm trying to figure that out, same as you." Secrets shimmered in his eyes when he looked back at her, but she wouldn't ask. Not tonight.

"Look at us, actually having a civilized conversation." She tried to laugh, tried to act like it didn't mean a thing. Like her heart wasn't about to explode any minute now. Like she didn't want him to take her in his arms again. Desperately.

His slow smile sent a fresh rush of feelings ricocheting through her entire body. "Yeah. Look at us." Tanner's fingers brushed her cheek. "For the record, I'm glad you got on that plane and came back here."

"You wouldn't have said that when I first arrived."

"No, I wouldn't have." His dimple deepened. "Not out loud anyway."

"Well." She shrugged, too aware of her heart's rapid rhythm.

"Now that you know my sorry story, I hope you'll forgive me for not keeping in touch. Updates on the number of pills I was taking and who shared what in the Honesty Circle that morning wouldn't have been terribly exciting."

"I would have thought so." Another smile sent her stomach swirling.

"Stop." Natalie laughed and shook her head. "I'm not falling for your charm. Besides, I already said you could drive the stupid car so you can quit trying so hard."

"Sorry to disappoint you, but I have no charm." Tanner ran a finger down the side of her face, sent a shiver down her spine. "And right now I couldn't care less about the stupid car."

"What are you thinking then?" *Oh, she really shouldn't have asked.*

He stared at her for a long moment, then sighed. "If you must know, I'm wondering whether you might let me kiss you without telling me I look like a Backstreet Boy."

He wanted to kiss her?

"Oh." Natalie took a step back, fear fluttering in her throat. "Um. No." Letting Tanner Collins kiss her would only add to her confusion. "That would be a terrible idea."

"Probably." He put his arms around her, placed his lips above her eyebrow, and pressed them against her skin, creating a pull of desire she couldn't ignore. "But I seem to be living a little dangerously this evening." His soft lips moved to explore the space between her eyes.

"Tanner," she breathed his name, hardly able to stand. She pushed her hands against his chest. "Did you have too much wine?" Because he simply couldn't be sober. A sober Tanner Collins would never dream of kissing her.

"Natalie." Tanner placed his hands around her face again, his gaze smoldering. "I don't drink. I taste it, but I don't drink it. I'm in full control of all my faculties right now."

"A vintner that doesn't drink? Now that's interesting."

"It's a long story."

"Tell me. It'll take your mind off doing something you'll regret."

"Some other time. And who says I'll regret it?"

"You will, Tanner. We both will."

"You don't want me to kiss you?"

Oh . . . she wanted him to. So much it scared her.

"I didn't say that." There was no point in lying. "But we're just getting to know each other again. It'll complicate things."

"Yeah, you're right." He stole further reasoning away by bringing his lips to hers.

The moment they connected, Natalie came alive. Electricity pulsed through her as she pressed closer to him. Accepted his kisses, welcomed them. While her brain told her to stop, her body did the opposite. She wound her arms around his neck, let her fingers drift through his hair, and lost herself in the fiery feeling of being wanted, needed.

He was gentle and sweet and she would have allowed him to kiss her all night, but he didn't. Instead, he drew back, blinked a couple of times, tipped his head, and waited.

"Say something." Her heart was about to jump out of her chest.

"Okay, you're right. That does complicate things." He cleared his throat and moved away from her.

"What?"

"I don't want you to think I'm trying to influence you about whether or not you shut down this place, okay? I fully expect you to make that decision regardless of how I feel. This doesn't change anything."

"Of course it doesn't change anything." It changes everything. Natalie reined in runaway thoughts, waited for her breathing to slow, and tried to extricate the memory of his lips on hers. "I told you it would be a bad idea."

He rolled his eyes and rammed his fingers through his hair. "You didn't like it?"

"Oh, please." He wasn't getting an answer to that.

A loud crack split the night, sending bright sparklers into the dark sky.

"The fireworks."

"Finally." Relief rang through his voice.

Knowing Grandpa, the show would be spectacular, but it wouldn't be able to compete with the fireworks she'd experienced moments ago. "We'd better get back," Natalie said. "Jeni will be looking for you."

"Jeni's probably asleep." He rubbed his jaw and shot her a sidelong glance. "Are we good?"

Natalie pushed aside longing, banished the thought of actually telling him how she felt, and nodded instead. "Let's just say we've satisfied our childhood curiosity and leave it at that."

The zing of more fireworks pinged through the air followed by a loud explosion of light.

"We what?"

She ignored him and walked as quickly as she could back to the safety of the crowd. Then she stopped. Sarah and a man who looked vaguely familiar were engaged in what seemed to be, from this distance at least, a rather heated discussion. "Who is that?"

Tanner turned to where she pointed. "I don't recognize him. Wait, I think . . ."

Natalie's memory clicked, and she gave a happy squeak. "That's my uncle!"

Twenty

IT WAS HARD TO BELIEVE HE'D BEEN IN EUROPE A FEW DAYS ago. Jeffrey almost wished he was still there. He'd walked the perimeter of the party undetected for quite some time. Watched the fight with guarded interest. Wondered what that was about, but he'd find out. Spied his father, some old friends he recognized, and finally found Sarah.

Lord help him, she was still so beautiful. Still capable of causing that dangerous knee-jerk reaction that sent his brain on a permanent vacation. It was all he could do not to stride across the grassy area and swoop her into his arms.

Eventually he'd approached her. And immediately regretted it.

Sarah's frozen glare was hardly welcoming.

"What are you doing here?" Sarah hissed. She scanned the crowd, no doubt sussing out his father's whereabouts so she could warn him that hell was about to freeze over.

"I came to see my dad. And . . ." Another explosion sent colors shooting across the dark sky, shook him senseless. Jeffrey breathed in and stared at Sarah instead. He needed to get a grip.

"Is Hal expecting you? I don't want you upsetting him." Sarah gripped her elbows, her eyes wide and filled with distrust. The white cardigan she wore over a pretty yellow top and navy capris didn't do much to hide the fact that she was trembling. The night air was balmy, in the high seventies if he had to guess, so he suspected her uncomfortable stance could be blamed purely on his presence.

"I should have called."

"You think?"

"Look, Sarah, we can talk . . . we should talk. But not here." He ran a hand down his face and felt air leave his chest. The adrenaline he'd been running on the last twenty-four hours was dissipating.

"There's nothing to talk about." Sarah veered her gaze. "No sense rehashing ancient history, is there?"

Jeffrey sighed and pondered a response. Came up empty.

"Jeffrey!" Somebody yelled his name and he silently thanked God for the interruption. He swiveled to see who the voice belonged to and grinned as his niece raced toward him. "Uncle Jeff!"

"Natalie Mitchell, you went and grew up on me." Jeffrey gave her a long hug, then stood back to study her. If his instincts were right, the smile she wore was taking some effort. Her eyes were red-rimmed, her cheeks splotchy. He wondered if the tall man tailing her had something to do with that. The guy who'd been in the fight. "You look just like your grandmother, gorgeous."

She rolled her eyes but her smile broadened. "That's what I've heard. What are you doing here? Did Grandpa know you were coming?"

Jeffrey ran a hand over his windblown hair and shrugged. "I decided to surprise him."

"He doesn't like surprises." The man standing behind Natalie spoke, looked him up and down, unsmiling.

"Should have figured as much." Jeffrey tried to keep his voice calm. "Neither do I. Have we met?"

"This is my son." Sarah moved to stand beside the man and slipped an arm through his. "Tanner Collins."

"Ah. Tanner. You were just a kid last time I saw you." Jeffrey extended a hand. Tanner shook it warily, gave off warning vibes. Sarah's son wasn't a kid anymore. Had to be at least six foot—and looked ready to take him down too. Jeffrey almost grinned. He'd be in for quite a shock if he tried. "Jeffrey Mitchell."

"I know who you are." And clearly knew Jeffrey and Sarah's history, if the stony look on his face was any clue.

"Uncle Tanner, you're missing all the fireworks!" A little girl ran up to their group, a larger man following, huffing like he'd just run a marathon.

"Thought she was asleep! She just took off on me."

"No worries, David." Tanner's smile came out as he lifted the child into his arms. "Sorry, princess. I got a little sidetracked. Let's go watch the show. Coming, Mom?"

"Gladly." Sarah shot him a parting glare and they were gone.

Jeffrey hadn't realized he'd been holding his breath until he let it out in a sigh of relief spiced with regret and a bunch of other emotions he didn't care to analyze right now.

Natalie stared after them, her face screwed up like she was try-ing to figure something out. Then she trained her gaze on him. "My imagination or did the air just warm up after they left?"

"Not your imagination." Jeffrey cracked a smile, flung an arm over her shoulder, and knew he'd found a friend. "Come on, darlin'. Buy your old uncle a drink and tell me what you've been up to since I last saw you."

Natalie's laughter didn't last long, but it sure made him feel good. "Since that was about thirteen years ago, Uncle Jeff, I think I'll find a bottle. But first, let's go find Grandpa."

"Uh, okay." He could argue, but she wouldn't understand. And maybe his gut was wrong. Maybe Dad would actually be glad to see him.

And maybe he'd actually sleep through the night without wak-ing in a cold sweat.

That hadn't happened in years.

Every muscle in his neck tensed as Natalie propelled him through the crowd toward a collection of picnic tables.

Hal's white head stood out amongst the dark-haired men

engrossed in their card game. Figured the old man would be playing cards with his cronies rather than working the crowd. He'd be doing the same. Bill was the schmoozer in the family.

"Grandpa, look who's here!" Natalie pressed forward. "Isn't this great?"

His dad turned, took one look at him, and his brows shot skyward.

Hal stared at him a long time. Jeffrey was usually pretty good at reading him, but tonight he was out of practice and got nothing. Hal's jaw twitched as he drew in breaths. The other men fell silent, all eyes on Jeffrey. For a moment he was back in Siberia, facing a potential firing squad.

Jeffrey shoved his hands in the pockets of his Levis and rolled back on the heels of his boots. "Hey, Dad. Long time no see."

"Long time no see?" Hal pulled his long legs over the bench and got to his feet. He was still a couple inches taller, his blue eyes just as piercing. Heart attack or not, the old guy looked good. "Is that supposed to be funny?"

"Not especially." Jeffrey cleared his throat, tried to smile but old anger tapped at his heart. "I would have been here earlier but my flight was delayed." Never give out useless information. There went that rule.

Dad's mouth formed a hard line. "Somebody else must have sent you an invitation, because I didn't."

Ouch. "No. I just . . . decided to come. Didn't know it was harvest celebration."

"Don't suppose you've ever heard of a thing called the telephone. You can even carry them in your pocket now. Got one myself." He pulled out an iPhone and waggled white eyebrows. "You ought to get up with the times, son. That way at least we might know you're alive."

The man still had the ability to make him feel like he was

fifteen and breaking curfew. Jeffrey clenched his jaw. "If I'm not welcome, I can go."

"Of course you're welcome." Natalie's worried gaze darted from him to his dad. She slipped an arm through Hal's. "Isn't he, Grandpa?"

"Sure. Since he's here." Hal still didn't smile but his eyes weren't quite so cold. "Maoilios is still your home, like it or not. Go grab something to eat. And try the Cab. Got a hint of chocolate this year. I think you'll like it." He turned back to his friends and sat down again. "Where were we?"

Right. Jeffrey ground the toe of his boot into the grass. He looked over at Natalie and smiled. "Want to show me where the food is? If there's any left, I'll make short work of it."

"Absolutely. And I'll see about that wine." She fairly skipped off ahead of him and Jeffrey had to laugh. At least one person around here seemed happy to see him.

❧

Early Wednesday morning, Jeffrey lay awake staring at the ceiling. Footsteps padded up and down the hall. Three thirty. He'd been home four nights and had quickly concluded that he wasn't the only one who slept sporadically. And since his father's snores were loud enough to wake the cats in the cellars down the hill, he'd put his finger on Natalie.

He noticed the shakes right off. The jumpiness, the way she tried too hard to hold a conversation. Watched her pick at her food and stare off into space when she thought nobody was looking.

He'd been in Moscow when they'd finally reached him that summer to tell him about Nicole. Hadn't been able to get back for the funeral. When he showed up at his brother's for Thanksgiving that year, out of the blue as usual, Natalie was a mess. He took

Bill and Jane aside and gently tried to explain that their daughter needed help.

Bill kicked him out.

There was little he could do. A couple weeks later he was back in the field. He had a buddy check up on them, found out Natalie had been admitted to a psychiatric hospital.

And now, all these years later, she was still suffering.

They had more in common than she knew.

At dawn, he hauled himself out of the bed he'd slept in for a lot of his life and got into the shower. Let the hot water pummel him and inhaled steam. Once dressed, he paced his room. Rifled through his drawers, put everything in order again, and his eyes landed on his revolver.

Technically, he wasn't supposed to be packing, but one thing he'd learned over the last thirty-some years was that you never went anywhere without protection. He checked the cartridge again, knowing he'd emptied it and stored the ammo up in the top shelf of the closet. Even doing that made him nervous. It would take approximately twenty seconds to sprint across the room, get the ammo, load, and shoot. But you could be dead in twenty seconds.

Brant had been right. He did need a vacation.

Downstairs, he scoured the hall, listened to the sound of a vacuum, and tried to determine which room Sarah would be in. Sounded like the living room. He went the other way and found sanctuary in the quiet kitchen.

Jeffrey paused at the refrigerator and studied the old photographs. His mother had loved to display family photos where she'd see them every day, along with postcards he'd sent from various stops around the world, and her typed-out Bible verses. She'd been gone five years, yet it all remained.

Coffee was still hot. He searched the cupboards, found his

favorite Lakers mug way in the back, poured, and gulped. Coffee could fix anything. Almost.

"Hope there's some left for me." Natalie entered the sunny room, a hand over her mouth as she stifled a yawn. She wore smart navy trousers and a navy and white striped sweater. Her hair was neatly styled and she'd applied some makeup.

Jeffrey poured her a cup and frowned. "Going somewhere?"

The past few days she'd been skulking around the house in shorts and baggy tees. He'd tried to get her to go into town with him for lunch, but she'd refused. The almost happy mood she'd appeared to be in when she'd first seen him on Saturday night had shifted with the wind, turned dark and stormy.

He was well acquainted with the mood swings too.

Natalie ripped open a packet of sweetener and sprinkled the white stuff into her coffee. "I have an appointment in the city."

"Business?"

She joined him at the kitchen table. Sat in silence, sipped her coffee, and finally shook her head. "Doctor's appointment."

Jeffrey pushed back his chair. "Hungry? I make a mean omelet."

"Sure, I could eat." She didn't look sure, but he went about fixing them food anyway, chopped, diced, grated up cheese, and soon had the ingredients in the pan. All the while Natalie sat at the table staring out the sliding glass doors.

He made more coffee and served breakfast. "So. Have you been dealing with PTSD since the accident?"

Natalie's hand stilled, fork in midair. Her eyes locked on him and widened with suspicion. "Who told you?"

"Nobody." Jeffrey ran a finger over the small crack in the rim of his mug. "Don't you know what I do, Natalie?"

"I don't remember. My dad always said you were a James Bond wannabe. I never knew what that meant. So what are you, a shrink?"

"Ha. That would be handy. No. I work for the FBI. I'm primarily posted overseas. Suffice it to say PTSD and I are old friends. I recognized your symptoms. I'm sorry."

"Seriously?"

"I'm on leave at the moment, but yeah."

She looked down at her plate and Jeffrey took the opportunity to study her. The way she held her head, her complexion, thick wavy hair, smile when she gave it, reminded him so much of his mother. It was one of the things he'd dreaded, coming home, having to walk through the house, her absence palpable.

He hadn't figured on missing her so much. Having Natalie around somehow made it bearable.

She met his gaze again. "Do you ever get over it or is this something I'm going to live with the rest of my life?"

Heckuva question, kid.

Jeffrey finished his meal and pushed his plate aside. "Some get over it. I can't say for sure whether you will or not. But it's good you're getting help. A lot of people are too afraid to even admit what's happening to them."

"I had to be hospitalized a few months after the accident." She told him what he already knew, her expression neutral. "Then I went to boarding school. I forced myself to live with it, to cope. Eventually it got better. Things were good for a while. I'd get flashbacks or the occasional nightmare, but I learned to handle it. I thought things would be okay, normal even. And then this year, at the beginning of June, it started again, worse than ever."

"Was there a trigger?"

Natalie shifted her gaze, her cheeks pinking. He'd take that as a yes, and she clearly didn't want to talk about it. "If you're not doing anything today, Uncle Jeff, do you think you could drive me into San Francisco? I'm having trouble in vehicles right now."

"Sure." He'd take any opportunity to get away from Maoilios for a few hours. Away from the awkward conversations he'd attempted with his father and the frosty stares Sarah threw his way when they crossed paths. "I'd love to drive you."

"Thanks."

When they finished eating, she gathered their dishes and headed for the sink. Jeffrey glanced down at his grubby Stones T-shirt and contemplated changing. As he got to his feet, Sarah's son—what was his name . . . couldn't remember—came into the kitchen. Jeffrey raised a hand in greeting. "Morning."

A curt nod was all he got in response.

Natalie turned from the sink, her face losing a little color.

Interesting.

"Ready to go, Natalie?" The guy rocked on his deck shoes, hesitation in his tone.

"What are you doing here, Tanner?"

Jeffrey backed up against the counter and watched them.

"It's Wednesday. Your appointment is today, right? I said I would drive you."

"And I texted you saying you didn't need to. Didn't you get it?"

"I did, but . . ." He scratched his head. "Are you seriously mad because I had to cancel Monday?"

Natalie yanked the plug from the sink and let the water out with a whoosh. "Cancel? You never canceled. You just didn't show up."

"What?" The kid narrowed his eyes. What was going on with these two? "You didn't get my message?"

"What message?" She put a few clean mugs away and banged the cupboard shut. "I waited around for two hours, Tanner. You didn't show and you didn't call, and no, I didn't get your message."

He strode across the room to the answering machine and flicked it on. It beeped and played one new message. *"Natalie, Tanner. Something came up. Sorry. Call you later."*

"You have quite a way with words." Jeffrey clamped his mouth shut. He hadn't meant to say that out loud.

Tanner rewarded him with a cold stare identical to his mother's. "Why is this any of your business?"

"It's absolutely not." Jeffrey couldn't stop a grin. This was the most entertainment he'd had in months. "Natalie, I'm going upstairs to grab a clean shirt. Ten minutes?"

"Thanks, Uncle Jeff."

He left her to deal with the surly Tanner Collins, certain she could manage perfectly well on her own. And if she needed him, she could yell.

⌒

"Natalie?" Tanner stood stiff, blindsided. "You asked him to drive you?"

"Yes." She poured the remainder of the coffee into the sink and set the pot in the dishwasher. "After Monday, I didn't know whether you'd remember. I know you're busy, so . . ."

"Well, I'm here. I cleared my schedule. We're good." Except they were so clearly not.

"I don't want to be a bother. I'd rather my uncle take me." She stood at the sink, her back to him.

"Look, I'm sorry you didn't get my message on Monday. The crusher broke down. I spent all morning fixing it, had to drive to Napa for parts. And Mom and I were up all Monday night with Jeni. She has strep throat. She's still in bed, actually."

"Jeni's sick?" Worry crept into her eyes. "Who's with her now? Your mom's here."

He nodded. "I know." He'd seen her polishing the dining room table on the way in.

"A sitter. For the day. Well, until Mom finishes up here."

"I see." She rounded the table the other way. "Well, you can go home and send the sitter on her way. I'm sure Jeni will be much happier if you're with her."

Tanner read the truth on her face, narrowed his eyes, and blocked her path as she headed for the door. "Is this about Saturday night?"

Satisfied their childhood curiosities, his rear.

He still couldn't believe she'd said that. And he knew she didn't mean it. Not if the way she'd responded to his kisses was any indication.

Her eyes faltered but her mouth formed a thin line of denial. "No, I . . ." She let go a sigh. "I'm sorry I thought you bailed on Monday. But maybe it was for the best. I'm not sure we . . ." She looked down at the floor. "Look, my uncle is taking me to my appointment. Let's just drop it. Tomorrow, I plan to concentrate on the winery again. I think I've come up with a business model that might work. We can talk then, and if you think it sounds viable, we'll approach my grandfather with it."

"O-kay." It was definitely about Saturday night. And she was blowing him off big-time. Confusion crashed through the hopes he'd had for today, carrying his good mood off at a clip. Had he been so off base about her?

"I'll be in touch later." She refused to make eye contact.

Tanner headed for the door. "Right. Have a good day." No point in standing there staring at her. He left the room, ignoring his mother who called out hello as he marched down the hall, yanked open the front door, and slammed it behind him.

Twenty-One

UNCLE JEFF WAITED FOR HER IN THE LOBBY WITH A STRAW-berry shake and a jelly donut.

"You remembered." Natalie smiled as they exited the building and headed toward the parking lot.

"Your mother hated it when I showed up and took you girls out. Said I was ruining your healthy eating habits."

"She was probably right about that." Natalie reveled in the sticky treat and the sweet goo that oozed into her mouth. She hadn't had a jelly donut in years.

Her uncle didn't visit often, but when he had, they'd always done something exciting. He'd take them places they would rarely go. Like the Bronx Zoo or the Hard Rock Café. Sometimes they'd take a carriage ride around Central Park. One day he took them to a racetrack and the horse they'd bet on won. Sometimes they'd just ride the Staten Island ferry. They'd people watch and make up wickedly funny stories, then laugh until their sides hurt. And they always took the subway.

Natalie eased into the passenger seat and caught her breath. "I think I just put on five pounds. Thanks." She licked white powder residue off her fingers anyway.

Uncle Jeff handed her a napkin. "Well, if you did, you could stand it." He snapped his seat belt in place with a smile. "How was it?"

"The donut or the appointment?" Natalie sipped her shake and fiddled with the radio while he slid his ticket into the gate at the front of the lot.

"Both."

"The donut was divine. The appointment . . ." Natalie pushed her plastic cup into the holder beside her seat. She listened to the radio and processed the past hour. "Good."

"Yeah?" He sounded a little skeptical.

Natalie turned toward him. "My doctor asked me something today I'd never been able to answer until now."

"What's that?" He maneuvered in and out of traffic, perfectly at ease behind the wheel of the Jag. She could easily imagine him zipping down the Autobahn in a red Ferrari.

She slid her thumbnail underneath her fingernails and thought about it. Saying it out loud would make it real. Make it so she hadn't imagined it. Make it so she meant it.

"He asked me if I wished I had died that night instead of Nicole."

Her uncle's short intake of breath was barely audible, but she'd caught it. He pushed up his shades with a sniff. "That's heavy. And?"

They stalled at a red light. Traffic was piling up. Horns blared. The sidewalks were jammed with people hurrying to and fro, jostling to get out of each other's way. She could just see the sky beyond the tall city buildings. A slight claustrophobic feeling began to simmer. How on earth would she ever assimilate to being back in New York?

For the first time, it dawned on her that she might not want to return.

"Natalie?"

She smiled at the concern in his voice. "No. The answer is no." The thought practically made her giddy. "For a long time I wouldn't have said that. I wish my sister hadn't died. More than anything. But I'm glad I didn't. I'm glad, for whatever reason, that I got a second chance."

Uncle Jeff pressed the gas again and reached across to give her hand a brief squeeze. "Me too, kid."

When they reached the Golden Gate Bridge he broke the silence again. "So, what's the deal with you and the angry dude?"

Natalie laughed, turning down the music a tad. "Tanner?"

"Right. Tanner."

"Yeah. Um . . . I don't know. He's been mad at me since I got here." Well, that was sort of true.

"What'd you do to him?"

"Nothing. Except . . ." She shifted in her seat and moved the vent in front of her, letting cool air hit her cheeks. The memory of the disappointment in Tanner's eyes that morning made her miserable. "My father wants to shut down Maoilios. Tanner thinks I'm going to do it."

Jeff gave a low whistle. "That explains it."

"He's got other things going on too." Not that she knew the extent of them. She was doing him a favor, really. He clearly didn't need more complications in his life.

"No, I meant . . ." He niggled his bottom lip and shook his head. "I called your father before coming out here. He wanted me to sell my Maoilios shares to him."

"Oh no." Natalie sighed and knuckled her forehead. She hadn't thought far enough ahead for this scenario. "He's serious."

"Apparently. Why?"

"The winery hasn't been doing so well the past few years. Well, since Grandma died, I guess. Grandpa brought Tanner on board as vintner a few years ago, and the numbers are slowly starting to pick up, but not fast enough for my father."

"Bill doesn't have much use for things that don't meet his expectations."

"Or people." Natalie said the words quietly.

She'd lived with the knowledge for years, just tried to side-step it and convince herself that if she tried hard enough, the truth could be altered. "You didn't say you would, did you, Uncle Jeff? Sell him your shares?"

"No way." Laughter shook his muscular shoulders. "I wouldn't sell your father the morning paper after I was done with it. He seems to think yours are in the bag though."

Natalie's throat tightened. Tears pricked and Tanner's words came back to her.

Where'd you go, Mouse?

"How bad are things?" Uncle Jeff asked. "Surely not dire enough to shut the gates?"

"I don't think so." Natalie toyed with the charm around her neck. "I believe things can improve. Tanner has some great ideas, and with a solid business plan, I think we'll see a dramatic change over the next quarter. Maoilios used to be one of the greats, back in the day. We need to put her back on the map."

"We?" He took the exit toward Sonoma, gave a slow nod. "You sound like you're pretty invested in the place, Natalie Grace."

Was she? Invested enough to go up against her father?

"I do own 50 percent," she mumbled. He overtook a truck and Natalie closed her eyes. They'd be off the highway soon enough. She could get through this. She trusted Uncle Jeff.

"Yes, you do," he said. "So your old man figures you'll cave, sell your shares to him, and he'll march in and shut down the whole place without batting an eye."

"Something like that, I suppose." Slow heat hit her cheeks. "But that's not going to happen. I want to convince him he's wrong." There. She'd said it. "Grandpa shouldn't be forced out of the business he built from the ground up simply because my father can't be bothered with it anymore. That's not fair to anyone."

"No, it's not. Putting people out of work is never a good thing." A smile caused the dimple in his cheek to jump. "Especially not tall and handsome vintners."

Natalie rolled her eyes. "This isn't about Tanner." Did that sound convincing? "I want Maoilios to succeed. Purely from a professional standpoint. Because I see the potential. Besides that, it's family."

"And you see this as a challenge."

He'd read her so easily. "I haven't felt this energized about anything in years."

Uncle Jeff pulled at his earlobe. "Any idea how many employees they've got on the payroll right now?"

"Not offhand, but it's a significant number. Of course they bring in extra workers over harvest. Tanner would have all that information."

He drummed his fingers to the beat of the music. "Are you really willing to go up against Bill on this?"

Talk about heavy questions.

"I'm willing to do the right thing. I don't believe shutting down the winery is it."

"There will be fallout."

"With my father there always is." She clenched her hands in her lap.

Was she really willing to go through with this?

Was she strong enough to suffer Bill Mitchell's wrath?

Well. She'd been doing that most of her life.

"Listen, kid . . ." Uncle Jeff interrupted her thoughts. "I don't know how long I'll be here, but you can count on me. I'll do what I can to help. Okay?"

"Thanks, Uncle Jeff." Natalie wanted to smile, but the realization of what she was planning hit her full force. "You want to talk to my father for me?"

His quiet laughter did make her smile. "If you really want me to."

"No." She exhaled and felt a little lighter. "I think, as strange as it sounds, that's why I'm here. To learn how to stand on my own, find out who I really am. At least that's what Tanner says."

"Sounds like Tanner and I might need to have a chat. If he's not too busy doling out advice to pretty ladies."

Great, now he wanted to play matchmaker. "Don't read anything into that, Uncle Jeff."

"Who me?" He chuckled. "There was a time when I would have been in his position, you know. Running Maoilios."

"No, I didn't know." She studied his handsome face. He had to be fifty-something but he looked younger. His thick, dark hair sported barely a hint of gray outside of the dusting around his hairline. He could give every actor who ever played 007 a run for his money. And he was the real deal. "Being James Bond held more appeal?"

Uncle Jeffrey's laugh sounded so much like Grandpa's. "We all make choices. I didn't think a life in Sonoma would make me happy."

"Or maybe you were afraid it would."

His smile broadened as she turned the tables on him. "Astute, aren't you?"

"Well, the tension between you and Sarah Collins isn't hard to miss. Story?"

"Long."

"We still have twenty minutes to home."

Her uncle ground out a sigh, kept his eyes on the road. "You really want to know?"

"Yes. If you want to tell me."

"Sarah and I met in high school. Dated through college. And then . . ." A cough stayed his words and she wondered if he'd continue. "I ended the relationship. On our wedding day."

"Oh." Shock skittered through her. She hadn't seen that coming. Natalie searched for the right words. Wondered if there were any. "Did you just leave or give her an explanation?"

"We talked. Or rather, I tried to talk, she yelled. And if the last few days are any clue, apparently she still hasn't forgiven me."

Natalie grinned. "But she got over you. I mean, at least she found someone else. Had a family."

"I hoped she'd find someone who could make her happy."

"I think she's been on her own awhile though." Natalie wasn't sure of the whole story and didn't want to delve further into topics that might lead back to Tanner. "You never married."

"Nope."

"I suppose your job isn't exactly conducive to a long-term relationship or a family."

"That would be correct."

"And I guess you leaving Maoilios didn't go over too well with Grandpa?"

"You could say that." His sigh was sad. "If you're looking for an explanation, I don't really have one. The only thing I can say is that, at the time, I believed getting married was a mistake, and I knew I had to get out before it was too late and I didn't have the guts to do it before that day."

Natalie pinched her lips and stared out the window. Of course he couldn't know how close to home he'd hit.

"Natalie?"

"Sorry." She debated not telling him. But there wasn't any reason to keep it a secret. "At the beginning of June, I found out my fiancé was cheating on me. So I guess I can empathize with Sarah."

"I'm sorry to hear that." He did sound sorry. "I wasn't cheating on Sarah."

"Maybe not. But you still broke her heart."

He pulled at his jaw, stared straight ahead. "It was a long time ago, kid. Please don't hold it against me. You're the only friend I've got here at the moment, and I sure don't need any more enemies."

"I won't hold it against you." Natalie decided to process their conversation later. She sent him a smile and felt better. "I need all the friends I can get too." The heaviness around her heart lifted the closer they got to Sonoma. Yes, she was invested all right. More than she'd ever thought possible.

Twenty-Two

THE DAY AFTER HER APPOINTMENT IN THE CITY, NATALIE SPENT all morning on her laptop, creating a viable business plan for Maoilios that even her father couldn't say no to. By lunch, she was more convinced than ever that they could make this work.

She sat out on the patio of her grandfather's home and surveyed the property, grateful that she was feeling more like herself, less anxious. And her appetite was back. Just about to go in and see about food, her cell phone rang. Natalie frowned at the screen but answered anyway.

"Hi, Dad."

"Natalie. I read your e-mail and I'm concerned." He didn't waste time. Natalie tapped her feet and willed her heart rate back down.

"What are you concerned about? I'm positive that with the plan I'm putting in place, we can succeed. Put Maoilios back on the map. We'll be back in the black by the end of the year; that should make you happy." And perhaps a little proud of me.

"I thought I was clear. I want that place closed."

Natalie swallowed, measuring her words. "I thought you'd agree with this plan, that you'd consider alternatives."

"I don't see the point. I appreciate the work, but you're wasting your time. I want you back in the office. You've been gone long enough now. I trust you're feeling better and ready to get back to work."

"Dad . . . I'm not sure I . . ." What could she say? Tell him she couldn't leave now because she was making progress with her new doctor and felt closer to normal than she had in years?

"What, Natalie?"

"I'm going to stay longer. Uncle Jeff just got here and I'd like to spend some time with him. And I'm going to keep working on bringing Maoilios back to life."

Her father snorted. "How ironic. A place that only breeds death. It's a lost cause. Give it up."

Natalie could count on one hand the instances she'd gone against her father . . . and wouldn't have to use all her fingers. But she wanted to fight for this. Even as her stomach tightened at his tone, her resolve strengthened. "I won't give it up, Dad. I can't." For so many reasons. Tears stung and she blinked them away angrily. "And since I am the majority shareholder, it's my decision."

A long silence stretched out. Finally, he sighed. "I have never understood you, Natalie. This is bad business, that's all there is to it. But since you seem determined to defy me, I don't suppose there's much I can do. Are you quitting your job?"

"What?" Natalie straightened, her throat dry.

"I assume, since you'll be working so hard with your grand-father, you won't be coming back to work for me."

Natalie watched the dogs race through the vines as a few work-ers headed down the hill. "I hadn't thought about it."

"Then I suggest you do. You have two weeks. I'll need your final decision by then. Stay out there and go down with that sink-ing ship or come home. Where you belong." He clicked off and left Natalie listening to dead air.

Well, then.

She stood, brushed off her jeans, and shook her head.

The line in the sand was drawn.

She'd just have to step over it.

❧

Natalie needed a break. After lunch, she decided to take Sarah up on her invitation to visit Jeni. Before she'd left last night, Sarah said she would be home that afternoon and had invited Natalie to come by.

The little girl was pleased to see her, and Natalie spent some time playing board games and reading with her until she started yawning.

"Need a nap?" Natalie stroked the blond curls and smiled as Jeni nodded. She tucked her into bed and went in search of Sarah. She found her out on their small back porch tending to her herb garden.

"Jeni's napping," Natalie told her, inhaling the strong scent of lavender and mint.

Sarah straightened and took off her gardening gloves. "She usually nods off for a bit around this time. The antibiotics make her drowsy." She moved to a small table and lifted a pitcher. "Iced tea?"

"Thanks." They sat and Natalie sipped the cool liquid, her mind still spinning from the conversation with her father. She turned to Sarah. "You've known my family a long time. Do you have any idea why my father wants this place closed down so badly?"

"Ah." Sarah set down her glass and frowned. "Still insisting on that, is he?"

"I'm afraid so. I thought . . ." She wasn't sure how much to admit. "Well, I thought if I proved him wrong, gave him a viable plan, he'd back down and actually give me some credit for the accomplishment."

Sarah fiddled with a ring on her right hand. "I know that Hal always thought the boys would stay here, that he'd pass the business down to them. Neither one of them was interested."

"I know. Uncle Jeff told me about . . . well, why he left, I guess. Because he wasn't ready to be tied down."

Sarah's eyes clouded. "I suppose you could put it that way. And Bill never came back after he graduated from college. Went straight to Wall Street and never looked back. Hal gave up trying to convince him after a few years. Their relationship has always been rocky, Natalie. I think Bill tried to stay on good terms, because of his mother mostly, bringing you out here for vacations. But since Nicole died . . . and then Grace . . . well, I'm not sure Maoilios holds any good memories for your father."

Natalie hadn't thought about it that way. "You think he'd shut the place down just because it holds bad memories?"

Sarah shrugged. "People deal with grief in different ways."

"Well, I'm quite optimistic about the future of Maoilios. Uncle Jeff agrees. He's willing to do all he can to help."

A small smile lit the other woman's face. "Is that right? What's gotten into him, I wonder? He hasn't wanted anything to do with the place in years."

"True," Natalie mused. "I wonder how long he'll stay."

Sarah gave a half laugh. "As long as it takes for the wind to change."

"I don't know about that." Natalie smiled and hoped the two would have a chance to talk. "I think he has some regrets."

"Don't we all." Sarah leaned over to stroke one of the cats prowling by her legs. "But then again, if I hadn't moved to Seattle and met Brian, I wouldn't have had Marnie and Tanner. Things worked out the way God intended. I have to believe that." Her voice cracked a little and Natalie caught the tears in her eyes.

"How's Marnie doing?"

Sarah's eyes flared, then dimmed. "You don't know?"

Natalie shook her head. Had something happened and nobody told her?

"Marnie's in a coma, Natalie. She's on life support and . . ." Sarah's face grew flushed, and tears trickled down her cheeks as she drew in a shuddering breath. "The doctors have done all they can. We're going to have to say good-bye. Soon. Tanner isn't taking it very well."

"Oh, Sarah." Natalie stared, unsure how to process the news, what to say. "I had no idea."

"Tanner doesn't like to talk about it. I thought maybe Hal might have mentioned it."

"No." She shook her head and wiped her own eyes. "Oh, I can't imagine. I'm so sorry. Those poor kids."

"I know. It's been tough on them. She's in a private acute care facility not far from here. Thankfully her father has been very generous. We could never . . . well, anyway. At first we'd hoped, prayed for a miracle. But now . . . it's not meant to be, I suppose." Sarah gave a small smile and patted Natalie's hand. "Tanner can come off a little rough sometimes, but he's got a lot to deal with."

"Thank you for telling me." Natalie's heart ached for all of them. Why did things like this happen? Why did God allow such senseless death? "I know what it's like to lose a sister."

"Yes." Sarah nodded. "Tanner blames himself for what happened to Marnie. There were things . . . well, no use rehashing it, but it's going to be difficult for him. He needs to forgive himself if he ever hopes to heal."

Natalie felt a chill run through her. She turned her head to avoid Sarah's gaze.

What are you really running from, Natalie?

Dr. Sherman had asked her that yesterday. She hadn't been able to answer him. It would be so easy to admit the truth now, to confide in Sarah, who'd become a friend in a short span of time. But how could she share that memory that kept her up nights; that one lapse in judgment, the tragic mistake she had yet to forgive herself for?

Apparently Natalie had more in common with Tanner Collins than she'd thought.

Tanner trudged up the front steps of the house and kicked off his boots at the door. Gwin bounded in with a bark. Probably hungry. Tanner walked down the hall into the living room to find his dog in Natalie's embrace. Jeni was stretched out beside her on the couch, covered in a blanket, with what looked to be a new American Girl doll. An open book lay on Natalie's lap.

Wonderful. He was so not in the mood to deal with his traitorous feelings when it came to Natalie Mitchell. Work was piling up, he was still exhausted, and the week wasn't over. The only good thing that had happened was Hal firing Leo Kastner on Monday.

"Hi, Uncle Tanner." Jeni coughed and held her arms out. "Wanna see my new doll? Miss Natalie brought her for me."

Tanner sent Natalie a curious glance as he bent to give his niece a hug. "How are you, Jeni Bear?" He pressed a hand to her forehead. Nice and cool.

"Nan says I'm all better. Hafta go to school on Monday." She scrunched up her nose.

Natalie pushed Gwin down and picked up the book. "School's not so bad, Jeni. Weren't you just telling me you got bored at home today?"

"Uh-huh." Jeni's grin slid out and warmed Tanner's heart. He'd freaked with how sick she was at the start of this. Of course, his mother downplayed it and said he was overreacting. He probably had been, but he couldn't imagine anything happening to Jeni. Or Jason. He'd make it to his nephew's game on Saturday if it killed him.

His gaze slid back to Natalie. Her face was shadowed in soft light that played with the blue in her eyes. A hesitant smile lifted her lips and sent a shiver through him.

Okay, she needed to leave.

Tanner straightened and crossed his arms. "What are you doing here?" Because that wasn't obvious.

"I came to see Jeni." She appeared a bit taken aback by his tone. "Where's my mother?"

"In the kitchen."

"Uncle Tanner?" Jason stood in the doorway, textbook in hand.

"Hey, bud." Tanner stifled a yawn, too aware of Natalie's stare. Too aware of her presence in his house. With his family. "What's up?"

"Math. Nan said I had to ask you. She doesn't know how to figure it out."

"Okay." He took a moment to catch his breath. "Let me feed Gwin, grab a drink, and then I'll—"

"I can help." Natalie beckoned Jason over. "Show me what you've got there, Jason."

"But we're reading, Miss Natalie," Jeni protested.

Natalie smiled and tapped Jeni's nose. "I know, but if we don't save some for later, we'll be all done. You can't rush a good book, Jeni. You need to savor it."

"What's that mean?"

Her brother huffed. "It means you need to enjoy it. Make it last." Jason rolled his eyes. "*S-A-V-O-R*. Savor. Spelling bee last week. Don't know why we need to memorize stupid words we're never going to use."

"Because it furthers your education, Jason," Tanner quipped. "You could grow up to be a Harvard graduate like Miss Natalie and use all sorts of stupid words."

A flicker of anger marred Natalie's features, but she lowered her head and studied Jason's textbook. Tanner snapped his fingers at Gwin and went into the kitchen.

His mother sat at the table. Working on her Bible study.

Guilt gripped him by the collar and gave him a good shake.

Tanner sighed. *Okay, God, I get it.*

"Hey, Mom."

"Hi, hon. How was your day?"

"Long." Tanner poured kibble for Gwin and refilled her water dish. Impatience stamped out his guilt and he turned back to his mother. "Why is she here?"

His mother hummed, wrote something in her study guide, closed the book, and set it aside with her Bible. Took off her reading glasses and smiled. "If you're referring to Natalie, she came over this afternoon to see Jeni. Brought her a new doll."

"I saw." Tanner opened the fridge and stared at nothing in particular.

He grabbed a soda and slammed the fridge door. "When are we eating?"

"Excuse me?" Her eyes narrowed as she sat back and folded her arms.

"What? I'm hungry." Fizz shot up his nose and he coughed. "Didn't know it was a crime to ask when dinner is." Tanner was fully aware he sounded just like Jason. He put down his soda and flicked through the pile of mail. Nothing from Seattle, thank God. "Any more unwanted phone calls?"

"Not this week." Her sigh rang around the kitchen. "I'm planning to call Rance and your father tomorrow."

Air whooshed out of him, and he slammed a hand on the counter.

"If you're finished there," his mother said pointedly, "you can set the table. And ask Natalie to stay. Hal was headed out to a new restaurant in town with Jeffrey."

Tanner shrugged off the request. "I'm sure Natalie will want to go with them." He strode to the door.

"Tanner." Her voice took a tone he knew better than to argue with.

"Mom. She doesn't need to be here." He couldn't take anymore.

"Maybe she does, Tanner." She pulled him back from the door, pinned him with searching eyes. "Natalie wants to give Hal and Jeffrey a chance to talk. She suggested they go out, had to twist both their arms but finally got them to agree. If you think for one minute I'm going to send her up to that big house to eat all alone, think again. Now go wash up, find a clean shirt, and find some manners while you're at it."

"Hey, I—" He lifted his hands in protest but she skewered him with a look that said he could argue all night, but he wouldn't win.

"Go."

Tanner marched to the bathroom and slammed the door. Sank against the wall and closed his eyes. *How much more, Lord?*

Twenty-Three

NATALIE HADN'T REALLY WANTED TO STAY FOR DINNER, BUT Sarah insisted. So she suffered through Tanner's dark looks and unnecessary comments, enjoyed Sarah's pot roast, and divided her attention between the two children.

Jason was a bright boy, but she sensed an underlying anger that seemed to be directed at his uncle, for the most part. Jeni wanted Natalie to stay all night. Natalie agreed to one more game of Candyland after dinner, but then said her good-byes and pulled on her jacket.

"Thanks so much, Sarah. Dinner was wonderful."

"We're glad you could stay. And you didn't need to help with the dishes." Sarah smiled and walked her to the front door. "Oh." She looked out into the dark night. "Where's your car?"

Natalie peered through the darkness. "It was such a lovely day, I walked down. I wasn't expecting to stay so long." A decision she now regretted.

"You can't walk back in the dark. Tanner, grab the flashlight, hon."

Tanner was sprawled in the La-Z-Boy, eyes closed, a discarded newspaper on his lap. His dark hair fell forward, his mouth slightly open in slumber. Natalie fought the urge to walk over there and brush his hair back. Considering what a jerk he'd been all night, she'd be more tempted to pull it, so she studied her sneakers instead.

"Tanner!" Sarah's voice rose as she tried to get his attention.

Natalie cringed. "Honestly, Sarah, don't wake him. I'll be fine."

Tanner sat up, pinching the bridge of his nose. "What? What's wrong?" His hair was still damp from the shower, mussed and curling attractively above one eyebrow.

"Natalie is leaving."

Heavy eyes blinked at them. "Okay. See ya." He flopped back in the chair and closed his eyes again.

"Tanner!" Sarah looked mortified but Natalie shook her head and stepped onto the front porch.

"Good-night, Sarah. I'll be fine, really." She bolted before Sarah could do more damage. She was almost to the end of the gravel drive when she heard boots crunching behind her.

"Natalie. Wait up." Tanner jogged up to her and matched her stride. He shone a flashlight around them before training it on the dirt road. Huddled in a UCLA hoodie, he smothered a yawn, still looking half asleep. Gwin ran circles around them and eventually bounded off into the vineyard.

"You don't need to come with me." Natalie pushed forward. The night air was cool and the full moon lit the path she turned down to take her through the vines.

Tanner gave a slight chuckle. "Oh, I do need to," he answered. "My mother won't let me back in the house if I don't."

"Then just stand out here for a few minutes. I don't need the light, and I've had enough of your pleasant company for one night."

He cleared his throat and gave a long sigh. "I'm sorry. I've been acting like an idiot. Can we start over?" He sounded so worn-out that Natalie simply shrugged, shoved her hands in the pockets of her jacket, and walked on.

When she couldn't stand the silence anymore, she spoke. "Well, I'm sorry if I was rude on Wednesday."

"Apologies all round then," he replied, eyes on the ground.

"Tanner . . ." She searched for the right words. "Your mother told me about your sister. I'm so sorry."

He exhaled, nodded, and ran a hand down his face. "It's hard for me to talk about. I probably would have told you at some point."

"I don't mind that you didn't." Natalie shook her head. "I just want you to know that I'm here, if you do want to talk. I don't want this awkwardness between us. We can't let one stupid mistake stand in the way of us being friends and working together to save the winery."

"Mistake?"

Was the man completely daft? "Saturday night. We kissed. That was a mistake. Forget it happened. Okay?"

Oh, but it had. And no matter which way she turned it, it still tipped her world.

Tanner picked up his pace and began to walk up the hill.

Natalie walked faster to catch up to him. "Tanner? Can we move on?"

"Ten steps ahead of you."

Okay, then. Good. "I found out my father asked Uncle Jeffrey if he'd sell him his shares in Maoilios."

A low rumble rose from the cavity of his chest. Natalie stole a glance at him. He bent to pick up a stick and threw it for Gwin. "Now what?"

"Oh, he's not selling." Natalie laughed, surprised she wasn't more afraid of what was coming. "I don't think there's much love lost between my father and my uncle."

"Or between Hal and his sons, by the sounds of it."

"True," Natalie surmised. "I know Uncle Jeff regrets leaving all those years ago. I hope he and Grandpa can improve their relationship."

"I doubt your uncle will stick around long enough."

"He does have a job, Tanner." Natalie watched his eyes narrow. "I guess you know the story between him and your mother."

"That he dumped her at the altar? Yeah, I know the story." Tanner whistled for Gwin and threw another stick.

"He just told me. I was a little surprised," she admitted. "I know they were young, but I felt for your mom. I know what it feels like to get jilted."

Tanner's angry sigh sailed through the night air. "Men who run away from commitment aren't worth the air they breathe. They have no concept of the devastation they leave in their wake when they walk out."

Natalie slowed her steps, catching the fire in his eyes. "Are we still talking about my uncle?"

He walked over to a row of vines and examined the leaves under the glow of his flashlight. She watched him carefully turn the leaf and check out the underside.

"What are you looking for?"

"Mildew. Bugs." He bent to snag a weed, yanked it by the roots, and tossed it onto the path. "Do you know how long it takes to get a first harvest, Natalie?"

"No idea." She shot him a tentative smile.

"It can take years. You don't use your first year's crop. The fruit is too small, not sweet enough. You have to train the vines, you see. You cut them back, tend to them, keep them free of bugs and disease. It's not a process you can just walk away from." He stooped low and came up with a few stray grapes that the pickers had left. Walked to where she stood and held a purple globe to her lips. "Taste."

Natalie opened her mouth to receive the morsel and allowed the flavor to saturate her taste buds. "Wow, that's sweet."

"Too sweet." Tanner munched on a couple of grapes and spat seeds. "When the fruit begins to ripen, we have to continually monitor what's going on out here. The ripening process is crucial to our end result. Veraison—when the grapes soften—is when the sugars accumulate, and the taste of the grape tells us when they're ready. You can't turn your back on it. Not for a minute."

"I suppose not." Natalie watched him pull a few more weeds

around the vines. "Rather like raising a family, right? You can't bring children into the world and then let them fend for themselves."

"No. You can't." He rose, brushed his hands over his jeans. "But it happens all the time."

"My mother had a string of nannies for us." Natalie wasn't sure where that thought came from. "I don't remember her ever reading to me or taking us to the park. When she wasn't traveling with my father, she was out at some meeting or other. We were paraded in front of their friends when it was convenient."

Tanner stepped a little closer. "My father left when I was ten." The pain in his voice was still raw.

Natalie frowned. Had they ever talked about it? "Why?"

"I suppose for the obvious reasons. My folks were fighting all the time." He started walking again, slower this time. "And my sister . . . had problems. I remember she had these intense mood swings. One day she was up, the next she wouldn't leave her room. After her first suicide attempt, I remember my parents arguing. She'd been diagnosed as bipolar. I didn't want to hear it, so I left the house. A couple months later, my dad was gone. And he took my sister with him."

"Tanner." Tears welled in her eyes. "That's terrible. I'm so sorry."

"I got over it." His stalwart expression said he hadn't. Not by a long shot. "My mom and I came back to Sonoma. My grandparents were still here. She started working for Hal that year, and we moved to Maoilios."

"Did your father visit or anything? Did you see your sister at all?"

"My dad tried to keep in touch, but I was pretty angry, I didn't make it easy. He remarried. Marnie visited a few times. When she got older, the visits stopped. My father tried to get me to visit them in Seattle. I never would because—"

"You were scared he wouldn't let you come back."

He stopped walking, stared at her for a long moment, his eyes flashing in the moonlight. "I never really looked at it that way, but maybe you're right."

"And you've never forgiven him for leaving."

He shrugged and glanced across the fields of vines, as though ghosts from the past would emerge any minute. "He basically abandoned me. That's not forgivable."

They approached the swing set on the lawn below the house. Natalie stopped and stared up at the big house, seeing ghosts of her own. A few windows glowed with soft light. "Your sister came back eventually though?"

"Yeah. Around the time your grandmother passed. I was on vacation. Came home and there they were, like they'd always been there." He shuffled his feet, hands still in his pockets. "Well, here you are." He tipped his head toward the house, unsmiling.

They were done talking.

Sorrow stretched between them, but she didn't know how to step around it. "Thanks for walking me."

Silence hovered, punctuated by Gwin's panting and the occasional cry of a night owl. Natalie hesitated, strange emotion sticking in her throat. "I do want us to be friends, Tanner. The truth is, Saturday night . . . you scared me," she whispered.

"I what?" His brows knit together.

She smiled and let her shoulders rise and fall. "The things you said. You were right. I don't let my guard down very often. Don't let anybody get close to me. But you . . . I don't know, for some reason I feel like I can talk to you. I always did."

"And this is a bad thing?" He stepped a little closer, almost smiling.

Natalie laughed. "Besides Laura, I don't confide in anyone. Don't become invested in relationships. To be honest, when I found out Peter was cheating on me, I was relieved. I was glad I wouldn't have to marry him, wouldn't have to keep pretending."

"Pretending?"

She waved a hand. "I didn't really love him. Not the way I should have. I tried to because I thought it could work, thought I could be the person everyone expects me to be. But here, this place . . ." Natalie walked the perimeter of the play set and drank in the solitude of the surrounding fields. "I don't have to pretend when I'm here. You made me remember that. And then you kissed me."

"Which was a mistake, as you've already pointed out." Tension edged his words and made her wonder whether she should go on.

Natalie stared at her feet and willed the tears back. "I wasn't expecting it. And I wasn't expecting to feel . . . the way I did. That scared me."

Tanner reached for her hands. "Why?"

"Because the things you said gave me hope." Slow tears warmed her cheeks. "For the first time in years, I felt like maybe I could get through this. Like I wanted to. Like maybe my life is worth living after all."

"I did all that, huh?" The warmth of his smile burrowed deep and watered the seeds he'd already planted. His hands moved up to rest on her shoulders. Hooded eyes bored into her and unlocked her secrets. "I'm sorry for all you've gone through, Natalie. If being here is helping, then I'm glad. But if it isn't, if it's too hard, then you should go. Forget about the winery. I'll figure things out on my own."

"No." She shook her head, unexpected joy filling her. "The thing is, Tanner, I want to stay. I want to save Maoilios. I think it's something I need to do. For me."

He held her gaze for a while without speaking. "Your father won't like it."

"I know." Stubbornness she didn't realize she owned stepped out of the shadows.

Tanner still looked skeptical. "Are you sure you can handle this, Mouse?"

"No." She wasn't. Not really. "But as long as I have my grandfather and Uncle Jeff supporting me, I think I can."

His smile came and went. "Do I get to be on the team?"

"Only if you want to be." He didn't need to know about the conversation with her father that morning.

"I love a good fight." His boyish grin made her laugh.

"Yes, apparently you do. But do try to keep your fists in check if he happens to show up, okay?"

"I'll do my best." Tanner stepped away from her, whistled for Gwin, and tossed the flashlight back and forth. "So. Still want to see those wineries?"

A flutter of excitement started and she smiled. "Still want to drive my Jag?"

"You know it."

"Well, I'm free next week. Let me know what works for you." This was not a date, Natalie reminded herself. This was business.

"I think I can clear Monday morning." Tanner's phone glowed in the darkness as he studied it. "Yeah, that would work."

"Good. It's a date." Natalie almost slapped her forehead. "I mean, it's not a date. It's . . . oh, you know what I mean."

"I know what you mean. It's a date that's not a date. Right?"

"Right."

"We could make it a date." His teasing tone brought heat to her cheeks.

Oh boy. Natalie's chest constricted as she forced herself to shake her head. "Not a good idea."

"Worth a shot though. I can see you blushing even in the dark." His wink sizzled through her and coaxed a smile.

"Good-night, Tanner."

"Good-night, Mouse." Tanner tapped two fingers to his forehead in salute. "Sweet dreams."

Twenty-Four

Nerves set up a trampoline in Natalie's stomach and began to bounce as she walked down the steps on Monday morning to where Tanner waited, leaning against his truck, two colorful travel mugs in hand, dressed in jeans, a rough-hewn sweater, and sneakers, looking like a movie star.

"Please tell me that's coffee," she mumbled, reaching for the mug he held toward her. "I didn't sleep well last night."

"Coffee. Strong." His chuckle wrapped around her like a hug in the crisp morning air. "I've been up since five."

"Aren't you special." Natalie grinned and waved a CD his way. "I brought the tunes."

"You what?" Tanner opened the passenger door as she handed over the keys to her vehicle.

Natalie laughed, got in, and buckled up. Tanner pulled off the thick blue sweater he wore over a white polo shirt, chucked it onto the backseat, and slid into the Jag. A look of awe swept over his face as he wound his hands around the gleaming wood and leather steering wheel.

"Sweet." He looked like a kid on Christmas morning.

"It's just a car, Tanner."

"Oh no, no, no. This is not 'just a car.'" His gleeful chuckle made her smile. She had to admit, the beige leather interior was impressive.

Once he started the engine, she slipped in the disc. As they pulled out of the driveway, The Spice Girls blasted from the speakers.

"Nooo . . ." Tanner's groan competed with girly shouts of "Tell me what you want . . ." *Seriously?* "Spice Girls? How old are you?"

"They were my favorite group in middle school." Natalie laughed and bounced in her seat. "You can drive, but I get to pick the music. The best of the '90s. All. Day. Long."

"Dang, girl. Your taste in music sucks. We should have taken my truck." The sides of his mouth twitched as he shot a glance her way. "Are you torturing me for any particular reason today or just for fun?"

"Just for fun." Natalie pushed her seat back a bit and sipped from her mug. The coffee warmed her, but the smile he sent her lit her soul.

It was going to be a good day.

～

After seeing several wineries and enjoying a leisurely lunch at one of them, it was time to head back. Natalie was itching to get onto the computer and put down some new ideas. She wrote furiously while Tanner drove them toward home.

"Oh." When she finally glanced up, she realized they weren't anywhere near the road to Maoilios. "Where are we going now?"

"You'll see."

"Okay." Natalie breathed deep and tried to enjoy the scenery while Tanner drove the winding roads, not saying much as she talked. They drove for almost an hour, the car taking them higher until eventually he pulled into a lay-by overlooking Lake Sonoma.

"Best view in town," he told her. "Come on."

They got out and Natalie found a picnic bench to sit on and stared at the red ball of fire in the sky with Tanner beside her. The setting sun stretched feather-like fingers of orange and pink toward the tops of the Douglas firs below. "It's beautiful, Tanner."

"One of my favorite spots."

"I can see why." Natalie smiled and turned to see Tanner watching her. "What are you looking at?"

"You." His finger brushed the side of her cheek, his touch sending a shiver through her. He was close enough to kiss her. If he wanted to. If she'd let him. He inched closer and Natalie's heart picked up speed. "I've been thinking about something," he said quietly.

"Okay. Do I need to take notes?" She shifted a little, trying to put a bit of space between them. His chuckle made her smile, but as he brought his hands around her face and threaded his fingers through her hair, her smile faded.

"I doubt it." He leaned even closer so their noses touched, his breath warm, inviting her mind to places it had no business going. "I think we should revisit the no-kissing rule."

"You do?" She was lost in his dancing eyes. Totally, completely, delightfully lost.

"I do."

"Tanner, I'm not sure. I—"

A low growl stuck in his throat as his lips tentatively touched hers. "You overanalyze, Mouse."

"One of us has to."

"Sometimes thinking is overrated." Tanner pressed his lips to hers, gently at first, until she relaxed against him and began to respond. Before she could process what was happening, Natalie melted into his embrace, gave in, and realized he was right.

Thinking was definitely overrated.

Tanner's kisses set her insides on fire. She ran her fingers through his hair, across his muscular back and down the arms that held her so carefully. His exploration of her mouth ignited feelings all too willing and able to push her toward dangerous territory.

"Tanner." Natalie broke away and caught her breath. "Oh boy."

"Yeah." He let out his breath and pressed his forehead against hers.

"I'm still not sure this is a good idea."

He pulled back a bit and his playful smile said he couldn't care less. "Live a little, Natalie. Admit you enjoyed it. I won't tell a soul, I promise."

She rolled her eyes and leaned into his embrace. "You're incorrigible."

"Dictionary."

"Whatever." Natalie gave a happy sigh and ran a finger over the veins of his tanned hand.

Tanner tipped her chin upward. "And just so you know, that kiss was not a mistake. The first one wasn't either."

She studied his serious expression. "Are you sure?"

He didn't answer her with words, just wrapped her in his arms again and kissed her until nothing else mattered. Natalie finally fought against foolishness and pushed her hands against his chest. "All right, I believe you."

He gave a low laugh. "Please don't fire me. I promise not to let this get in the way of doing my job." Tanner threaded his fingers through hers and she suspected he was only half joking.

Natalie grinned and shook her head. "I won't fire you. But I'll probably have to fire Candy."

"Candy? Why is that?"

"Because I think she has her sights set on upper management."

"Oh, does she now?" Tanner laughed. "I don't think she's at all suitable for the position. That job requires somebody uber-organized to the point of annoying, who has very odd taste in music, and knows exactly how to press my buttons."

Natalie giggled. "I don't do that on purpose. Not all the time." She placed a hand against his cheek and watched the golden flecks in his eyes. "Thank you for bringing me here. For . . ." Why was it so hard to voice her feelings? "For believing in me. You do, don't you?"

He nodded. "I do. And I think we're going to make a great team." The light in his eyes faded as the sun dipped lower. "What I'm going through, losing Marnie, maybe losing the kids . . . having you here is making life a little easier."

"That's something I didn't think I'd ever hear you say." They shared a laugh, then sat in silence until finally Natalie had to ask. "Can you tell me what happened, Tanner? With your sister? Your mom told me she's in a coma, in a long-term care facility, but I don't know the story."

Tanner rubbed the bridge of his nose. "Okay." He sighed and stared at her through tired eyes. "It was early August. We had a few friends over for a barbecue. Marnie skipped out halfway through. The kids were frantic. We didn't know where she'd gone. She didn't answer her cell. I made up some excuse about her going to see a sick friend." He pulled his arms up and locked his hands behind his neck.

"I got real good at that the past few years. Telling them things that weren't true." He trained a steady gaze on her. "Along with the bipolar, Marnie had other issues. Drugs, alcohol. She'd go off her meds without warning. She called me later, at around two a.m. Wasted. Wanted me to come get her." He closed his eyes and leaned forward. "I was angry, and you can probably imagine how the conversation went. I told her to get a cab. The next call I got was about an hour later. From the cops."

Natalie's heart thudded against her chest. "She drove."

He lowered his head. "She drove. Rammed through a guardrail on Highway 1. She was unresponsive at the scene, but still had a pulse. The damage to her spinal cord was too severe. She never regained consciousness. After a week we were told if we wanted to keep her on a ventilator, she'd have to be moved to a facility that could care for her. I guess we all hoped she'd pull through some-how, beat the odds. The latest batch of tests they ran last week showed still no brain activity."

"Oh, Tanner." She reached for his hand.

"I don't drink now because of Marnie. I just figured it was bet-ter for the kids. They've seen enough. Although some days I have to admit I'm tempted, but I don't ever want to be out of control around them like she often was." He draped an arm around her shoulder.

"You're a good man, Tanner Collins." Natalie leaned against him, wishing for the right words. "What comes next?"

"We let her go. My mother wants to do it now, before the holi-days. Says it'll be easier on everyone. She's already called my father and Rance, the kids' father." He jumped down and walked the area, kicking small stones around. "I don't know how to do this." His ashen expression, the haunted eyes, everything about him said he held himself responsible.

She could tell him any number of possible scenarios he'd probably heard before. Tell him he could have picked Marnie up and still gotten into an accident. Tell him Marnie could have been run over crossing the street.

But she couldn't tell him her own story.

Couldn't tell him that sometimes things just happen, mistakes are made, and you somehow learn to live with the consequences.

Instead, she took the few steps needed to bridge the gap between them, slipped her arms around him, and held him again. "I'm so sorry, Tanner."

He released a shuddering sigh as he hugged her back, buried his face against her hair, his lips resting at her temple. "She's already gone," he rasped. "I know that, but I just don't know how to let her go, emotionally, I guess."

Natalie nodded and raised her eyes to his. "Letting go means releasing the responsibility. And you can't do that because then, how would you be punished? Knowing she's still here physically, seeing her like that, that pain is what you deserve. Right?"

Tanner's eyes flared, his rugged features shadowed in orange. "That's an awfully accurate analysis." A smile flickered and faded.

"I've spent a lot of years hanging out with shrinks." Tears blurred her vision. "But that's how I feel too. Letting go of Nic, saying that awful night was an accident and nothing more, that frees me from guilt. Why didn't I die too? I ask myself that a lot. At least I used to. But I'm learning that somehow it doesn't matter. I need to get over it. I know that, but I haven't quite figured out how either."

"We make quite a pair, huh?" He cradled her face, his stare so intense she felt she would melt under it. He brushed aside her tears with the base of his thumbs. "Maybe we could figure it out together?"

Natalie lifted her chin slightly. "Maybe."

He covered her hand with his. "Somehow I knew you'd understand."

Oh, she could love this man.

Maybe she already did.

Fresh tears pricked and she blinked them back. "Will the kids' father take them?"

Tanner's mouth turned downward. "I don't know. Jeni doesn't even remember Rance. She was barely two when they left Seattle. Jase is just angry. I don't want that scumbag in their lives. I'll do everything to make sure he stays out."

She recognized the stubborn anger and knew there was no point in explaining that in most cases, the biological father would win if they went to court. "Well. Let's hope things don't get ugly."

It was getting dark; they needed to go. Natalie held out a hand. "Give me the keys."

"What?" The space between his eyes got smaller.

"I want to drive home. Since we're working on getting rid of our demons, I figure it's the perfect opportunity. If I can get us back to Maoilios without turning into a blubbering, incoherent mess, I'll be one step closer to normalcy."

Tanner fished the car keys from his pocket and dropped them into her hand. "And I think I just got a little crazier."

"Oh, come on, Mr. Collins." Natalie flashed a smile. "You like to live on the edge. Get in the car."

Natalie drove with hesitation at first. She hadn't driven since her panic attack on the way back from San Francisco, but slowly, giving herself an internal pep talk the way her doctor had instructed, she gained confidence, loosened her grip on the wheel just a tad, and began to enjoy the drive. Mostly she enjoyed knowing Tanner sat beside her, a satisfied smile set in place.

Twenty-Five

TANNER SAT AT HIS DESK IN HIS OFFICE ON THURSDAY MORN-ing, trying to concentrate. He had to admit, Natalie's system of tracking their sales and orders made things easier, and he hardly missed his old dinosaur of a computer. Yes, having her around was definitely making life easier. In a lot of ways.

A grin escaped as he thought about their time on the mountain on Monday. Funny thing was, he hadn't seen it coming. Over the weekend he'd convinced himself that she was right, they should be friends, nothing more. It was a practical decision and one that made the most sense. Yet by the end of that day, having had more fun with her than he'd intended, he'd known the whole friendship thing just wasn't going to fly. And the way she'd responded to his kisses told him she felt the same.

And it was ridiculous.

What could he possibly offer someone like Natalie Mitchell?

She was getting calls from her father. He was pressuring her to change her mind, do things his way. He wondered whether she was strong enough for this fight. As much as Tanner didn't want Bill Mitchell to win, he was beginning to care more about Natalie's well-being than the future of Maoilios.

Tanner groaned and scrubbed his face. He couldn't afford to give away a piece of his heart when there was so little left of it in the first place.

But . . .

Get over it, doofus. He could almost hear Jason saying it out loud.

Sometimes the kid gave great advice.

Juan Carlos, one of the younger employees in the yard, burst into his office, waving a cell phone. "Tanner! *Hubo un accidente—* it's Miguel, come on, man!"

"What kind of accident?" Tanner bolted after Juan Carlos, sweat slipping down his back. "Did you call Hal?"

"*Sí.* He wasn't at the house but I left a message with Mister Jeff." They hopped into the truck and Juan Carlos floored it out of the gates of the property. Fifteen minutes later they pulled up to the scene.

A Maoilios flatbed lay on its side in the ditch. The heady stench of wine permeated the air. Police and ambulance personnel were already there, and Tanner caught sight of Miguel being lifted onto a stretcher.

"Miguel!" Tanner raced to him, looked him over, and breathed relief when his friend flashed a weak smile.

"Tanner . . . I don't know what happened, man. One minute I was driving along, the next I was in the ditch. Man, the wine—"

"Don't worry about the wine." Tanner clasped Miguel's hand and shook his head. "You hurt? Did you get knocked out?"

"He was coming around when we got here, conscious but loopy," one of the paramedics said. "His leg's broken. His shoulder, too, and we'll treat him for a concussion."

"Tanner?" Sheriff Grimes crooked a finger. Tanner nodded, patted Miguel's hand as they wheeled him to the waiting ambulance.

"Hey, Sheriff." Tanner greeted the older man, his heart still pounding.

"Sorry about the wreck."

"Yeah, well." He sighed and hooked his thumbs through his belt loops. Tried not to look at the boxes of broken bottles strewn on the field beside him. Flies were already swarming and a couple buzzards inspected the area, flying low, then swooping upward. How many boxes had been in that delivery? Fifty, a hundred? Twelve bottles in each box.

"Miguel's okay. That's what matters."

"Yup." The sheriff scratched his jaw. "If it wasn't for his Medic-Alert bracelet, I would have done a blood alcohol. His sugars were way low. You know he's diabetic, right?"

"Shoot. Yeah." Tanner set his jaw. "He's not always the best at checking his levels or taking his insulin. I'll have a chat with his wife." This was not what they needed right now, but the damage was done.

"Okay. Well, we'll just call it an accident. No other vehicles involved, thank God. And make sure he knows how serious this could have been. I don't want this to happen again." He strode off, leaving Tanner with the urge to puke up the three cups of coffee he'd downed that morning.

Tanner stiffened as he watched Natalie's car and Hal's truck park on the side of the road. Hal headed toward the ambulance and Jeffrey and Natalie jumped out of the Jag and headed toward Tanner.

"Tanner!" Natalie saw him, broke into a run, pulled up short an inch away. "You're okay."

Tanner frowned and dipped his head.

For a moment there, he'd thought she was about to launch herself at him.

"Ye-ah. I'm okay." He scanned her face, caught the fear in her eyes. "I wasn't driving. It was Miguel." A completely inappropriate smile tickled his lips at her stricken expression. Tanner put a hand over his mouth and massaged his jaw. She was getting really good at letting her guard down.

"Oh." Color rapidly returned to her cheeks. "How is he?"

"Shaken up, but not too badly injured. Could have been worse."

"That's good. So you're okay?" Her hands fluttered a little, like she wanted to make sure for herself, and she shoved them in the pockets of her jeans.

"I'm okay." Tanner bit his cheek and fought a strong urge to put his arms around her. But with her uncle watching them with obvious interest, he refrained.

"I'll go check on Miguel then."

Jeffrey cleared his throat as Natalie hightailed it toward the ambulance. "The message we got wasn't clear. Just that there'd been an accident."

"She really thought it was me?" Tanner didn't have to ask, but Jeffrey's nonchalant shrug was the confirmation he needed.

"It would seem so."

The guy's knowing smile irked him, and Tanner bit back a smart remark. "Well, anyway . . ."

"What happened?" Jeffrey stalked the area, taking it all in.

Tanner tried to put thoughts of Natalie out of his head. "Miguel's diabetic. Apparently his sugars were low; he must have passed out behind the wheel."

Jeffrey took off his sunglasses and frowned. "That's unfortunate. What are you going to do about it?"

Tanner stared. "I'll talk to him but there's not much else I can do. This'll probably get him to start taking things more seriously."

"If you fired him he'd definitely take things more seriously."

"Well, that's not going to happen." Tanner shoved his hands in his pockets. "It was just an accident."

"And what did it cost you?" Jeffrey swept an arm toward the overturned truck and shook his head.

Tanner tried to ignore the disapproval on the man's face. "Look, maybe this isn't how you'd run things, but we're a family here. I'll talk to Miguel and make sure it doesn't happen again. But I won't fire him."

"Fair enough." Something passed across Jeffrey's face, regret, sorrow maybe. Tanner didn't know and didn't care. Then the man clasped his shoulder and smiled. "I'll go see where my dad is." He strolled off and Tanner looked toward the ambulance to see if Natalie was still there.

Oh no.

She hadn't made it past the overturned truck.

She stood on the side of the road, staring at the wreck, her face gray.

He got there fast. "Hey, hey. Look at me." Tanner turned her to face him instead. He slid his arms around her, pulled her close, and felt her trembling.

"Don't let go," she whispered.

"Not a chance." He breathed her in, his heart aching.

"I thought I could handle this." She stared up at him through wide wet eyes. Then she crumpled against him.

Tanner held tight and rested a hand on the back of her head. "It's okay, Natalie, nobody got hurt. You listening to me?"

Slowly she lifted her head, fear still stamped across her face. "Is he really okay?"

"Yes. A few injuries. Nothing life threatening."

"Okay. And I'm glad that you weren't—" She jumped as the ambulance wailed off. Her nerves had to be shot. "Has anyone called Iliana?" She disengaged herself from him and did a remarkable job of pulling it together.

Tanner checked his cell. "I don't know. She teaches at Jason's school. I'll see if I can get hold of her. I should probably get down there and drive her to the hospital."

"She'll be upset. I'll come with you."

"Are you sure?"

"Yes." Natalie glanced backward, and he watched a shudder rip through her. "How many cases did we lose?"

"I was trying to remember. I'll have to check the inventory." Tanner hesitated and shifted his gaze under her stare.

"A significant loss?"

She was good. He clenched his jaw, put a hand under her elbow, and directed her toward his truck. "We'll make up for it." They'd better. Or Bill Mitchell just might get his way after all.

⁓

Natalie and Tanner waited with Iliana until Miguel was moved from the ER to a room upstairs. David arrived, and Natalie stood in a corner of the room listening to him pray with Miguel and Iliana. Hal and Jeffrey stood on the other side of the bed. Her grandfather's head was bowed. Jeffrey studied his cell phone.

Tanner stared out the window, stance stiff, arms crossed against his chest, his mouth tight. One dirty boot tapped quietly against the shiny linoleum floor. She could see that he wanted to be anywhere else but in this room.

She'd almost thrown herself at him in relief when she'd realized that he was safe. A stupid lapse in self-control. The last thing they needed was for her uncle and grandfather to get wind of the shift in their relationship. Besides that, Natalie wasn't ready to figure out her feelings for Tanner Collins.

She had enough to deal with.

Natalie let herself out of the room while they prayed and wandered the halls of the hospital. She intended to make her way downstairs and wait outside. Everything here brought back horrific memories. The sight of her sister, life gone from her, cleaned up and waiting alone in a single room as they all traipsed in to say good-bye . . .

The image quickened her pace and heightened her need to leave the building.

As she reached the elevator, an overhead sign caught her eye. *Chapel.*

Natalie pressed the Down button and waited. Her eyes lifted to the sign again. Frustration kicked against some inexplicable force that drew her toward the two wooden doors at the end of the hallway.

"What do You want from me?" she murmured.

Inside the chapel, the air was cool, the room lit with soft light from half globes positioned along the walls. About twelve wooden pews with red cushions led up to an altar, a large gold cross atop it.

Natalie's breath hissed out of her like air released from a tire.

She took a seat in the front pew, clutched her elbows, and battled an overwhelming urge to sink to her knees.

She was so tired of feeling alone. Feeling helpless. Trapped in the life she'd thought would make her happy. Or, at the very least, make her parents happy. From the moment Nicole died, Natalie's feelings no longer mattered. *She* no longer mattered.

Except perhaps to God.

"You know what I've done," she whispered. "How can I accept what You want to give me?"

Mercy. Forgiveness. Love.

Redemption.

Lately, when sleep stayed away, Natalie padded through the darkened house, crept downstairs, and spent time in her grandfather's study. Over the past few weeks, she'd read more books on faith than she'd known existed. At first she'd picked up a couple of titles by sheer curiosity. *Mere Christianity, The Pursuit of God, The Case for Christ* . . . She'd read each at least twice, looking up quotes in the Bible Laura had given her. She'd found a couple of authors whose words resonated. Spoke to her soul. And she could no longer refute the message.

Yet something still held her back.

She leaned her head against the hard pew, released the stress of the day, and let the tears trail down her cheeks. A peace surrounded her, sheltered her, and waited for her to claim it. Perhaps God understood her hesitation. Expected it. If there were no coincidences, as her grandfather was so fond of saying, then her reluctance to fully commit was no surprise to Him.

She wondered what a new life filled with purpose and meaning might look like. Or would she continue to live her life like a ship sailing with no particular port in mind.

The doors creaked open, but Natalie didn't move. Didn't open her eyes when she heard steps thudding down the aisle, stopping at her pew. And didn't dare move at the sound of Tanner's long sigh as he lowered himself beside her and slid an arm around her shaking shoulders.

"Hal and Jeffrey went home. I thought you might have taken off, but Jeff had your keys. He took your car. I told them I'd find you and bring you home."

"Sorry." Natalie sniffed and wiped her eyes. "I just couldn't stay in there. Didn't mean to worry anyone."

"No." He slipped his fingers through her hair and massaged the back of her neck. "You never do."

Natalie gave an involuntary shiver. "How did you know where to find me?"

"A hunch." Strong fingers deepened their pressure and forced her tight muscles to relax. "You getting any answers?"

"Not yet." She smiled and leaned into his touch. "Does God really care about us, Tanner? Does He love us more than we can ever comprehend?"

His hands moved to her shoulders and he pressed, working out the kinks. "Yes. I believe that. I don't always act like it, or understand it, but I can't dispute it."

Natalie propped her elbows on her knees, her eyes burning.

She could tell him the whole story now, see what he would do with it. But she didn't have that courage.

"Since coming to California, I can't stop thinking about the night of the accident." It was as close to the truth as she was willing to get. "I don't know how to get past it, Tanner."

He stopped the pressure of his fingers and sat back, one hand warm against her back. "I know that feeling all too well, Mouse."

She turned her head, her eyes catching his. "You do, don't you?"

Tanner didn't say anything for a long moment. His eyes misted over and he chewed his lip, finally reached for her hand. "I need to go see my sister. Make my peace."

"What happened wasn't your fault. Get rid of that guilt, Tanner. Say good-bye knowing you're free of it."

"Come with me."

Natalie shook her head, her heart breaking for him. "You have to do this on your own. Don't wait. Don't make any more excuses. Just go."

He brought her hand to his lips and kissed it. "All right. Tomorrow morning then."

"If my prayers will make a difference, you'll have them."

He smiled and wiped his cheeks. "They will."

"I guess you won't really be alone after all, will you?" Warmth she couldn't explain flooded her as she spoke the words.

Tanner pulled her close and kissed the top of her head. "No, I won't. Thanks for the reminder. Come on, let's get out of here."

⌒⏑

The next morning Tanner stood beside Marnie's bed. He'd wanted to argue with Natalie last night, put this off again. But as usual, she was right. Tanner sensed it the moment he'd walked in here.

It was time.

Tanner pulled up a chair, reached for Marnie's limp hand, and held it in his. "I guess this is it, huh?" He sniffed, ignoring his tears. He sat awhile before he could speak again. "I'm sorry, Marn. I should have listened to you that night. Should have come to get you." He gave a deep, shuddering sigh. "But I didn't. And I have to live with that. But something tells me you'd want me to get over it, to move on."

"Hold a grudge much, Tanner?" Marnie grinned and tapped his foot with hers.

The summer night was warm, and they sat out on the deck, sipping wine and catching up. Marnie was having a good month and Tanner was glad. Life was so much easier on them all when she stayed on her meds. He didn't know how long it would last. In the three years since she'd moved back to Sonoma, he'd lost count how many times he'd gone out looking for her, finding her in one bar or another, sometimes not finding her at all.

"I'm only saying if Dad hadn't left, maybe things would have been different."

"Things wouldn't have been different." Marnie pushed long curls behind her shoulders and nailed him with those clear eyes that saw right through him. "Things might have been worse. Moving didn't make me better. You know that."

He sat in silence, not sure what to say. "Will it always be like this?"

"Maybe." She shrugged, her eyes glistening under the glow of the moon. "All I know is, I needed to get back here, to Mom. She'd make sure the kids were taken care of. Their father can't do it and I . . . Sometimes I don't trust myself with them."

Tanner knew. He'd seen her flares of temper, watched Jason flinch at her touch and Jeni snuggle in closer to his mom when the winds changed and the other side of his sister showed up. It broke his heart, but he'd vowed from the beginning that his first priority would be to protect his niece and nephew.

"I hate it." Marnie swiped the back of her hand across her eyes. "I hate that they're scared of me sometimes. I love them so much, but I can't . . . I can't stop things once they start. I need you to make sure they're safe, Tanner. Do whatever it takes, whatever you need to, okay?"

Tanner stared at her, his chest tight, his breath coming hard and fast. He put an arm around her shoulders and pulled her against him, nodding as she gave way to sobs. "I'll look after them, Marn. I promise."

Whatever it takes . . .

Tanner wiped his eyes and got to his feet, his head pounding, heart heavy, but his load a little lighter. He placed Marnie's hands one over the other atop the light blanket that covered her motionless frame. Inhaled and tasted the salt of his tears as he managed a last smile for her and bent to kiss her cool cheek. "Rest well, sis. I'll take care of things here."

He straightened, took a final glance around the room, and accepted what would come.

The next time he stood here, it would be for the last time.

But he'd gotten his chance to say good-bye, made his peace.

His focus now was on the kids.

Twenty-Six

JEFFREY STOOD IN THE SMALL GRAVEYARD ON FRIDAY MORN-ing, zipped up his beige Windbreaker, and huddled against the mid-October wind that nipped his heels. The sun was just cresting over the rows of grapes. Soon the day would warm, but for now he'd enjoy the chill in the air.

He knelt beside the granite headstone and ran his finger over his mother's name.

GRACE CONSTANCE MITCHELL
BELOVED WIFE
CHERISHED MOTHER
SAFE IN THE ARMS OF JESUS

He hesitated over the Scripture verses. Jeremiah 29:11 and Romans 10:13. He knew the first one from memory. *"For I know the plans I have for you," declares the Lord* . . . but he stalled on the second. Jeffrey fished out his iPhone and clicked on his Bible app. Couldn't remember when he'd last used it.

As soon as he scrolled to the verse, he knew it.

"Everyone who calls on the name of the Lord will be saved."

Everyone?

He sank to his knees, his eyes burning.

After everything he'd done, he wouldn't be included on that list. He'd turned his back on his family, betrayed the woman who loved him.

Killed people.

Committed murder under the guise of serving his country, doing his job.

Sometimes he'd pulled the trigger to save his own life. Sometimes he'd pulled it because he could. Sometimes . . . *God forgive me* . . . because he'd wanted to.

He pinched the bridge of his nose and listened to his ragged breathing.

His shoulders shook with the effort it took to contain his sorrow.

Jeffrey inhaled the scent of the soil and the sweet smell of grapes that still lingered on the vines. He wished God would show him what to do next. He placed a hand on the dry ground beneath him, felt the life of the land pulse through him like an electric current.

And then he felt the thud of boots coming up behind him.

He didn't have to turn to know his father crouched next to him. He rested a hand on Jeffrey's shoulder and uttered a thick sigh.

"Your mother loved you very much, son. And she was proud of you. We both were."

Jeffrey lifted his head and looked into his father's eyes. "Were you?"

His dad sank to his knees and flashed a withering smile. "Did I wish you had stayed here, worked the vines with me? Sure. But over time, I came to realize that you needed to create your own life. Not the one your mother or I thought you should have, but the one you wanted. Even if you were making a mistake, I knew we had to let you go. And you did well, son. The work you did over there, that was important."

Jeffrey stared, realizing for the first time that perhaps his parents really had been proud of him. "I came to love it," Jeffrey told him. "I even met someone eventually. Lisa. We worked in the field together for years. She wasn't much like Sarah, but she was passionate, brave. I thought I loved her enough to maybe bring her home one day."

"Why didn't you?"

Jeffrey released a broken sigh. "She was killed. Ten years ago. I almost quit then, wanted to give it up and come home, but I became consumed with revenge. So I stayed."

"Did you find them?"

"Yes."

Dad's eyes shimmered with understanding. "And did it help you? Did it validate your grief?"

"No." Jeffrey shook his head and blinked moisture. "It only made it worse."

Dad nodded somberly and picked at a few blades of grass. "Do you remember when I used to take you and Bill hunting?"

"Sure." Jeffrey shrugged. They would make the five-hour trip north every year to the rustic cabin in the Marble Mountains. The area was stark, cold, and beautiful. But he'd enjoyed it mainly because he got to hang out with his father.

"I remember the day you shot your first buck. Do you?"

"Yeah." He'd been about ten or eleven. At first he thrilled to the thought. Imagined going back to school and bragging about it. Maybe take pictures for them all to see. But he'd locked eyes with the animal, and somehow he couldn't do it. He wanted to put the gun down and run. Then Bill nudged him, called him a wuss, and Jeffrey pulled the trigger. Bill and Dad ended up skinning the thing. Jeffrey hadn't touched venison since.

"I guess hunting was never my thing."

"Your brother enjoyed the kill. You didn't. I saw it in your eyes that day. After that, I was happy to let you fish while we went out. I didn't force you to shoot again. A man has to make his own way. And you were making yours. Which is why your career path always baffled me."

Jeffrey nodded. "Yeah." He flexed his fingers and watched a flock of birds descend on the copse of cypress trees at the crest of the hill.

After he fled California, he'd met up with a buddy in London. Simon introduced him to some friends and the next thing he knew, Jeffrey was so deep in the world of espionage he didn't think he'd ever get out. "I suppose I chose it because it was something so far beyond what I thought I would ever do. I left home because I wanted more. I didn't want to do the expected thing, work for you, marry Sarah, and have a family. As crass as it sounds now, the thought of that life was stifling. I was a stupid kid who didn't value what he had. I thought I could reinvent myself. I did it so well I forgot who I really was."

"And where you came from."

"Yes." He ran a hand down his damp face. "The last mission I led ended badly. I wanted to resign, but my boss convinced me to take leave and reassess. I . . . I've been a bit of a mess, for years actually. PTSD, same as Natalie. Funny, huh?"

"No." Silence ran along with the stream at the bottom of the hill. "What is it you want, Jeffrey?" Dad asked. "More importantly, what do you think God wants for you?"

Jeffrey studied his mother's headstone through a haze of tears. "I'd like to be happy. And I think . . . perhaps I could be happy here."

"All right." Dad nodded. "It's never too late to start over."

He met his father's eyes, incredulous. "Would you have me? Would you let me come back here and work with you?"

"Of course I would. But maybe I'm not the only one you need to ask." His father's knowing look brought a smile.

"In case you hadn't noticed, Sarah isn't talking to me."

"Sarah has a lot going on. I think you'll find she needs you more than she's willing to admit."

"You think she'll forgive me?" He needed to believe that. Needed to believe second chances were possible.

"I suspect she already has." They stood together and Dad squeezed his shoulder with a smile. "Now that you know what you want, son, it's time to go after it."

❧

Jeffrey found Sarah in the kitchen after lunch that day.

"Thought you didn't work Fridays."

She looked his way. "I don't. But I had to take a couple days off when Jeni was sick, so I'm catching up."

"Need some help?"

"Suit yourself." Her reply made him grin. It was a start.

He joined her at the sink and grabbed a plate to dry. She moved about the kitchen putting things away and obviously trying to pretend he wasn't there.

Finally she spoke. "How do you think things are going with the vineyard? Has Natalie decided what to do yet?"

He placed a couple glasses in the dishwasher and turned to face her. "I think she has."

Hope lit Sarah's eyes. "Does she want to stay?"

"I'm not sure she knows that yet. But I suspect your son wouldn't complain if she did."

"No, he probably wouldn't."

Her smile tugged at his heart and made him want to take her in his arms. He shoved his hands in the pockets of his jeans instead.

"And you, Jeffrey? Your father seems to think you might be staying awhile."

"Well, that depends on your definition of awhile."

She rolled her eyes in familiar fashion. "Which means you have no idea."

"It means I'm doing some thinking."

"Well, if you are planning on staying longer, could you please stop stalking me?"

"I'm not stalking you." He chuckled at the pretty flush rising in her cheeks. "If I was stalking you, you would have no idea I was doing it."

Sarah dried her hands on a tea towel. "Of course I wouldn't. I imagine you're well trained in all manner of stealth, aren't you, Jeffrey?"

Now he felt his own cheeks heat. What was wrong with him?

He smiled anyway and watched light dance in her brown eyes.

The years had been kind to her. More than kind. In his estimation, she was even more beautiful than she'd been as a young girl. Hardly a hint of gray in her honey-colored hair, and only a few laugh lines around her eyes.

He wondered what Sarah saw when she looked at him. Not the virile young buck she'd planned on marrying, that's for sure. Probably the washed-up old guy he felt like most days.

"How's your shoulder?" She backed up against the counter and crossed her arms.

"My what?"

"You've been favoring your right arm since you arrived. And judging by the slight limp and the bruise along the left side of your face that's just starting to fade, I'd guess you were in a heck of an accident. Or something. Is that why you came back here?"

The question hit him like an unexpected strong wind.

Jeffrey rocked back on his heels. How could she read him so easily after all these years?

"I can't really talk about it." He couldn't blurt out his failures, his fears. Couldn't admit he'd been wrong on so many levels.

"Sorry I asked." Sarah brushed past him to the door.

"Wait." Jeffrey reached for her arm.

She tossed him a hard look over her shoulder. "You were never too fond of intimate conversations and, given your current line of work, I assume that hasn't changed."

"Sarah." Jeffrey refused to let her go. He held her hands in his and pulled her closer. So close he could see her tears shimmering, threatening to slip down her cheeks.

"Don't, Jeff." Her lower lip trembled. "Whatever you're about to say, don't. Too much time has passed. It's too late."

"I don't believe it's ever too late to say you're sorry." His voice thickened with unexpected sorrow, and he managed a weak smile. "You have no idea how long I've thought about this moment. Talked myself out of it. Said the same as you, that it was too late. Whether it means anything to you now, I truly am sorry. I can't change how I treated you. I abandoned you on what should have been the happiest day of your life, but I can tell you this, I've regretted it every day since."

"I don't believe you," she whispered.

He held her hands and waited until she looked at him. Wet trails marked her cheeks. Jeffrey sighed and wished he could make things right. "I know you got on with your life—married and had a family. But I didn't. I left my life here. With you. I know I won't get a second chance, I've accepted that. But I need to ask for your forgiveness. I don't deserve it but—"

"Stop." She shook her head, drew in a breath, and finally smiled.

"What?" Jeffrey battled confusion.

"It's already done," she said, placing a hand against his chest.

"What is?" He wondered at the peaceful look that broke through her tears. "I don't understand."

"I know." Her smile grew braver. "Why don't we go sit outside. I'll explain."

They sat in a shady section of the patio and Jeffrey listened to her story, hung on her every word, and reiterated the fact that he was a first-class fool.

"So, that's how Tanner and I ended up back in Sonoma." Sarah dabbed her eyes with a Kleenex. "I feel like I failed my daughter, Jeff. I was a nurse. I should have been able to deal with her illness. Instead, I pushed her away, lived in denial pretending it wasn't happening. I have so many regrets, especially now, when I won't get the chance to make things right with her."

"I'm so sorry."

She met his eyes, sighed deep, and smiled. "Letting Marnie go will be the hardest thing we've ever done, but I trust God to get us through." She squeezed his hands with a laugh. "When you first showed up, I questioned God. I couldn't understand why, at this time, when I'm already dealing with so much, but maybe—" Her voice hitched and her anguish tore through him.

"Maybe I'm here because you need someone?"

She nodded and Jeffrey stood, pulling her to her feet and into his arms. He held her as she cried. And in that heartbreaking moment, he made his peace.

With his own past.

With God.

And he made a promise that whatever came next, he would never let this woman down again.

Twenty-Seven

NATALIE AND TANNER SPENT THAT SATURDAY TOGETHER. Went to Jason's game, took the kids out for burgers, and later, Tanner picked her up for dinner. A real date, he promised.

Sarah had said she was waiting to hear from Tanner's dad, wasn't sure what day he and Rance would be arriving, and Tanner didn't want to talk about it. For a few hours, they let reality slip away and relaxed in each other's company over good food and an excellent bottle of wine—from Maoilios, of course.

They pulled up to Grandpa Hal's just before ten. Natalie noticed the strange car in the driveway at once. "Who's here at this hour?"

Tanner shrugged but a frown crested his forehead. "Guess we'll find out."

As soon as they entered the foyer, Natalie heard voices, one of them Sarah's. "What's going on?"

Tanner set his jaw and strode ahead of her.

They found Grandpa, Uncle Jeff, and Tanner's mom in the living room. Sarah was in conversation with two men Natalie had never seen before. Everyone in the room turned their way as they entered.

"Oh no." Tanner exhaled and leaned over his knees like he might pass out.

Uncle Jeff was by his side in an instant. "Take it easy, kid." He placed a hand under Tanner's elbow. Natalie held his other arm, her heart pounding. She caught the flash of anger in Tanner's eyes as he straightened and stared at them.

"Tanner." The older of the two men stepped forward. "It's good to see you, son."

His father.

Natalie moved a little closer and studied the man. It wasn't hard to see where Tanner got his good looks. He was about Tanner's height, dark hair flecked with just a few gray strands. Dressed in a three-piece suit and shiny black shoes, he could have walked into one of her company board meetings and been right at home.

The other man was younger, in his thirties maybe, dressed in faded jeans, a black T-shirt emblazoned with the emblem of some band she'd never heard of. Tattoos curled around both biceps and a diamond stud sparkled from one ear. He caught her staring, narrowed a pair of startling blue eyes, and crossed his arms.

Not terribly friendly, whoever he was.

"Natalie." Grandpa Hal cleared his throat, stood in front of the two men. His eyes were clouded with worry. "Allow me to introduce you. This is Brian Collins, Tanner's father. And this is Rance Harper. Marnie's husband."

"Ex-husband," Tanner ground out.

"Dude, chill," Rance said, emitting a frustrated-sounding sigh.

"You're kidding, right?"

Natalie prayed Tanner wouldn't take a swing at the guy. "I'm Natalie Mitchell, Hal's granddaughter." She wasn't sure it was nice to meet them, so she didn't say so. She shook hands instead. Then she glanced at Sarah. Her stricken look told the story.

Told her why they were here.

It was time to let Marnie go.

The older woman's face displayed more sorrow, fear, and pent-up emotion than Natalie knew what to do with. She moved toward her and embraced her in a long hug.

Sarah sank against her and choked back a sob. "I tried calling Tanner's cell . . . tried to find you earlier."

"Didn't check my messages. Sorry." Tanner cleared his throat. "Where are the kids?"

"Upstairs. We were over here watching a movie," Sarah explained. "I didn't know they were coming in tonight."

"We were able to find an earlier flight. I did leave a voice mail." Brian shot Sarah a look of concern.

"Well, I didn't get it."

"Have the kids seen them?" Tanner's voice held a frantic edge but Sarah shook her head.

"The kids were already asleep when they arrived."

"Good." Tanner folded his arms, still glowering.

"Okay. Why don't we all take a seat?" Grandpa shot Natalie a pointed look and she nodded. Took Tanner's hand and tried to coax him to a chair, but he shook her off.

"I don't want to sit. I want them to leave." He pointed at his father with a trembling hand.

"Tanner, they need to be here," his mother said. "You know that."

Brian Collins raised his hands in surrender. "Son—"

"Don't call me that." Tanner took a step forward and Hal moved to stand between Tanner and his dad.

"Tanner, you need to calm down." He placed his hands on Tanner's shoulders and waited until he looked at him. Natalie watched fear replace his fury.

"Did something happen today?" Tanner's voice trembled, moisture pooling in his eyes. "Is Marnie gone?"

"No, sweetheart. Tanner . . . come sit." Sarah patted the spot beside her on the couch and Tanner lowered himself down and put his head in his hands. Sarah wrapped an arm around his back. "I know it's hard. But you knew this was coming. We're talking about Monday. But Rance has power of attorney. He—"

"What?" Tanner's head shot up and he glared at his sister's ex. "That's not possible."

"Actually, it is. Because I'm still married to Marnie." Rance sniffed and ran a hand down his face, his eyes moist. "She left me, but we never officially divorced."

Tanner shook his head. "I don't believe you. Mom, she said, they . . . she . . ." Tanner leaned back against the couch and rubbed his face, his chest heaving. Natalie's heart broke for him.

"Marnie said a lot of things that weren't true, Tanner," Sarah said. "I didn't know there wasn't a divorce either."

Tanner skewered Rance with a glare. "So you want to come in now, sign a piece of paper, and be done with it? You've got two kids who haven't seen you in years. How do you explain that?"

"Tanner." Brian slid off his jacket and loosened his tie. Let out a breath and glanced at Rance. Natalie noticed a flash of gold on Brian's left hand. "When Marnie left Seattle, we didn't know where she'd gone. She didn't head straight here. It took weeks to track her down. She drove the kids all over the place. They lived out of their car . . . it was the middle of winter. We're lucky they made it down here in one piece."

"I'm not asking you," Tanner snapped. "I'm asking him. Your kids have been here five years. Where have you been?"

The guy let go of a long, sad sigh. "I was pretty messed up when Marnie left. It took me a few years to get my head on straight. I'm not proud of it, but that's who I was back then. A friend finally convinced me to get help. I'm clean now. And I knew they were safe here. Happy. I didn't want to confuse them, I guess. I figured until I could get my life together, they were better off without me."

"They are." Tanner's stare never wavered. "They don't need to have their lives turned upside down again. And they'll have to lock me up before I let some drug addict take them out of my home."

"Whoa, back up." Rance held up a hand. "You don't know me, man."

"I don't need to know you."

"Yeah, actually you do." Rance let out his breath and scanned the room. "You're right. I was a druggie. Marnie had her issues, but so did I. I didn't think I wanted to be a dad. Sure wasn't ready for the responsibility. But I'm not that man anymore. I've been clean going on two years now. I have a good job, and I'm ready for that commitment. And, like it or not, they are my kids. You can't stop me from seeing them."

"Nobody's stopping you." Tanner's dad placed a hand on Rance's arm and gave him a look of warning. "Tanner, I realize this is a lot to take in, son, but—"

Tanner shot to his feet. "If you call me that one more time, I swear I'll—"

"Tanner, stop!" His mother rose and grabbed his arm. "Losing your temper isn't going to solve a thing. Now look, it's late, and we're going to have a hard day tomorrow with the kids. I suggest we call it a night."

Tanner shook her off and stormed from the room. A moment later the slam of the front door shook the house.

❧

Sunday was excruciating. He didn't know how he sat through church that morning. They made a sorry bunch, the lot of them, wiping their eyes and sniffing through the sermon. Jason kept staring at Rance, seated across the aisle and three pews down. Tanner wanted to drag the man out of the sanctuary by his collar. Natalie kept squeezing his arm, like she could read his mind. Which she probably could.

Lunch was painful. For some reason his mother insisted on inviting his father and Rance to join them. And then, that afternoon, they sat down together and explained to Jason and Jeni what Tanner suspected they already knew.

Tomorrow they'd say good-bye to their mother.

That evening, Tanner trekked down the hall to the kids' bedrooms, his heart thundering. Wondered how fast he could pack their stuff and head for the border after the funeral.

Jeni was asleep, her arms wrapped tight around her teddy bear, Gwin sprawled at the bottom of the bed. Tanner picked up a few books off the floor and set them on her bookshelf. Scanned the outfit laid out for the following day, his throat burning, a pink skirt with a white T-shirt with big pink and red flowers over it, Jeni's favorite.

Tanner leaned over his niece and laid a hand on her head. "God, help me," he breathed out. Tears stung and warmed his cheeks as he watched Jeni roll onto her back, a sleepy smile on her lips. Her eyes fluttered and opened for a split second.

"Uncle Tanner?"

"Shh. Just saying good-night, princess. Go back to sleep."

Jeni sat up, sleepy eyes wide and red-rimmed. "Mama's gonna die," she whispered.

"I know." A tear slipped down her cheek as he brushed her hair back.

She smacked his hand away.

"You said the doctors would make her better!" Huge gulping sobs erupted from her tiny chest. "You promised!"

Tanner stared at her in horror. "Jeni . . . I . . ."

What? What could he say or do to take her pain away?

He *had* promised.

She inched up the bed and clutched her teddy bear in a choke hold, eyes flashing. "You said you *always* keep your promises. Why'd you lie? Make them do it, Uncle Tanner! Make my mommy better!"

"Baby, I can't." Grief squeezed all the air from his chest. "I'm sorry I promised you that. I shouldn't have."

"But you did." Jeni turned her back on him and burrowed her

face in the pillow. Tanner put a hand on her back and she scooted away. "Leave me alone!"

"Jeni, I'm sorry." He wanted to scoop her into his arms, hold her, and make it all go away. But all he could do was sit there while she cried.

Once Jeni's breathing slowed and she sank back into slumber, Tanner backed out of the room.

They'd probably be up with her through the night. Lately, thanks to Jason talking about Rance, she'd started having nightmares, dreaming about people taking her away.

There was no way to fix this.

How would any of them get through the next day and what was to follow?

Light glowed under Jason's closed door. Tanner inhaled and pushed the door open.

Jason sat on his unmade bed, still dressed in the day's clothes, knees pulled to his chest as he glared at the wall in front of him. Tanner took a look at the empty shelves and stepped around landmines of Legos, books, Pokémon cards, and the contents of Jason's closet. The kid had done a bang-up job of trashing his room.

A flash of memory let him see himself at ten years old, having done the very same thing the day his father and Marnie left. Tanner knew this kind of pain.

"Hey." Tanner sank down beside Jason, put an arm around his nephew's trembling shoulders, and pulled him close. He shut his eyes at the sound of the first sob.

There was nothing he could say, nothing he could do to take it away. He prayed through the stifling silence and wondered whether God would grant them a miracle. Not that he deserved it, but it sure would be nice. Because life was crashing down around him and he wasn't sure how he was going to make it through the next forty-eight hours.

"I don't want to go tomorrow." Jason wiped his eyes and released a shuddering sigh.

"Me either." Tanner tightened his hold and rested his chin on Jason's sweaty head. "It's gonna be hard, Jase, but we need to let her go."

"Why didn't God just make her better?" Jason lifted his chin and stared up at him through defeated eyes. "I asked Him every day. Why didn't He listen?"

Tanner clenched his jaw and blinked. "He did listen. But sometimes God allows things we don't understand. Things we don't like, things that don't make sense. But that doesn't mean He doesn't love us. Doesn't still want the best for us."

"How is this the best?" Jason stuck his bottom lip out, his eyes filling again.

Tanner swallowed the burning acid in his throat. "Remember that day last year, we were fishing in the river and you lost your footing?"

"Yeah."

It had been the end of winter, but the sun was out and Tanner figured it'd be fun. But Jason waded out too far and slipped. His terrified yell turned Tanner's blood cold. Next thing he knew, Tanner was up to his neck in icy water, gripping his nephew's hand, and trying desperately to inch back to the riverbank before the rushing water took them both under.

"Remember how I grabbed your hand that day, Jase? How I promised I wouldn't let go?"

Jason shrugged. "I remember being scared and screaming at you to not let me go."

"And I didn't, did I?" Tanner ran a hand over the boy's mop of brown hair. "What did I tell you, do you remember?"

Tears shimmered on Jason's blistering cheeks. "You told me to trust you."

"That's right. And that's what I'm asking you to do now, bud. Trust me. And trust God. He's not going to let go, and neither am I."

Soulful eyes studied him, filled with more questions than Tanner had answers for.

Then Jason finally asked the question Tanner knew was coming. "Is my dad going to take us away?"

Panic clawed its way upward and Tanner was back on that riverbank, trying to pull Jason to safety. "I don't know, Jase."

"You don't know? You mean he could?" The boy's eyes widened and Tanner fought hard against the urge to lie and tell him absolutely not.

"Let's wait and see what the next few days bring, bud."

Jason fingered the soft blanket and heaved a sigh. "Can't we just stay here with you and Nan? I don't care if you never come to another game. And lots of dads work all the time. It'd be okay."

Tanner's laugh was short and shaky. "But I'm not your dad, Jason."

Jason rubbed his eyes, his stare ripping Tanner's heart in half. "I know, but you could be. You could marry Natalie and you guys could adopt us."

Tanner about fell off the bed. "Marry Natalie?"

"Why not?" Jason's watery smile said it was the perfect solution. "You guys like each other. Don't you?"

Oh boy. "It's not that easy, Jase." But it was surprisingly easy to imagine. Tanner sighed. "Look, Nan and I want you and Jeni to stay with us, if that's the best thing. Right now we don't know if it is. We don't really know your dad, and he doesn't know us. We have to figure it all out. So we're just going to have to take it one day at a time, okay?"

"No!" Jason pushed against Tanner. "You can't let him take us, Uncle Tanner! You can't!"

"Jase, please . . ." Tanner's vision blurred as he reached for his nephew. "I don't know what to do."

"Well, you're supposed to! You're supposed to look after us. Not let anything bad happen to us. You can't let him take us. There must be something you can do!"

Tanner held the boy tight and let him cry. He wanted to cry, too, just as hard. Jason leaned against Tanner's chest and finally gave a tiny whimper. "This is freaking messed up."

"Yeah." Tanner cradled his hand around Jason's head and nodded. "It is."

Messed up didn't come close.

As he stood on the porch later, angry tears running down his face, Tanner shook his head at the night sky. This was worse than any punishment he'd ever conjured up for himself.

Watching the kids live this nightmare, unable to ease their pain, faced with the possibility of having to let them go . . .

If he had to let them walk out of his life . . . it would kill him.

And . . . if he simply let them go without a fight? If he walked out of theirs?

Then he'd be no better than his own father.

Twenty-Eight

HE'D EXPECTED RAIN. ON A DAY LIKE TODAY, THUNDER-storms would have been appropriate. Instead, bright sun streamed through the striped curtains of the quiet room where Tanner and his family gathered. One last time.

Papers were signed. The doctor and nurses had disappeared, and now his mother stood beside Marnie's bed, her arms around Jason and Jeni. She spoke in soothing tones, letting them know their mother was in no pain and that she would soon be with Jesus.

Tanner's shoulders shook and he gulped air. How was his mom not a complete wreck?

He couldn't even get one word out.

And if that infernal machine beeped once more, he'd hurl it to the floor.

Jason glanced his way through stormy, tear-filled eyes. Tanner's father and Rance had already come in and now waited outside, giving them this time alone. Tanner was grateful for that. He summoned what little strength he had left, went to stand beside Jason, and his nephew fell against him, his thin frame wracking with sobs.

"I know, I know." Tanner held tight, his eyes flooding.

God, get us through this. Let it be over.

Let them be okay.

Jeni tugged on his arm. "Uncle Tanner, can you pick me up?" she whispered. "I want to give Mama a kiss."

He hoisted her up and Jeni leaned over, smoothed back Marnie's hair, and kissed her forehead. "Bye, Mama. I love you."

Jason cried harder, and Tanner heard his mother struggling to hold in her sobs. He held Jeni close against him and felt her tears on his neck as she buried into his shoulder. "Okay, sweetheart." He met his mother's red-rimmed eyes in silent question and she nodded.

"You take the kids outside, and I'll let the doctor know."

Tanner was never so glad to leave a room in all his life.

He still held Jeni, and Jason clung to his arm. As they approached the small waiting area, Rance and Brian got to their feet. Rance took a couple steps forward and Tanner shook his head. The guy got the message and let them pass.

Down in the large foyer, Tanner caught sight of Hal, Jeffrey, and Natalie.

His eyes filled again as she walked quickly toward them, and Jeni lunged for her.

Tanner hugged Jason close and wished his mother would hurry up.

There was only so much a man could take, and he'd reached his limit today.

⌒

Later that afternoon, Tanner sat alone on his back porch. Gwin rested her head on his knee, gazing up at him through mournful eyes. He ran a hand over her soft coat, completely numb.

The back door creaked open and he knew it was Natalie before she sat down.

"Hey." She wound her fingers through his, rested her head against his arm, and gave him that smile he was starting to wonder if he could live without. "The kids are watching a movie and your mom's resting."

Tanner nodded, his throat burning. "I didn't expect you to come today. You didn't have to."

"I know." She sniffed and blinked tears. "But I couldn't imagine being anywhere else."

He sighed and slid his arm around her. "Thank you. I'm glad you were there. It meant a lot to the kids. And my mom. It wasn't too much?"

"Tanner." She wiped a tear off his cheek and placed her hand against his face. "I'd do anything for you."

And somehow he knew she meant it. The words resonated, filled the hole in his heart, and almost made him smile. Words wouldn't come, so instead, he leaned in, kissed her softly, and they sat in silence as the sun went down.

⌒

Two days later, following the funeral service, friends and family gathered around a cleared patch of land by the small lake on the property where white swans swam and ducks dove for fish, and they planted rose bushes, lilies, and lilacs.

Marnie was gone.

A lot of people came to pay their respects. All the employees at Maoilios. The friends Marnie had made during her time with them. The kids' teachers, people from church.

David gave a brief sermon, but Tanner couldn't remember a word of it. Marnie would be cremated, so they'd ended up here on Hal's property at the kids' request. Later, they'd have a quiet family dinner. Which included his father and Rance Harper.

Tanner held Jeni in his arms as they watched Miguel and a couple other guys fill in dirt around the new plants.

"These pretty flowers are going to grow and bloom and whenever we come down here, we'll think of Mama in heaven," Jeni explained. "And one day when I'm old and all grown up and shriveled, with lots and lots of grandchildren, I'll see her again."

Tanner nodded, his vision blurred, but he mustered a smile for his niece. What he wouldn't give for just an ounce of that childlike faith.

"Don't be sad, Uncle Tanner. Mama's happy now." Jeni wrapped her arms around his neck in a hug as Tanner saw Rance heading toward them.

"Hey, Jeni." Rance settled a foot away. Didn't try to touch her. "You doing okay?"

Jeni nodded and stuck her thumb in her mouth. Tanner's heart clenched. She hadn't sucked her thumb in almost a year.

Tanner looked at Jeni. "Sweetheart, how about you go help water the flowers, huh? Looks like Miguel has an extra watering can over there just for you." Jeni gave him another hug before she wriggled down and ran off to the flower garden.

"She's shy," Tanner muttered, not sure why he was bothering.

"She doesn't know me yet." Rance turned the diamond stud in his ear. "They're going to need some time. I understand."

Tanner scuffed his shoes and stared at the swans in the pond.

"You holding up all right, Tanner?"

"Sure." He blew air through his lips, his jaw tight.

"Your friend David seems like a great guy. Good preacher."

Tanner shoved his hands in his pockets and set a scathing glance on the man about to ransack his life. "No offense, but I really don't feel like talking to you today, Rance."

Tanner walked off. Out of his peripheral vision he watched Jason kick a ball around with some of the older boys while the younger kids chased the dogs and played tag.

The garden had been Natalie's idea.

She'd sat beside him during the service, held his hand, given him the strength he needed. She'd been there for him the past few days; so much a part of his life now that he wasn't sure what it looked like without her. He watched her talking with his father and Hal. Dressed in a simple black dress, a thin gold belt buckled around her waist, and black pumps, she was the picture of elegance. Always gave off that vibe, the way her grandmother Grace had. Her hair curled neatly around her face and she played with her necklace. When she glanced his way and saw him looking, she flashed a smile that pulled one from him in return.

Funny how one smile from her could reach right through him and turn on the lights, even on the darkest of days.

Tanner wasn't quite sure when he'd fallen in love with Natalie Mitchell.

Or what he was going to do about it.

First he had to get through what he feared was coming.

He was going to lose the kids.

Rance's first meeting with Jason and Jeni had been more than awkward. They'd been quiet, Rance a little wary, and Tanner hadn't made it any easier, looming in the back of the room. But the guy showed up faithfully every day.

Jeni was unsure, but it wouldn't take her long to warm to him. Jason might need more time, but Tanner saw an innate curiosity there, recognized that deep-seated longing the boy had to know his father.

He'd once fostered the same feelings.

He told Natalie he'd sell everything he owned to fight Rance in court if it came to it. She thought he needed to give the man a chance. But Tanner knew where the kids belonged. Where they'd be happier. And that was right here on Maoilios.

With him.

As the days passed, that conviction began to waver.

Who was he to stand in the way, denying Jason the second chance he himself had never had?

That question robbed him of sleep and haunted his waking hours.

But he wasn't quite ready to go there. He didn't trust Rance Harper. Not yet.

And Tanner's heart began to harden against the pain headed his way.

"Hey." Jeffrey approached him. "Nice service."

"Yeah." Tanner messed with his hair. He needed a trim. If he'd shaved that morning, it'd only been out of habit; he couldn't remember doing it. "Thanks for coming." Tanner hadn't failed to notice the support the man had given his mom these past few days. More than he'd been able to.

"You doing okay, Tanner?"

He'd be a lot better if people would quit asking him that. "Hanging in."

"Good." Jeff clapped him on the shoulder. "So, thought you might like to know I've done a little digging on your man over there." He tipped his head in Rance's direction.

Tanner's smile tickled. "I'm starting to like you, Mitchell."

Jeff grinned, fished out his phone, and scrolled down the screen. "Don't get too excited. Harper's story checks out. He was a small-time dealer when he and Marnie met. She got pregnant at eighteen. They got married at some point, looks like around the time Jason was born. I gather they were both pretty strung out until she left Seattle. That seemed to shake him up. He did two years in and out of rehab, but eventually it stuck, seems to be squeaky clean now. Works for his brother's advertising agency, doing quite well by all appearances. Has his own house, a mortgage, a few debts but he's paying them on time. Leads worship at his church."

"Wonderful." Tanner put on a pair of shades. "Any women?" The guy had to have a weakness.

"One. A 'close friend.' Kate Thomas. Single. Couple years younger than him. Kindergarten teacher. Loves kids, dogs, and her elderly grandmother. Goes to the same church. The perfect match, apparently. But from what I've heard, the relationship has been kept low-key, given that Rance was technically still married. No sign of them sleeping together or anything that might go against the Good Book."

"What about his past?" Tanner knew he was reaching. Floundering in the clear waters of truth, trying to muddy them up for the sake of his selfish heart. "Surely a judge wouldn't just hand the kids over to a drug addict?"

"Tanner." Jeff's smile bordered on pity. "He's clean. Gets tested once a week. He's got accountability partners up the wazoo, gives talks against the evils of drugs in high schools. Volunteers with youth groups and young-adult ministries. You can fight this, spend months in court, and bankrupt yourself on legal fees, but chances are good it'll still go in his favor. He's their biological father, clean and sober. He's got a lot of influential references. Your father, for one."

"My father doesn't know the first thing about raising a family." Tanner kicked at a rock and sent it flying toward the pond.

"That's not entirely true." Jeff pulled a folded piece of paper from his suit jacket and slowly opened it. "Brian remarried a few years after your parents' divorce was finalized. You knew that, right? You have three half-siblings. Two brothers and a sister."

Tanner knew.

His mother had tried to talk to him about his dad over the years, but he shut down every time she broached the subject. He didn't want to know anything about his father's new family. Wouldn't open his letters or take his calls.

When Marnie came home, she'd wanted to show him pictures. He wouldn't look at them, but snuck into her room one day when she was out and took a gander anyway. They told stories of a life he'd had no part in, hadn't wanted to be part of. Eventually, he let her tell him about his brothers, Timothy and Scott, and his sister

Chelsea. She'd be in middle school by now, the boys in high school or graduated.

"They still live in the same area? He and Rance?" He couldn't even say his father's name. Clouds trailed across the sky and provided shade from the sun. Tanner focused on the kids, forced himself not to move forward and intervene when Rance approached Jason and they started kicking a soccer ball back and forth.

"Same neighborhood. Rance spends a lot of time with them. They're close." Jeff held out a printed photograph of his father's family. The family Tanner knew would embrace Jason and Jeni in a heartbeat. His hand hovered over the paper. He saw himself in his brothers' grins, saw Marnie in the way the younger girl's eyes sparkled, and wondered, for a fleeting moment, what it might be like to meet them.

He pulled his hand back. "Throw it away." Tanner shook his head and walked off.

He couldn't handle anything else today.

He was done.

Twenty-Nine

IT HAD BEEN A LONG, EXHAUSTING WEEK. AFTER MARNIE'S funeral, Natalie spent as much time with the kids and Tanner as she could. Friday arrived too quickly, and as expected, the call from her father came.

Natalie had made her decision. Maoilios would stay open.

Dad did not take the news well.

Their conversation ended with him hanging up on her.

As Saturday morning dawned, an unfamiliar feeling flooded her. Something she hadn't felt for so long that she couldn't really be sure she was feeling it now.

Peace.

She *was* doing the right thing.

Early morning sun filtered through the cypress trees that crested the hills around the house. Off in the distance a lone tractor chugged along between the rows of grapes, the dogs running behind it. She caught a flash of the blue UCLA cap Tanner often wore and grinned. Did he ever sleep?

At the breakfast table, the calls began. Dad wasn't giving up. Natalie tried to focus on her eggs and not on the fact that both her grandfather and uncle were scrutinizing her. When her cell buzzed again, she rolled her eyes.

"You gonna answer that, kid?" Jeffrey sipped his coffee, his steady gaze fixed on her.

"No. It's not important." She bit into a slice of toast, her mouth too dry to swallow.

Her phone kept buzzing.

Sarah hovered by the sideboard, raised an eyebrow when Natalie looked her way. Natalie shrugged and managed a smile. "Grandpa, can you pass the coffee, please?"

He filled her cup, his eyes narrowing as her phone vibrated on the table. "Natalie Grace, somebody is awfully persistent. Who's bothering you at this hour?"

"More like harassing," Uncle Jeff stated, buttering his toast. "Do I need to handle this?"

"Handle what?" Tanner strode into the dining room, whipped off his cap, and wiped his brow with the sleeve of his sweatshirt. "Morning, all." His eyes immediately found hers. "What's wrong?"

"Nothing." She answered too quickly, too loudly. She picked up her coffee cup again, her hand trembling.

He dropped into the chair beside her, concern rippling his forehead. "Who's harassing you? Your ex?" Her phone vibrated again. Tanner glared at it. "Is that him? Give me the phone."

"Oh, settle down." Natalie sighed, grabbed her cell, and powered it off. "It's just my father." She took another gulp of coffee and waited until Tanner sat back. Sarah served him his plate and took a seat at the far end of the table.

She took a deep, calming breath, pushed her plate away, and nodded. "Since you're all here, I want you to know I've come to a decision regarding the vineyard."

Tanner's fork stilled in midair. Everyone stopped eating and stared at her.

"As you know, my father thinks we should shut down Maoilios. Although he seemed determined, I thought once I came up with some viable numbers, he'd change his mind. He hasn't." She exhaled and ran a hand over her hair. Her grandfather sat back, arms folded, a tiny smile playing about his lips. Natalie sent him a grateful look.

He knew. Probably had known for years that this day would come.

That she wouldn't let him down.

"Grandpa, when I first arrived, I asked you something. Remember?"

His smile stretched. "You wanted to know why your grand-mother left you her share of the winery."

Natalie nodded. "And you said I'd have to figure it out for myself."

"And have you?"

"I think so." She placed her hands on the rough-hewn table. Memories danced around her—family dinners with her grand-parents and Nicole, often Tanner and David, too, on summer nights when rain kept them inside. Conversations so lively sometimes it was all she could do not to put her hands over her ears.

Every room in this house held a special moment, a time when Natalie could remember what it felt like to be truly happy. To belong.

To be free and at peace.

Over the past several weeks, she'd found that feeling again.

"What are you getting at, kiddo?" Jeffrey's fingers drummed a beat on the table.

"Last night I informed my father that we are not shutting down Maoilios." The proclamation should have made her smile, but she was still battling her father's harsh words.

You've let me down again, Natalie. Well, I can't say I'm surprised . . .

Tanner's fork clattered onto his plate. He pushed his chair back and ran a hand over his face. "Thank You, Jesus."

"Indeed." Sarah sent her son a sharp look. "Natalie, sweetheart, are you sure?"

"She looks sure to me." Tanner shot her a sidelong glance. "You're sure, right, Mouse?"

Grandpa Hal tipped his head, victory shining in his eyes. "Of course she's sure."

Uncle Jeff gave Sarah a wary look. Natalie couldn't read him. Tanner's mother lifted her hands with a small smile. "Look, I know you're all concerned about the vineyard. So am I. But I'm more concerned about how this might affect Natalie."

"Thank you, Sarah. But I'm fine." Natalie tapped a finger on her phone. "I'm out of a job, but other than that . . ." Her voice took on a tremor as reality set in.

"Wait, what?" Tanner rested a hand on her back, his touch warm through the cotton blouse she wore.

Natalie sighed. "Two weeks ago, my dad gave me an ultimatum. Do what he wanted or seek employment elsewhere. I didn't do what he wanted."

"Two weeks ago?" Tanner's face grew stormy.

"Well, that's not the end of the world," Uncle Jeff said. "Because from what I've seen, you're needed out here."

"I'll second that." Grandpa Hal nodded. "But let's take one step at a time." His iPhone rang out in a chorus of *The Sting* and he raised his eyes to the ceiling when he looked at the screen. "Now he's trying me. Excuse me, everyone, I'll handle this."

Natalie exhaled and put her head in her hands as her grandfather left. "I feel like I've just started World War III."

"You're doing the right thing." Uncle Jeff rose and began to clear the plates. Sarah was quick to get up and take them from him.

"Natalie won't be the only one out of a job if you don't let me do mine," she told him. Jeff backed off with a smile, which to Natalie's surprise, Sarah returned as they headed to the kitchen.

Natalie was half out of her chair when Tanner cleared his throat. "Natalie, wait."

A reticent sigh slid out of her as she met his questioning gaze. "What?"

"Why didn't you tell me?"

"Because you had enough going on. And it wasn't important." She moved toward the door.

"Not important?" He pushed his chair back so quickly that it tipped backward, landing on the rug with a thud. "Natalie, stop! Maybe we should rethink this. I mean, is this worth losing your job over, creating a rift between you and your father? What are you going to do, stay here and run the place?"

Natalie squeezed her eyes shut. Seriously? She turned on her heel to face him. "Yes, Tanner. That's exactly what I plan to do. You know, I just put everything on the line for you. I thought you'd at least be happy about it. But you still don't trust me, do you? I don't know why I expected you would."

"Wait. Back up." Tanner pushed up his sleeves, rounded the table. He tipped his head and narrowed his eyes. "Did you just say you put everything on the line . . . *for me?*"

⌒

"Natalie?" Tanner waited for her answer, a sick feeling swirling in his stomach. "Are you doing this for me?"

"Of course not." She shook him off, pressed her lips together. "I just meant that this is your livelihood, that you love Maoilios just as much as my grandfather does. We've created a plan that I'm convinced will be profitable. There's no reason to close."

"Okay." He didn't believe her. Not for a second. Her eyes refused to connect with his. "That's not what it sounded like."

"I know what it sounded like." When she finally looked at him, he saw a hint of anger in her eyes. "But that's not what I meant."

"Good. Because I wouldn't want you to make that kind of decision out of some misplaced loyalty to me." Did he just say that? Tanner wanted to shove a fist in his mouth.

"Misplaced loyalty?" Natalie clamped her hands on her hips and her eyes flamed.

Oh, this was bad. Very bad. "I didn't mean it that way. I meant . . . I—"

"Do you honestly believe for one minute that I would make a business decision purely based on emotion?"

"Look, all I'm saying is . . ." He raised his hands and gave up. He had no idea what he was saying.

"How about you stop questioning this and get on board?" She poked him in the chest. "What happened to *Do I get to be on the team?*"

"Natalie." Tanner sighed her name as she stalked across the room.

She threw him a glare over her shoulder. "I have things to do, Tanner."

"So do I." But he wouldn't be able to focus on anything until they cleared the air. "I just don't want you to do something you're going to regret in a few days."

"My mind is made up. If you don't want me here, be honest."

"Did I say I didn't want you here?" Tanner rolled his eyes.

"You don't seem exactly thrilled by the thought."

"I haven't had a chance to process it." He ran a hand down his face to hide his smile as she made a slow turn.

"Then by all means, process away." Natalie left the room, slamming the door behind her.

Oh no you don't.

Tanner raced after her. She was already out the front door, cresting the hill, and making her way toward the stream at a slow jog.

Her soft cries carried backward on the wind.

When he reached her, she whirled to face him, tears streaking her cheeks. "Leave me alone!"

"No." Tanner steadied his breathing and caught her by the arms. "Tell me why you're upset. Tell me."

"This is ridiculous."

Tanner tightened his grip. "Tell me."

Her gaze faltered but her glare scorched him. "I'm upset because it feels like you still don't trust me!"

"I don't trust you? You're the one who didn't tell me your father threatened to fire you over this!"

"I didn't tell you because I knew you'd freak out. Just like you're doing now!" Natalie shook her head, her eyes flashing in the sunlight. "I've lived most of my life trying to please people, Tanner. And I'll be hanged if I add you to that list. So you're either on board or you're not. Which is it?"

Tanner gave a low chuckle. It probably wasn't the smartest response, because her glare grew fiercer, and it was all he could do to not sweep her into his arms.

"Did you really stand up to your old man?"

"Yes." A fleeting smile came and went. "He wasn't expecting it. But I'm tired of doing things his way. Tired of worrying whether he'll approve. I don't think I'll ever make him happy. And I guess I'll just have to live with that."

He risked taking a few steps toward her. "You want to talk about it?"

"Not yet." She scrubbed her face and gave a half laugh. "But I think this has taught me that it's time to face the truth. Because that's the only way I'll let go of the past."

"What truth?"

Natalie shook her head. "Don't ask. I'm not ready, okay?"

"Okay." Tanner frowned, but realized there was no sense in pushing. He closed the gap between them and took her hands in his. "I'm proud of you, Mouse."

Tears wet her lashes again. For a moment he thought she was

going to say more, but she only smiled, squeezed his hands, then let go.

Tanner watched her head back to the house, his heart beating a little erratically. Something else was going on here, but he couldn't force it from her.

Letting go of the past.

Well, that sounded good.

If only he could do the same.

Thirty

NATALIE MADE A PANICKED PHONE CALL TO LAURA AT TWO a.m. that Sunday morning. Blurted out the whole story through gulping sobs, and waited for her friend to speak through the silence.

"Oh, Nat." Laura's sleepy sigh reached through the miles in a gentle hug.

"I'm tired of keeping this to myself. Tired of knowing that every time my dad looks at me, he knows, he blames me." Natalie swiped tears and stared at the full harvest moon out her window, illuminating the long rows of now barren vines. "I just want to be done with this."

"Then be done with it," Laura said. "Just tell them."

"I know. I need to." It was the only way, yet she couldn't stop shaking. "I'm so afraid."

"Don't be, Nat." She could almost see Laura's smile. "You're stronger than you think. You can do this. I believe in you."

"Okay." Natalie sniffed and tried to stop her tears. "Thank you."

"Can I pray for you?" Hesitation hovered in Laura's question and made Natalie smile.

"Actually, I was going to ask if you would."

ℚ

Sleep refused to come and at around five a.m. Natalie crept through the dark house to the kitchen, and soon sat with a spoon in a carton of chocolate ice cream. She turned on the radio to drown out the silence, keeping the volume low so as not to wake anyone. A rap on the patio door sent her spoon flying as she whipped her head around, wondering how fast Uncle Jeff could get down here if she screamed.

Tanner peered through the sliding glass door at her, Gwin beside him, her tail wagging.

Natalie let them in, her heart still pounding. "You scared the crap out of me!"

"Sorry. I was just getting up, let Gwin out, and saw the light on. Hal's not usually up quite this early. Is everything okay?" He shook droplets of rain from his hair. She tossed him a tea towel and retrieved her spoon from the floor.

"Of course everything's okay. I'm always up at five a.m. eating ice cream for breakfast." She plopped into her chair with a new spoon and slid another across the table. "Have a seat."

Tanner took a few bites of the Häagen-Dazs, then sat back, his steady eyes intent on pulling the truth from her. "What's going on, Nat?"

Natalie set her spoon down. Put the lid on the ice cream, put it back in the freezer, and returned to the table. "It has to do with the accident. The night Nicole died."

Tanner edged his chair closer and took her hand. "Tell me."

She nodded, prayed to get through it without breaking, prayed he'd still be holding her hand when she was done. "It was Nic's idea to sneak out of the house. I didn't want to. My parents had gone to the coast for the weekend. My grandparents were asleep. Nic wanted to take Grandpa's Jeep out. She found the keys. We drove around for a while. It was crazy, scary."

Natalie gripped Tanner's hand tighter. "I don't know how she knew how to drive but she was pretty good at it. After a while, we pulled over and Nic said it was my turn." She looked down at the scratched oak table, heard his short intake of breath.

"I said no, but you know how she was. I figured what was the harm, and I sort of wanted to. So we traded places and I took the wheel. I had no idea what I was doing and she kept yelling at me to go faster and faster and . . ." Sad laughter bubbled up. "It was kind of fun, you know? Driving, doing something I wasn't supposed to be doing . . . but then . . ." Natalie closed her eyes and fought the image.

She couldn't do it. Couldn't relive it.

"What happened, Nat?" Tanner crouched in front of her, placed his hands on her knees. "Tell me what happened."

Tears streaked her cheeks as she locked eyes with him. "There was a deer. It came out of nowhere. I didn't see it until it was right in front of me. I tried to swerve and I guess it ran off, but I . . . couldn't . . ." Couldn't breathe. Couldn't say the words. Couldn't let the truth be told.

Tanner wiped her tears and waited.

Natalie nodded. "The Jeep flipped. We were both thrown. I don't remember anything after that. Just waking up when the ambulance arrived and seeing Nicole . . . she was just lying there against a tree, like she was asleep. But I knew. I knew I'd killed her."

"Nat." Tanner pulled her with him as he stood, slipped his arms around her. She stayed there for a while, waiting for her sobs to subside. When she raised her head, he moved her hair off her face and placed a gentle kiss on her forehead. "Go on." He sensed there was more.

"I remember seeing the flashing lights, the sheriff. He wanted to talk to me there, but I was pretty out of it. I . . . I told them Nicole was driving." She raised a trembling hand to her mouth. "I was so scared. I thought I'd go to jail or something, so I lied. When my parents arrived, I told my father that I was the one driving, that I'd lied to the police. And he . . . he said it didn't matter. He said I should stick to that story and not tell the truth. It would be our secret. And it was."

"All these years." Tanner's eyes held contempt. "How could he let you live with that?"

"I don't know." She could only speculate. "I suppose in his mind, he was protecting me. Saving me from further questioning, maybe even getting charged, who knows. It doesn't matter why now. But it drove me crazy. Literally."

Regret weighed her down and overpowered the relief of telling him.

"I never wanted anyone to know. I was so afraid of what people would think. But I don't care anymore. I can't live with the lie. And I know the only way I'm ever going to move on is if I face it, finally tell the truth."

"Nobody would hold you responsible. Okay, you lied, but you were thirteen years old. It was an accident, Natalie!"

"I know." Moisture pooled at the corner of her mouth. "But I think my father always blamed me for my sister's death. He can barely look me in the eye whenever someone talks about her."

"And nothing you do is ever good enough for him." Tanner swore, broke away from her. He paced the kitchen, placed his hands against the counter, and lowered his head.

"I'm sick of it, Tanner," she confessed, the awful reality riding the waves of her emotion. "I can't make him happy, can't make him love me any more than he's capable of. But I can tell the truth. And maybe that's the only way I'll ever get over what happened. What I did."

"Truth is always a good thing." His voice caught as he turned to face her.

She nodded. "I need to tell Grandpa and Uncle Jeffrey. And my mother. I don't think my dad will like it, but that's too bad." A cool breeze floated through the open window and Natalie shivered. Tanner walked toward her, wrapped her in his arms again, and kissed her tears away.

"You don't have to go through it alone." The light in his eyes told her he meant it, told her she should never have listened to her fears.

"I don't know what they'll say," she whispered. "I've been so afraid of this all these years. I've . . ."

"Turned it into an even bigger lie." He blinked, a sad smile resting on his lips. "You're not guilty of anything, Natalie."

"Only of not telling the truth." She nodded, putting her arms around his neck. "But I know I have to let this go."

"That's the hardest part, isn't it?"

Natalie met his eyes and nodded. "Tanner, you need to do the same. You're not responsible for what happened to your sister. It's time you believe that."

His smile flashed for an instant. "I suppose next you're going to tell me to make things right with my father."

"Well, there's an idea." Natalie grinned and ran a hand down his arm. "I can't be the only one having all the fun."

◞

Jeffrey stood at his bedroom window as the sun went down that Sunday evening and watched Tanner walk the rows of vines. He'd always loved the view from his room, regretted taking it for granted. Regretted a lot of things. But maybe second chances really did exist.

If he was getting one, and he wasn't entirely certain of that yet, but if he was, he'd take it. And this time, he'd do it all right.

It had been a crazy day. After they'd all gone to church and finished lunch together, Natalie announced she had something to tell them. He couldn't imagine what else was coming after her decision to keep Maoilios open, and he certainly wasn't expecting to hear that she'd been the one driving the night her sister was killed.

Jeffrey sighed deep and massaged the back of his neck. Secrets.

He'd kept enough of them. Knew what they could do to a person. His heart broke for Natalie, for what she'd obviously suffered keeping that truth to herself all these years. And he couldn't for the life of him imagine why Bill had let her.

But it was done now, and Natalie was on the road to making her peace.

Sarah came into his line of vision, heading toward home, and he smiled.

Perhaps he needed to do the same.

Make his peace.

He pushed up the window and stuck his head out. "Sarah! Wait up!" He grinned at her startled expression as she turned to look up at the house.

A few moments later, he stood in front of her, out of breath.

"What's gotten into you?" A breeze blew around them, lifting her hair away from her face. "Are you all right?"

"I am." His bad leg hurt like the dickens from running down two flights of stairs but he tossed that thought aside. "I just . . . I wanted to ask you something."

Sarah stood back and folded her arms, the barest of smiles touching her lips. "And that would be?"

Jeffrey exhaled, tamped nerves, and went for it. "You know I came out here on leave. Needed to get my head together. But I also needed to make things right. With my dad . . . and also with you. Dad and I have talked, and we're making progress. And now with Natalie intending to stay, well . . . Sarah, I think this is where I need to be. I want to stay."

She blinked a couple times, her eyes wide. "You're going to quit your job?"

"I am." Saying it out loud sealed the deal. "I'm going to talk to my boss tomorrow. I want to stay here, work with my father. But I need to know if you'd be okay with that."

"And if I wasn't?" She was actually grinning at him. Jeffrey couldn't stop a chuckle.

"Well, I'd probably stay anyway."

Sarah rolled her eyes and moved a little closer. "I'm happy for you, Jeff. I know this will please Hal. And Natalie needs you too."

"And you, Sarah? Do you think that maybe one day you might need me again?"

A laugh slipped from her lips, hinting at old sorrow. But she gave him the smile he'd carried in his heart all the years they'd been separated. "I'd say it's a distinct possibility."

"Sarah." Her name caught in his throat as he cupped her face, met her eyes. "I've never stopped loving you. And if you give me this chance, I promise I'll never leave you again. I'll never let you down again."

She nodded, tears streaking her cheeks. "I must be losing my mind."

"No." He laughed. "We've got a few good years yet, darling girl."

"Then we shouldn't waste a moment."

"You always had the best ideas." Jeffrey pulled her closer, brought his lips to hers, and finally kissed her the way he'd been dreaming of since he first saw her again.

Sarah drew back, her cheeks high with color, but her eyes shining with hope. "Welcome home, Jeff." She traced a light finger across a faded scar on the side of his face, one of many she'd see if all his plans fell into place.

But for now, for today, this was enough.

Thirty-One

ON MONDAY NIGHT, NATALIE WAS COMFORTABLY SETTLED ON the sofa with a bowl of pasta and a new journal. It always helped her to put her thoughts to paper. Grandpa Hal was out with friends and, in a surprising turn of events, Uncle Jeff and Sarah were going out for dinner.

Natalie planned to use the night alone to gather her thoughts and pray. That made her smile. Learning to rely on God wasn't easy, but it gave a comfort and peace she hadn't imagined possible.

She wished Tanner would do the same. He'd said he needed to catch up on some work tonight, but she knew he was sulking. Rance was taking the kids out for pizza. Nobody had said it yet, but they all knew Rance and Brian were leaving in a few days, and Rance's hope was that the kids would come and live with him.

The doorbell jarred her out of her musings. Maybe Tanner had decided he wanted company after all.

But Rance stood there, and she saw her uncle and Sarah pulling up in Sarah's SUV.

"Hi, Rance." She looked toward his rental. It was empty. "Where are the kids?" Her pulse picked up at his anxious expression.

"Um. They're not with you, are they?" he asked a little warily, his eyes worried.

Natalie shook her head, fear creeping upward. "What's going on?"

Rance ran a hand down his face. "Oh boy. Sarah and Jeff were out on the front porch when I arrived to pick them up. When she went inside to fetch them, they weren't there. We searched all the rooms. They must have snuck out the back, through the garden. We were hoping they'd be here."

"No." Natalie let out a long breath. "Oh no."

Rance cleared his throat. "So, um . . . Tanner wouldn't . . ."

"No, he wouldn't," she answered quickly. Still, a vision of Tanner hightailing it to the Canadian border with Jason and Jeni wasn't hard to imagine. "Come on in. Let's make some calls."

She tried Grandpa first. He was reasonable. Didn't panic. But he didn't have a clue where the kids were. Sarah thought they may have gone to a friend's house and began calling around, but the reality that they'd run away was starting to set in. Finally, all out of options, she leaned against the kitchen counter, took a breath, and called Tanner.

He answered on the fourth ring. "Couldn't live without me for one night?"

"Uh, yeah. Where are you?"

"In the lab. Where am I supposed to be?"

Natalie's heart thumped harder. "The kids aren't with you are they?"

"I just told you, I'm in the lab. The kids are with their . . . Rance. Did you forget about that?"

Natalie closed her eyes. "Tanner, I think we have a problem."

~

They split up to search the property. Natalie called Brian at his hotel, and he quickly arrived. Tanner went back to their house, found Jason's piggy bank intact. The thought of Jason and Jeni wandering in the dark was enough to drive them all insane.

"This is your fault, Harper!" Tanner stormed across the living room, having returned to Hal's with no news. "If something happens to those kids, it'll be on your head."

Rance simply stood there and let Tanner rail.

"I'm going to check the barn and the fields again." Tanner slammed outside.

Rance started to follow, but Brian intervened. "Lets you and me drive around town once more." They left Natalie standing alone in the living room. Sarah and Jeffrey were searching the gardens. Grandpa had come home and was making more calls. Out in the vineyards, workers walked through the rows of vines with flashlights, yelling the kids' names.

"Oh, God, please let them be okay," Natalie breathed out. "Please."

At the far end of the room, Gwin sat in front of the bookcase, her tail thumping against the rug.

"Oh my gosh." Natalie clapped her hands. Of course! The bookcase.

The section on wheels sat slightly out of place. Behind it, she knew, was a small, concealed door. Behind that, the winding staircase led to the turret.

She pushed the bookcase aside and wondered how they'd done it, because even on wheels, it was pretty heavy. "Please don't be locked." She jiggled the handle, and to her immense relief, the door creaked open.

Natalie ducked through and made her way up the steep cement steps.

When she reached the round room at the top of the stairs, she was out of breath and had to wait a moment to let her eyes adjust to the dim light. A musty smell crinkled her nose, but she smelled something else too. The distinct cheesy scent of Doritos.

"Shoot." Jason's voice reached her first.

"Natalie!" Jeni scrambled up and flung herself at Natalie.

"Oh, Jeni." Natalie crushed the little girl against her. "Thank God." She leveled her gaze on Jason, huddled in one corner of the room. "Do you have any idea how worried we've been?"

"You don't—" he began.

"Stop." Natalie held up a hand. "Don't say another word, young man." She punched Tanner's number into her phone. He picked up at once. "Got them. In the turret. Yes, they're fine. Okay." Jeni clung around her waist, her small frame trembling. Natalie hugged her again. Kissed her and breathed silent prayers of thanks. "Jase?" She met his eyes over his sister's head.

"Yeah?"

"Downstairs. Now."

Five minutes later, Tanner burst into the house, followed by Rance, Brian, Sarah, and Jeffrey. Grandpa Hal was already in the kitchen fixing hot chocolate.

Jeni ran to her uncle and Tanner swept her up with a groan of relief. "Jeni Bear, are you okay?"

"Uh-huh."

"You scared us all silly, baby." Tanner sounded on the verge of tears and Natalie pushed back her own. Rance seemed to be having trouble, too, and she saw Brian push him toward a chair.

Tanner set Jeni down and she ran to her grandmother. Tanner focused on Jason, his eyes blazing. "Let me guess. Your idea?"

Jason huddled in a navy Gap hoodie, kicked the backpack by his feet, his face dark.

Tanner crouched and placed his hands on the boy's shoulders. "Why would you do something like this? I was just about to call the sheriff. If Natalie hadn't found you, there would have been cops all over the county looking for you! Do you understand that?"

"Yes, sir."

"Do I get an explanation?" Tension smacked Tanner's words

and Natalie hoped he wouldn't lose his temper. Much as Jason deserved it, anger probably wouldn't help right now.

"We don't want to go to Seattle," Jason said, his lower lip starting to tremble. He glanced at Rance and gave a shrug. "Sorry."

"You don't want to go to Seattle." Tanner straightened and tipped his head back. "Awesome. Well, okay, Jason. I guess you're calling the shots from now on, huh? I don't want to go to work tomorrow. So I'll just stay home. Okay with you? Oh, and I don't want to pay the bills either. So we won't have any electricity next month. Okay with you?"

"Tanner . . ." Sarah stepped forward, her mouth pinched. Jeffrey grabbed her hand and made her stay put.

"You don't get it," Jason mumbled. He crossed his arms and stared at his sneakers.

"No, I guess I don't." Tanner swore under his breath, but the room was so quiet everyone heard. "But guess what, neither do you. Did you think for one minute how Rance might feel tonight, getting to the house to pick you up and finding you gone?"

"No, sir."

"Did you think about your sister, how traipsing off into the night might make her feel?"

"No, sir." Tears formed in the boy's eyes.

"Or the rest of us? Me, Natalie, your grandparents? Did you give any thought to how frantic we'd be, not knowing where you were? You're a smart kid, Jase. You know the dangers. We've been looking for you for two hours! You know what can happen in two hours, Jason?"

"Okay, Tanner." Natalie didn't want to intervene, but Jason was starting to cry. "He gets it."

Tanner took a breath and placed a hand on Jason's shoulder. "Apologize."

"Sorry." Jason didn't lift his head. Tanner did it for him.

"Not to me. Your father is over there. Go and apologize to him."

Natalie wiped her eyes as Jason shuffled over to where Rance stood. She had to give the guy credit for maintaining his composure.

"Um." Jason's voice cracked a bit. "I'm sorry for running away from you. I won't do it again. And if we hafta go live with you, then I guess that's okay. If Uncle Tanner says so." He sniffed and knuckled his eyes.

Rance nodded and put a hand on his son's shoulder. "I was really worried, Jason. I'm glad you're both okay. But I'm not going to make you guys do anything you don't want to do, all right?" He crouched a bit, brushed Jason's cowlick back, and smiled. "Let's talk about it some more. We'll figure out a plan that makes everyone happy, okay?"

"Maybe." Jason shot a timid glance at Tanner, then looked back at Rance. "I got a soccer game tomorrow night. You can come if you want."

"Thanks, Jason. I'll be there." Rance straightened and Jason shrugged, walked back to Tanner, and looked up at him with the most forlorn expression Natalie had ever seen.

"I'm sorry, Uncle Tanner."

"Me too, bud." Tanner exhaled, pulled his nephew against him, and held him as the boy cried.

Thirty-Two

TANNER SAT BY THE FIRE IN THE LIVING ROOM ON THURSDAY night and studied the flickering flames. He couldn't sleep, so he lit a fire and thumbed through the pages of his Bible.

He needed wisdom. Direction.

He was all out of answers.

Maybe God would finally come through with some.

He couldn't stop thinking of what might have happened to Jason and Jeni had they ventured farther than Hal's the other night. He understood their fears. Yet as each day passed, he knew they were avoiding the only reasonable decision.

Exhaustion fell heavy and he closed his eyes. Saw Rance piling the kids into a cab, saw himself running after them, yelling at them to stop, his mom yelling at him to stop . . .

Déjà vu.

But it wouldn't be like that.

Didn't have to be like that.

If only he'd cooperate . . .

"Tanner?"

Tanner startled to his mother's voice. Daylight streamed through the windows and the fire was out. He must have dozed off.

She was dressed, her hands around four stacked shoe boxes. "Have you been sitting here all night?"

"Most of it." He stretched his arms and tried to loosen the aching muscles in his neck.

"Thinking about the kids?"

"Yup."

"It'll work out. We need to trust God in this."

"I'm trying, Mom, but it's not easy." Some days he had more faith. This week, with reality looming, his faith was dwindling.

Mom placed a couple of cardboard boxes with the orange Nike stripe on the floor by his chair.

"Shoe sale?" He tried to smile. "Did you get those for the kids?"

"No. They're for you." She rested a hand on his arm until he looked her way.

Did he need new running shoes?

Maybe he did.

He'd tie them tight and let them take him far away as fast as possible from this nightmare that had become his life. But mom's expression told him there were no shoes in those boxes.

"Mom?"

"Your dad's letters."

The letters that came without fail—once, sometimes twice a week, for years—since the day his father left.

The letters Tanner never read.

Refused to open.

Eventually they stopped. His dad still called, and Tanner's mom would force him to the phone, but over the years, he'd done a good job of pushing his father from his life and refusing all invitations to take part in his.

"Why did you save those?"

"I thought you might want them one day."

"I don't."

"Tanner."

Determination in her tone dragged his eyes upward. "Do we have to do this?"

"Yes." She lowered herself onto the footstool beside him and placed her hand on his knee. "You've blamed your father all these years, and I'm ashamed to admit, I let you. But there's more to it than you know."

Tanner sat up in his chair, his mouth suddenly dry. "What are you talking about?"

"Do you remember much about how Marnie was before they left?"

"A bit." He wanted to slam the brakes on this conversation before it got started.

His mother sighed. "I refused to accept her bipolar diagnosis. For all my medical training, I couldn't deal with her. I was in denial and it drove your dad nuts. He insisted on getting Marnie the help she needed. There was a clinic he'd found, but it was near your grandparents, across the state. He wanted us to move there, thought having their support would be good. I argued that there were plenty of places in Seattle she could get treatment. I didn't want to move." She wiped her eyes. "I was being stubborn. For a lot of reasons. But one night while you slept, we found Marnie in your room. With a knife."

The room shifted. Tanner stiffened, nausea rising. "Would she have . . . hurt me?"

"I don't know." Mom shrugged. "I lost it at that point. Your father and I had reached an impasse. I basically told him to take her and go. Our marriage was over by then anyway, and I wanted it to be. He knew I'd never stopped loving Jeff. I loved your dad, in my own way, but—"

"You kicked him out?"

"It was a terrible time in my life, Tanner. I've regretted my actions ever since. The truth is, I turned my back on my own daughter. And my husband."

Tanner shook his head, tears pricking. "Is that why you let her come back to stay with us? To make up for it?"

"In a way. I didn't deserve a second chance with her, but I got one. I'll always be grateful for the few years we had with Marnie, tumultuous as they were." Her smile inched out. "Tanner, your dad didn't abandon you. He wanted to protect you."

Tanner shook his head. "What does it matter now? We don't have a relationship." He'd taken care of that.

"But you should have one." She gripped his arm, her eyes shining. "Like it or not, Tanner, the kids are going to end up in Seattle. You're going to have to spend time with your dad, and Rance, if you want to see the kids."

Mom rose and backed off. "Your father and Rance leave on Saturday. Brian and I have had a chance to work through things and get some closure. He hoped to do the same with you. But you're still pushing him away. Sweetheart, I'm asking you . . . give him a chance. Forgive him. Forgive us both, and move on."

Tanner stared at her, old bitterness biting. "He's moved on fine without me. What's the point?"

Mom leaned forward, brushed his hair back, and kissed him on the head like she had when he was a kid. "The point, my love, is that he's still your father. And he loves you."

$\backsim$

It was late afternoon when Tanner pulled into the parking lot of the Sonoma Mission Inn and Spa. The sprawling pink hotel always caught his eye. It had a great restaurant, and he'd wanted to take Natalie there for dinner. Maybe when all this was resolved, he would.

He locked the truck and trudged toward the entrance. Inside the large foyer a fire burned in a massive stone fireplace. Guests milled about, some wearing white terrycloth robes, headed for the spa. Others lounged on comfortable sofas. The place looked like something out of *Lifestyles of the Rich and Famous*. He was so out of his element.

Natalie wouldn't be. He rolled his eyes. Could he stop thinking about her for five seconds?

"Tanner?"

He turned at the voice and knew at once he wasn't prepared for this.

Rance.

"Are the kids okay?" The man pushed up the sleeves of his sweater, concern creasing his brow.

Tanner cleared his throat and nodded. "They're in school. They're fine." He swallowed down second thoughts. "We need to talk."

"Okay." Rance eyed him, wary. "You want to sit?" He indicated open doors that led out to a patio.

Outside, Tanner pulled up a metal chair and sank into it. The day had turned gray, threatening afternoon rain. There was an old man swimming in the pool nearby, nobody else around.

Rance broke the silence. "I'm really sorry about Marnie. The whole situation." He propped his elbows and rested his chin in his hands. "I screwed up big time with her."

Tanner clenched his jaw.

"After I got clean, I imagined coming down here. Asking her to forgive me, starting over . . . we even talked a few times. Did she tell you that?"

This was going to be harder than he thought. Tanner let out a shaky breath. "The only things Marnie said about you aren't worth repeating."

"Yeah, I figured." The guy had a nice smile. Warm and . . . like it or not, honest. "Funny, I was just headed up to my room to give you a call. I wanted to talk to you too."

Tanner crossed his arms. "You first then."

Rance smiled again. "So here's the thing." He splayed his hands on the table. "I won't bore you with the whole God-brought-me-out-of-darkness spiel. I realize you could probably take me to court, fight for custody of the kids, and I imagine you've thought about it." He lifted a shoulder in resignation.

"The truth is, I was a lousy father, a lousy husband, and part of me was relieved when Marnie left. I couldn't take the drama anymore. I was too wrapped up in my own world to worry about my family. By the time I came to my senses, it was too late. But I prayed for a second chance. Prayed for a way to make things right. Losing Marnie completely wasn't what I had in mind." He sniffed and pinched the bridge of his nose. "I don't want to lose my kids again. I want to make a life for them, a good one. But I won't take them from you without your blessing. I'm not going to rip a family apart just because I'm legally entitled to do so."

Tanner sucked air and stared at the man across the table.

Was Rance Harper really willing to walk away from his children if they'd be happier here? Was anybody really this good?

"Have you talked to the kids, Rance? Asked them what they want?"

"Yeah. We've talked." His eyes shone with moisture. "They're confused. They're kids, Tanner. They love you. They love their grandmother. This is the only home they can remember. What am I supposed to do? Be the bad guy and force them to get on that plane with me?"

That was exactly the traumatic scene Tanner imagined.

He sat through the silence and watched a small sliver of light slice through the gray clouds.

"What if I brought them?" It made more sense now than in the dead of night when he'd first considered the idea. "I could stay long enough to ease them into the transition. And afterward . . . I could visit some weekends, if it was okay with you. They're good kids, they'll adjust quickly . . . but that way it won't . . ." He looked down at his hands, his eyes stinging. "It won't seem like I'm abandoning them." His throat filled with fire, making further speech impossible.

"Are you serious?"

Tanner tried to gauge the guy's reaction. "Yeah."

"You would do that?" Rance's eyes widened. "What about the winery?"

"Jeff and Hal can man the fort while I'm gone. It wouldn't be for long. Maybe just until the New Year." Tanner leaned in a bit. "But there's something—"

"What if I relapse?" Rance said it for him. "I pray against that every day, Tanner. Trust me, if it happened, you'd be the first one I'd call."

"Okay." He wasn't completely at ease yet, but it would have to do. "I'll start making plans."

Rance scratched his head and frowned. "You talk to your father about this?"

Tanner let go a sigh and managed a smile. "He's next on the list."

⌒

"Tanner." His dad opened the door to his hotel room and backed up. "I didn't expect to see you."

"No, I'm sure you didn't." Tanner scuffed his boots on the carpet and stared at his mirror image. "I was hoping we could talk."

"Come on in." They walked through the large suite and Brian pointed to the sitting area. "Have a seat." His father lowered himself onto the sofa, brushed fluff off his jeans.

"I'll stand." Tanner saw the open suitcase on the bed, heard the hum of the AC click on, and tried to organize the things he needed to say. "I just talked to Rance."

Brian pulled at the collar of his black polo as Tanner shared the plan. "I think you've made the right decision," he said when Tanner finished. "It'll be easier on the kids for sure."

"Yeah, well. It's not exactly what I want, but at least they'll know I'm not walking out on them." Tanner exhaled and squeezed his eyes shut. He hadn't meant to say it that way. Or maybe he had.

His dad gave a slow nod. "You know I live right around the corner from Rance in Seattle?"

"Yeah." Tanner decided to sit after all. "I know."

He studied his father's face, trying to remember what he'd looked like years ago. Remembered going fishing with him, driving around in the truck, the windows open, tunes blasting . . .

"I didn't leave because of you, Tanner."

"I read your letters." As if that explained it.

"My letters?"

"The ones you wrote me. Every week from the day you left." It had taken hours, reading through them. Reading them again, trying to make sense of it all. Tanner could get up, leave the room, and pretend everything was fine. But it wasn't. Wouldn't be until he said this.

"You hadn't read them before now?" His father sat forward. "I'm not following you."

"No, I never read them, okay?" He felt fifteen years old again, glaring at the answering machine. Wishing Dad would quit already with the annoying messages. "I was mad at you. I told Mom to throw them away." Harsh laughter shot from him. "But she didn't. She saved them. Every single one. Every letter, every card, every picture. You really don't know when to quit, do you?"

"I guess I don't." His smile wavered. "It wasn't what I wanted, Tanner. I never planned to leave. Not like that."

Tanner knew. Knew so much more now, more than he wanted to. "Mom told me the truth." He ran a finger over the soft material of the armchair. "Told me she couldn't deal with Marnie, that she basically kicked you both out." All this time he'd blamed his father for leaving, for abandoning him. For breaking up the family. But his mother shared that blame.

And Tanner needed to forgive them both.

"I accepted the marriage was over," his dad said, "but I could have insisted on you seeing me. But I wanted to protect you from Marnie. She was just too unstable for too many years."

"You had other kids." It wasn't meant to be an accusation but it sure sounded like one. Felt like one.

His father flexed the fingers on his left hand, light bouncing off his thick wedding band. "Susan and I did everything we could to keep Marnie with us. In the end, we had no choice. After we moved back to Seattle, we found a state home not far from us. She came to us on weekends."

"She never told me that." Tanner barely recognized his own voice. How would he get through the rest without totally losing it? "She had bad times here, too, when she came to live with us. I learned to deal with her, loved her anyway." He gripped his knees and grappled with grief. Let the loss surface. "She tried to get me to go see you, meet Susan and the kids. She always wanted to make things right."

Brian dropped his head. "I feel like I failed her. Failed all of you."

Tanner mentally ticked off a thousand reasons why he could agree with that statement. Waited for his anger to rise, ready to make a smart remark.

But none came.

"I don't want to live in the past anymore, Dad."

His father lifted his chin, tears shimmering. "You've held on to this a long time."

"Yeah." Tanner sniffed, gave a wry grin. "I guess I don't know when to quit either."

"Seems like now might be as good a time as any."

"That's what I was thinking." He breathed relief at the smile on his father's face. But they weren't quite there yet. "I hope you can forgive me for shutting you out of my life. I'm not saying it'll be easy, but if you're willing to give me a chance, I was hoping we could start over."

"There is nothing to forgive, Tanner," his dad said. "If anyone should be asking for forgiveness, it's me."

Tanner ran the back of his hand across his eyes and gave a nod. "Consider it done."

Dad rose, stood before him, and extended a hand. Tanner stood and clasped his father's hand in his. And then he allowed his father to draw him into a firm embrace, warmth flooding through him. This was more than he'd hoped for, prayed for, or dared to dream about. At best, he'd planned to leave this room with a bit of his burden lifted. But it had disappeared completely.

And Tanner was finally free.

Thirty-Three

NATALIE WOKE, A SCREAM STUCK IN HER THROAT. ANOTHER nightmare.

When would they end?

She glanced at the clock on the bedside table and groaned. Five a.m. Wednesday morning.

She was turning into Tanner.

Wonderful.

She dressed, pushed her feet into her sneakers, and tiptoed downstairs. The dogs rose when she reached the kitchen, their tails wagging. "All right." Still dark out, she grabbed a flashlight and headed for the door. "Come on."

The early November air was filled with a briskness that brought a frown to Tanner's face along with rumors of a harsh winter. Natalie prayed it wouldn't happen. Since they'd made the decision to take the kids to Seattle, he'd been spending as much time as possible with them. They'd taken them on picnics, to the movies, even to the mall at Jeni's request.

Natalie was proud of Tanner for going to talk to Rance and to his father. The two men had flown back to Seattle, but all of them were working on fixing a date for the move that would be best for the kids. Probably at Thanksgiving break.

And now that Natalie had made her decision regarding Maoilios, it was time to deal with the rest of it.

Time to face the past and finally free herself of the guilt she'd carried over the years.

Natalie walked the rows of vines and eventually settled on the swing set. The dogs chased rabbits while she watched the lights come on in the house at the end of the road. Ten minutes later, Gwin bounded toward her with a bark. The other dogs joined in and they raced off down a row of vines. Natalie raised a hand as Tanner approached through daybreak's mist.

"You're up early." His smile slid out, soon smothered by a yawn.

"Couldn't sleep."

"You been talking to my vines, Mouse?"

"No." Natalie stifled a giggle. "Is that what you do?" She could actually see him out here in the dead of night, coaxing the grapes along.

"Sometimes." He shrugged and came to stand in front of her. "And if they can't hear me, I guess God can, so the conversation isn't completely one-sided."

"Good to know." Her smile didn't last long. The ominous feeling that had been shadowing her loomed large. She wiped her cheeks and veered her gaze.

"Natalie? Come here." He held out his arms and she moved into them, burrowing into his soft fleece and the shelter of his embrace. "What is it?" He stepped back, tipped her chin, and frowned. "Why the tears?"

She filled her lungs with sweet air. "I don't know. I . . . I just feel like things are ending here."

"Ending?" Tanner shook his head, cradling her face in his hands.

She nodded, wrestling with her thoughts. "I need to go home, Tanner. I need to talk to my parents. Tell my mother the truth about the accident. Wind things up there officially. It's the right thing to do."

He studied her carefully. "But you'll come back. Right?"

"I was planning on it." She allowed a smile. "But I am wondering if you'll be here when I do."

Tanner grinned. "You're getting pretty good at reading me."

They walked up to the patio and sat together on the bench. He wrapped her in his arms, and they watched the sun push upward over the hills, blanketing them in soft reds and yellows. He smoothed her hair and kissed the top of her head. "We've decided to take the kids to Seattle just before Thanksgiving. Mom will come home after that, and I'll stay on longer."

"Okay." Natalie laced her fingers through his and studied the veins in his hands. Met his searching eyes and wished things could be different. "What do they think?"

Tanner frowned. "They're okay. They understand he's their dad and why it's right. They're upset about leaving here, obviously, but I'm sure once they get there, they'll settle quickly."

The sorrow in his voice brought fresh tears to her eyes. "Do you think . . . I mean, have you considered moving there?" She almost dreaded the answer.

He sighed and leaned back against the bench. "In my less rational moments, yeah. But my life is here, Nat. I couldn't give this up. They'll be okay without me. Not sure I'll be okay without them, but . . ."

Natalie wrapped her arms round him. "I'm sorry."

"I know." He breathed a sigh. "As much as it hurts, I feel at peace with it."

"I envy you that," Natalie whispered. "I think that's why I need to go home. So I can finally put the past to rest."

Tanner sat up a bit and met her gaze. "You can do this, Natalie. It'll be fine."

"I hope so." Natalie smiled. "I guess we'll have to leave Uncle Jeff in charge while we're gone."

"I think he'll actually enjoy that." Tanner gave a mischievous grin. "I've a feeling he's sticking around, winery or not."

"He and your mother do seem happy." Natalie was thrilled

for both of them. "Well, we have a lot to do around here, that's for sure."

They'd found the perfect spot for a tasting room. Down by the lake. It wouldn't be large, but the initial plans the architect presented were exciting. She was looking forward to stepping into this new world, looking forward to making a life here.

But there was something she needed to do first.

One final thing.

Natalie rose and held out a hand. "Walk with me?"

They walked the long road she and Nicole drove that night. Natalie had avoided it until now. It was a back road, so there hadn't been a need to travel it. But now, as she placed one foot in front of the other, Tanner by her side, she let the memories come.

"I started to speed up here. It was one of those still nights where you could hear the world breathing." She pushed her hair back and gave a small laugh. "My grandmother used to say something like that. *Listen real close and you'll hear the angels sing.* I didn't hear any angels that night."

Tanner wrapped her in his arms and she leaned against his solid chest, drawing strength from him. "We didn't make it very far. Just over there." Natalie pointed, stared through her tears at the spot still seared in her mind. She blew out shallow breaths and removed her hand from his. "That's where the deer came out of the bushes."

She could still see the animal, the wild, frightened eyes as she tried to slam on the brakes, Nicole's scream as she lunged for the steering wheel as Natalie realized that in her fear she was pressing the gas pedal and not the brake.

"*Stop, Nat, the brakes! HIT THE . . .*"

"Nicole tried to stop the Jeep, but we were going too fast. It was too late." Natalie drew in a shuddering breath, crossed the dusty road, and crouched in front of the tree. "It was right here."

She placed her hand on the damp grass around the trunk. She

lowered her head and let her tears fall. Birds in the branches above began their morning songs. The sun crested over the hill and lit the vines and the moss on the tree. The early mist pushed higher.

"I'm sorry, Nic," she whispered, her throat burning, but her heart ready to be relieved of the ache. With trembling hands, she undid the necklace that had once belonged to her sister, and placed it deep within the roots of the old cypress. "I'm so, so sorry. But I need to let you go now. It's time to say good-bye."

Tanner moved in behind her and held her through sobs that sucked all the guilt and heartache from her. Eventually her tears subsided, and a blessed feeling of peace settled over her.

When she dried her eyes and turned to face him, he kissed her. "Okay?"

Mutely, she nodded, gaining strength from his quiet smile. "Thank you for being here."

"Thank you for letting me." Tanner pulled her close to claim her lips again. "How am I supposed to live even a day without you?"

Natalie smiled. "You'll figure it out. And by the time you get back from Seattle, I might already be back here. Home."

"Home." His smile faltered as he drew a shaky breath. "I'm holding you to that, Miss Mitchell. And believe me, if you take too long, I'll come get you."

"Promise?"

"Count on it." His next kiss was filled with a future she didn't know for sure belonged to her yet, but she clung to him and claimed it anyway.

෧

"All set then?" Grandpa Hal wandered into Natalie's bedroom and took a look around. Natalie nodded as she zipped her suitcase. A shaky sigh trembled off her lips when she turned to face him.

"You understand why I have to go, don't you?"

"I do." He took her hands in his gnarled ones. His blue eyes glowed with compassion. "I made a lot of mistakes with my boys, Natalie Grace. Lately, with Jeffrey home, I'm starting to work through them, make up for them, I hope. But your father . . ."

"I know. He's stubborn."

"He blames me for a lot of things. Your grandmother's death. He thinks I should have done more. Been more proactive with her care, even though she was refusing more treatment at the end. I'm not sure we'll ever get past that."

"I know. But I pray you will," Natalie told him. "And pray for me, Grandpa. Pray I can get through this."

"I will, darlin'." He placed a kiss on her forehead. "And I'll also be praying you come back to us soon. Back home where you belong."

"Thank you for everything." Emotion made speech difficult. "I feel like I've found myself again here. I won't lose sight of that a second time."

His smile sent a ripple of wrinkles across his weathered brow. "Did I ever tell you what Maoilios means, Natalie Grace?"

She shook her head.

"It's an old Scottish Gaelic name. It means 'Servant of Jesus.'"

Natalie returned her grandfather's smile and squeezed his hands. "That's perfect."

Regret flickered over his face. "I haven't always lived up to the name. Some folks might think it an inappropriate name for a winery, but your grandmother didn't. She said it would help remind us that, in all things, we are to serve the Lord."

"I'll remember that."

He laid a hand on her head. "Peace be with you, Natalie Grace." Natalie closed her eyes, received her grandfather's blessing, and embraced a new true sense of belonging.

Thirty-Four

WHEN SHE'D CALLED TO LET HER MOTHER KNOW SHE PLANNED to come home, Natalie wasn't sure what reception she'd get. Whether her father would even welcome her.

He hadn't said much when she'd arrived late that Friday evening. Her mother offered tea, food, asked after her grandfather, but conversation was stilted and uncertain. And her father kept casting wary glances her way.

Like he knew why she was here.

The next day, after an early breakfast with Laura that gave her the encouragement she needed, Natalie joined her parents for lunch. It was a crisp day, but the sun was shining. They sat in the glassed-in porch off the kitchen, and Natalie surveyed the long garden where she and Nicole used to play.

"Do you remember the year Nicole decided she was going to break the record for turning cartwheels?" The memory came out of nowhere and brought a smile. Natalie turned to her parents and took in their startled expressions.

Dad slowly lowered his dessert fork onto the white china plate, crusted with leftover chocolate crumbs, a mix of horror and bemusement on his face. Mom sat back a bit, hesitation hovering.

"She never broke the record, but she sure had fun trying." Her mother's whisper wound around them like fine silk.

For the first time in years, Nicole's memory was invited in.

Accepted.

Natalie's eyes smarted, but she smiled anyway. "Grandpa

reminded me of that summer he and Grandma took us to the beach for the weekend, and we found out I was allergic to clams."

Her mother's sudden giggle filled the emptiness in the room. "Oh, your sister was upset. Didn't understand why we felt you had to come home, *'Okay, she almost choked to death, but now she's fine!'* she kept saying. I had a feeling she was more annoyed that you were getting all the attention."

"That would be Nic." Natalie touched the bare spot at her throat where her sister's necklace had sat. "I wonder what she'd be doing now."

Dad chuckled, the sound so unexpected and startling, that they both turned to look at him. His eyes shone with years of unspoken grief. He gave a resigned shrug, as if he knew it too. Knew it was time to let it go. "She'd either be running for president or heading up a corporation larger than mine."

"Really?" Natalie shook her head. "I'd always envisioned her working with you."

"I don't think so. Your sister would have run her own show." His unguarded smile was so foreign that it took Natalie a moment to recognize it.

"Maybe so." She sat back in her chair and watched a pair of white mourning doves flutter around the birdbath beyond the patio. They settled on the rim and took turns pecking at the water. "It doesn't hurt so much anymore," she said quietly, "talking about Nic. Remembering."

"We should never have stopped." Mom sniffed and wiped her eyes. "Why did we?"

"Because of me." Natalie took her mother's hand and squeezed tight. "Because after Nicole died, I couldn't cope, and every year since then has been a battle. But I think I'm finally ready to let go. I've started to heal."

"Natalie." Dad's brow furrowed, his tone rife with warning.

She'd known he'd object. But she needed to do this, whether he approved of exhuming the past or not.

"It's okay, Dad." She concentrated on her mother instead. "Mom, I need to tell you something."

"What is it, sweetheart?" She sat forward, concern in her question. "Are you having troubles again? I knew it, Bill, I told you—"

"Jane." Dad cleared his throat and crossed his arms. "Just listen."

Natalie's heart thudded, but she pictured Tanner sitting beside her, silently supporting her. And she forced the words out. "Mom, the truth is, I have been having trouble again. After Peter . . . well, things started, the nightmares, the flashbacks. I didn't tell you because I didn't want you both to worry, and . . . I wanted to handle it myself this time."

"Oh, Natalie." Memories of the past raced across her father's face. "I'm sorry."

"We shouldn't have sent you out there!" Mom's eyes grew wide. "If I'd only known—"

"No." Natalie shook her head. "I'm glad I went. I needed to. I've been seeing a psychologist in San Francisco, and I've made real progress. I understand now where my inability to let go of what happened comes from. It's my own guilt. And I need to be free of it."

"Guilt?" Confusion narrowed Mom's mouth. "I don't understand."

Natalie avoided her father's gaze, pushed back fear, and pressed on. "There's something else you don't know, Mom. About the night of the accident. I told everyone Nicole was driving. But that's not the truth. The truth is, I was."

The room stilled as silence thickened the air. Dad let his breath out in a rush and Mom sat back with a small cry. But she didn't let go of Natalie's hand. She squeezed tighter.

"You were driving?"

"Yes. Nicole was, at the beginning, but then I took a turn. And I . . . I couldn't stop the Jeep." She inhaled and let her breath out, forcing calm. "Afterward, I was so afraid . . . I told the police it was Nicole, I didn't know what they'd do if—" Her throat clogged and she couldn't finish. Could only stare at her mother in a silent plea for forgiveness.

"Oh, my darling girl." Mom's eyes spilled with tears as her face crumpled. "Why? Why would you keep this to yourself all these years?"

Natalie wiped her eyes and moved her plate aside. "Once I'd said it . . . I didn't know how to take it back. And afterward, I—"

"Afterward, Natalie never told the truth because I told her not to." Dad's low voice rumbled across the table. He raised his hands and gave his head a slow shake. "God help me, I thought it was the right thing to do. I thought by protecting you, we could keep you safe. But that's not what happened, is it?"

Tears crested Natalie's cheeks as her resolve to stay strong disintegrated. "I've lived with the guilt of it ever since. And there were times I didn't think I could. Times I didn't want to. But I'm starting to see my way past that now. I want my life back. Going to California showed me that. And the place to start is here. By telling the truth. And asking for your forgiveness."

They sat in heavy silence a moment, both staring at her, broken.

"Natalie, there is nothing to forgive." Her mother finally leaned forward and kissed Natalie's cheek. "It could just as easily have been you. Or both of you. I'm sorry if I . . . if I've pushed you away over the years, Natalie. I suppose that was my way of coping. But you're right. It's time to start over. Can we do that?"

Natalie nodded and stared in surprise as her father stood and rounded the table to join them.

"It's high time we started being a family again," he said, a genuine smile lighting his face and taking years off.

As Natalie allowed her parents to embrace her, she felt a release she'd never known before. True freedom, without condemnation, without judgment. Only love. And forgiveness. And there, in the fullness of that moment of redemption she'd long believed out of reach, Natalie heard her sister's laughter.

Sweet, sincere, and rejoicing with her, as she claimed the greatest gifts she'd ever known.

⌐2⌐

Shortly after Thanksgiving, she'd sold her apartment and was getting on a plane in a few days, heading back to California. For good. And although they'd had some serious talks while she'd been home, Natalie knew there were still things left unsaid.

She found her father in his study. "Dad? Got a moment?"

"Natalie." He looked up from his laptop. "All packed?"

"Yes." She pushed her hands into the pockets of her long cashmere cardigan and sank into a leather chair. "I leave day after tomorrow."

"So you won't be coming back to work after all."

Natalie tossed him a grin. "You fired me."

He waved a hand. "Details. It's my company. If you want your job back, it's yours."

"I don't." Natalie studied the large family portrait above the mantel. The last one taken before Nicole died. "It's time, Dad. Time we all move on."

"I know." He nodded. "You were good at what you did, but I suspect your heart was never fully in it, am I right?"

"As always."

"Ha. I think we've proven I'm not always right. I suppose that boy has something to do with your decision to go back to California?"

Her smile came unbidden, even as she shook her head. "Well. Maybe. But Tanner is in Seattle at the moment. He'll be there until after Christmas, I think."

He studied her over silver spectacles. "Good thing Jeffrey showed up when he did then. At least that confounded winery won't crash into the ground completely."

"No, it won't." Natalie crossed her legs. "You've seen last month's financials."

"I have." His eyes gleamed with unexpected pride. "I should have let you do your own thing years ago."

"I wouldn't have been ready." They shared a smile and Natalie prepared herself for what she needed to say. "Dad, I'd like to ask if you'd consider coming to Maoilios for Christmas. You and Mom."

"I see." His smile faded and he pressed his knuckles together. "You don't ask for much, do you?"

Natalie sighed. She hadn't expected it would be easy. "Well, Grandpa says he'd love to have you. Will you at least think about it?"

"Hmm?" He looked up again, like he'd forgotten she was still in the room. "I suppose so."

"Good." She hesitated, but needed to get this over with. "So why did you want Maoilios shut down so badly? Why were you so against me trying to make a go of it? Why do you seem so angry with Grandpa?"

"Ah. So many questions." Her father pushed back his chair and stalked the room. Stood at the mantel and stared into the fire. Eventually he turned, his eyes cold with memory. "Do you know what it was like for us, Natalie, to get that call in the middle of the night, telling us our daughter was dead? It could have been both of you, God forbid, but you were spared. I trusted him, my own father, with my children and he let me down! How did they not hear you leave the house that night? Start the Jeep? How did my daughter die on his watch?"

"It wasn't their fault," Natalie choked out. "It was just an accident. An awful accident that nobody saw coming. You can't continue to hold it against him. Don't you see that?"

He gave an anguished groan. "Bah. I suppose I was so hell-bent on getting rid of the place because I thought that would get rid of the memories."

"I figured as much. But I don't think it's that easy, Dad." Natalie sent him a sad smile.

"No, I don't suppose it would have been. But I blamed them, and myself, especially for what happened afterward. I shouldn't have told you it was okay to lie, Natalie. I'm sorry for that. And I'm sorry for being so hard on you all these years, sorry if you felt I thought it was your fault. It was my own guilt I was acting on."

Natalie sat very still in the shower of his words. Wondered if he really meant them. "Grandpa knows you blame him. He also thinks you hold him responsible for Grandma's death. Is that true?"

Her father lifted his head, his face ashen. "She had cancer, Natalie. They refused treatment because he said they'd prayed about it and felt it was God's will that she die peacefully. Garbage."

"She'd already had years of chemo, Dad. She was tired. Grandpa said she was ready. They both were."

"I wasn't."

The clock on the mantel ticked out time. Time she couldn't turn backward. Somehow they had to find a way to put aside the memories, pick up the broken pieces of their lives, place them on the pyre of past mistakes, and watch them burn to ash.

Natalie got to her feet and met her father's eyes.

"Life is short, Dad. Make your peace with it."

He crossed the room to where she stood, hesitated, then put his hands on her shoulders. "Wise words from someone who could barely say 'boo' to a bee a few months ago."

She nodded. "I guess I've finally grown up." Memories sang

now, reminded her of the man he'd once been, the father she'd adored and looked up to.

And forgiveness fell like sweet rain upon the thirsty ground of her soul.

"I don't blame you for what happened, for keeping my secret." Somehow she smiled through tears. "I love you, you know. You're my dad. Wherever I go, you'll always be welcome."

He raised a trembling hand and placed it against her cheek. "Thank you, Natalie Grace," he said at last. "You carry your grandmother's name with dignity and honor. She would have been proud of the woman you've become. I am."

"Really?" Natalie's smile broadened.

"Always have been." His crooked grin reached back to happier times. "And you're right, I am still your father. So I expect that boy to come and talk with me before the two of you run off into the Sonoma sunset."

"Daddy." Laughter spilled from her lips as she drew him into a hug. "I think you'll find Tanner to be a man of impeccable character. But don't tell me if he talks to you. I'm not getting my hopes up."

"Well." He looped his arm through hers and they walked from the room together. "If he lets you go, he's a fool. But I foresee a wedding on the horizon."

"You do, do you?"

"But for heaven's sake, don't let your mother drag you to that awful designer who made your cousin's bridesmaids dresses last year. Absolutely hideous."

Their shared laughter made her smile. "Dreadful. Purple. Almost neon. I felt like we should all be wearing sunglasses."

"We should have been. That's the Harris family for you. I had a flask of Scotch in my pocket the entire day. Don't tell your mother."

"Dad." Natalie shot him a grin and he lifted his eyes heavenward.

"All right, all right. No more secrets. Tell her if you must."

Thirty-Five

NATALIE SWIRLED THE RED LIQUID, HELD IT TO THE LIGHT, sniffed, and tasted. Grandpa Hal did the same, and they grinned at each other.

"Well?" Uncle Jeff waited, clearly impatient.

Grandpa Hal took another taste and put the glass down. "You've still got it, son. That's really quite superb."

"Thank you." Jeffrey smiled, rounded the counter, tidying up after the last customers. Christmas carols played softly from the overhead speakers. "It's Tanner's formula. I just fiddled a bit." He looked good, tanned, rested, and very much at peace. In the short time she'd been back, Natalie had noticed a big difference in Sarah too. She was practically glowing.

Jeffrey washed glasses and Hal picked up a towel to dry them. They'd set up a makeshift tasting room on the property while the new one was being built. It would be a pine-paneled, sunny place with big windows and a view of the lake. Word was getting out and visitors were steadily increasing. So were profits.

"Since you're both here," Natalie said, gauging their moods, unsure what their reaction would be. "I've invited my parents to join us for Christmas. I spoke to my mom last night and it sounds as though they're coming."

Hal stopped drying and raised bushy brows. "Is that so? Bill agreed?"

Jeff shook his head. "Don't get your hopes up, kid."

"I just wanted you to know. So you can be nice." Both men gave her an eye roll and she laughed. The holiday would be an interesting one. Her thoughts turned back to business. "Tanner's going to flip when he sees how much work they've done on the tasting room already. They're doing a great job."

"And when *is* Tanner coming home?" Grandpa Hal wanted to know.

Natalie sighed and reached down to pat Gwin. The moment she set foot on Maoilios, the dog had abandoned Sarah and hadn't left Natalie's side. "I'm not sure. From what he told me last night, probably after Christmas."

"Hope it's sooner." Her uncle put a couple glasses away. "Now that business is picking up, we could use him."

"The kids have settled well, but I don't want to rush him." But her heart picked up speed at the thought of seeing him again just the same.

Uncle Jeff gave her a knowing smile. "Sometimes a man needs a push in the right direction, Natalie. Take it from one who knows."

"He'll be back when he's ready." Despite missing him with an ache she hadn't anticipated, Natalie had never felt more at peace.

The only thing now that would make her new life complete was still in another state.

∾

Natalie helped Sarah clear the breakfast dishes, shoving down disappointment. Her parents had arrived yesterday, but dinner had been awkward. Her father and grandfather seemed to be tiptoeing around each other, avoiding any real conversation, and Natalie was beginning to dread Christmas tomorrow.

"You can't force it, honey." Sarah poured her another cup of coffee after they finished the dishes. "At least they're here. That's progress. And if they stay a few days longer like your mother wants to, you never know. They could end up talking, sorting through things."

"I suppose." Natalie stood at the sliding glass door, pushed her hands into the pockets of her jeans, and watched the dogs run circles around each other. She could almost see Jason and Jeni out there with them. "It's so strange, the kids not being here. You must miss them so much."

"I do." Sarah joined her and pushed the door open to let in the fresh morning air. "I thought about joining them for Christmas. But Jeff and I will fly up for a visit in the New Year. They're adjusting to life in Seattle so well, and being with Rance. His girlfriend is lovely, Jeni's taken to her quickly."

"You think they'll get married?"

"Oh, I'm sure. Soon, I hope. I think Marnie would approve."

"I'm glad. And what about you?" Natalie turned her thoughts to happier topics. "You and Uncle Jeff certainly seem cozy these days."

"We'll see." Sarah's cheeks bloomed with a pink hue and Natalie smiled.

"You deserve a happy ending."

"Doesn't everyone?" Sarah studied her carefully. "What is it? You seem more at peace than I've seen you, but I get the sense there's still something bothering you."

"It's silly." Natalie shrugged, staring at the floor.

"Then it must have something to do with Tanner. And I doubt it's silly at all."

"Sarah . . ." She tried to find the words. "How do you know? I mean, when you really love somebody? And whether they feel the same?"

Tanner's mother nodded, her eyes shimmering. "I'm not sure there's a right answer to that. I suppose all I can tell you is that you just feel empty without them. Nothing really feels right until you're together."

"That's what I was afraid of." Although she and Tanner talked almost every day, Natalie's fears had grown. What if . . . heaven help her . . . what if she'd fallen head over heels in love with Tanner Collins and he didn't love her back?

⌒

Maybe they just loved to argue. It was the only logical conclusion. The three Mitchell men argued about everything and anything. And they seemed to enjoy it.

"Are we seriously going to just sit here while you three fight over the best way to carve a turkey?" Natalie threw her napkin down on the table. Bad enough she hadn't heard from Tanner all day, but now the Christmas dinner Sarah and her mother had worked so hard to prepare was getting cold.

"I'm doing it," Hal growled, standing at the head of the table, carving knife and fork in hand. "It's my house."

"And here we go." Bill poured more wine. "Your house, your rules. Your way or the highway."

"Which you never respected anyway," Jeffrey put in, grabbing the bottle from his brother.

"Like you did? Please. You were grounded every weekend."

"Actually, I think that might have been you, William." Hal pondered over the bird, turning it this way and that.

"It's not going to fly away," Jeffrey told him, his tone hinting aggravation. "Just carve it or we'll be having it for breakfast tomorrow."

"Well—" Natalie's mother smiled brightly, her hands around a large casserole dish. "We can at least get started on the vegetables. Natalie? Mashed potato?"

"Sure." She plopped a blob on her plate and glowered at it. The red and green candles in the silver candelabra were dripping wax. Colorful shiny balls, pinecones, and sweet-smelling branches of evergreen were placed carefully around the beautiful red and white flower arrangement in the center. Natalie was tempted to hurl a few pinecones at the three stubborn men.

"From the top down. Why don't you just let me do it?" her father muttered, still watching Grandpa and the golden-brown bird. "This is why Mom always carved. Now I remember."

Grandpa Hal's blue eyes flashed in the way that it was hard to tell whether he was humored or angry. "This is why we stopped inviting you for holidays. Now I remember."

"Stop it," Natalie scolded, already exhausted. "It's Christmas."

Jeffrey muttered something under his breath and Natalie saw Sarah shoot him a dark look. "What time is it, anyway?" he grumbled. "Are we missing the game?"

"It's ten to three," Natalie's dad replied. "And yes, we are missing the game."

Out in the foyer, the dogs began to bark. A door slammed and made her jump. Natalie heard the thud of boots coming down the hall, and then Tanner's face appeared around the half-open door to the dining room. "Smells good in here. Got room for one more?"

"It's about time," Uncle Jeff grumbled. "We've been stalling."

"Got here as soon as I could." Tanner strode into the room, his grin wide. "Lakers are winning, by the way."

"All right!" Grandpa Hal clapped a hand on Tanner's shoulder. "Welcome home, boy. Now we can eat."

"Merry Christmas, all!" Tanner kissed his mother's cheek, shook Jeffrey's hand, and nodded toward Natalie's parents. He glanced her way, probably waiting for her to introduce him, but she couldn't speak.

All she could do was stare.

Disbelief coursed through her and suddenly everything made sense. "That's why you haven't been returning my calls?"

"Airplane mode. Then we got stuck in traffic. It is Christmas, you know."

Natalie pushed her chair back, her eyes blurring. She could barely breathe. Tanner was here. Standing right in front of her. "Did you all know about this?" The laughter that filled the room as she walked on unsteady legs toward Tanner confirmed it. "How . . . did you . . . get here?"

He met her halfway. "David picked me up. I invited him to stay but he had other plans. Anyway . . . hello, Mouse."

"Tanner." She moved forward a bit hesitantly, but his arms came around her the next instant and swept her into a tight embrace. Natalie laughed through tears and pulled her arms free to wrap them around his neck.

He was really here. She let her fingers brush the back of his neck, felt his heart beating against hers, and welcomed his kiss. A kiss that went on just a little longer than it should have.

"Ahem."

They broke away from each other laughing. She held Tanner's hand tight and walked him around the table to meet her parents.

And then, at last, they got to eat.

∽

Jeffrey entered the small graveyard the day after Christmas and pulled up short. His brother stood in front of Mom's grave. He hadn't expected that. Hadn't expected anyone to be up this early. The sun was just cresting the horizon line. And he didn't know whether to stay or go.

Until Bill turned to face him with a questioning look.

"I can come back," Jeffrey offered.

"You're here now." Bill moved aside, his smart loafers kicking a few pebbles across the grass. Jeffrey nodded and went to stand beside him.

"Good dinner yesterday, huh?" Lame. But when was the last time he and Bill had actually talked about anything?

"Once we finally got to eat it. Thought that boy was never going to get here." An uncharacteristic chuckle filled the air. Jeffrey stood back a bit and studied his brother, taking in the changes the years had brought, but seeing a new light in his eyes.

"You okay, Bill?"

"Meh." He shrugged, his smile fleeting. "I'm an old man who's wasted far too much time dwelling on the past."

"You're not that old."

"Sixty next year."

"Well, crap." Jeffrey gave a long whistle. "That means I'm almost fifty-seven. How'd that happen?"

"Who knows?" Bill sighed and bent to brush a few leaves off the headstone. "Lord, I miss her. You think she'd be proud of us, the way our lives turned out?"

A lump pressed against his throat and Jeffrey pushed it down. "I've asked that question a few times. I'm not sure I know the answer."

"I know the answer." Boots crunched over the gravel and Jeffrey turned to see their father walking toward them. "May I join you boys?"

The lump pushed harder. What in blazes was wrong with him? Good thing he'd retired. He'd be useless in the field in this state. Jeffrey cursed his lack of control and pinched the bridge of his nose.

"The more the merrier," Bill said drolly. Jeffrey snorted and Dad rolled his eyes.

"You always did have the strangest sense of humor, son."

Bill stiffened a bit, but a small smile came and went. Jeffrey watched the two of them with guarded interest. Wondered if they'd ever move beyond the barriers of time and misunderstanding that kept them apart.

Dad cleared his throat, stared at the grave for a long moment, and then nailed them with sharp eyes. "Your mother loved you both. And yes, she would have been proud of you. What she wouldn't have been proud of is the way we've let our relationship fall apart."

That was true, but neither of them seemed in any rush to confirm it.

Bill rocked on his heels and stared across the rows of empty vines.

Jeffrey fiddled with his watch and realized it had stopped an hour ago.

"Maybe we can talk about that sometime," Dad suggested.

Jeffrey caught Bill's surprised look and smiled. "Maybe."

His brother ran a hand down his face and gave a slow nod. "Maybe. But not right now."

"No. Not right now." Dad crouched to pull a weed and rose with a creak. "I'm just happy to have you here now, both of you."

"Going to have lunch with that boy today," Bill spoke quietly, giving a slow grin. "I'm assuming he has a question he wants to ask me. What should I say?"

Jeffrey and Dad laughed and Bill's eyes sparked with mischief. Dad's face displayed a rare joy Jeffrey hadn't seen in some time. He was suddenly very glad he'd made the decision to stay in California.

"Normally I'd say give him a hard time," he told his brother. "But Tanner's been through a lot lately. The kid needs a break."

"That's what I hear." Bill nodded and thrust his hands into his suede jacket. "Well, he's not going to know what hit him once we're done, I'll say that."

"Now what are you up to, William?" A hint of concern was creeping into Dad's eyes. Bill looked at his watch, looked at both of them, and raised a brow.

"If you can indulge me in some time and a coffee back at the house, I'll tell you."

Thirty-Six

TANNER WALKED THE PERIMETER OF THE LAKE AND WATCHED the two swans swim across the still water. He had a couple of hours to himself before he was due to meet Natalie for dinner. His mind was still reeling from today's lunch with Bill Mitchell. Still trying to process everything he'd been through in the last few months. Still trying to figure out how Natalie Mitchell had waltzed into his life and turned it upside down so completely that he could barely breathe when they were apart.

A smile slid over his lips as he crouched by the water and skimmed a stone. He checked out the new blooms in Marnie's garden and thought about seeing Jeni's face yesterday, when the moment finally came and they called his flight. How she'd clung tight around his neck, then looked back at him through those big solemn eyes. "Don't you worry 'bout us, Uncle Tanner. You gots things to do now."

Even Jason had seemed okay with him leaving. Tanner had enjoyed watching his nephew's relationship with Rance develop, and as each day passed, he grew more certain he was doing the right thing. The kids would be fine.

They didn't need him anymore.

"It was a season of your life, Tanner," David had said in the car yesterday. "A good one. Necessary. But it's time to move on now."

Indeed. And somehow, he knew Marnie would expect nothing less. He'd kept his promise. He'd taken care of the kids. And now it was their father's turn.

His cell rang in the pocket of his jeans and he fished it out. "Hey, Miguel."

"All set here, Tanner. You ready?"

Tanner blew out a breath and squeezed his eyes shut a moment. Then he nodded and gave a laugh he was glad nobody was around to hear. "Oh, yeah. I'm more than ready."

⌒—

Natalie smoothed down the new cashmere sweater-dress she wore, enjoying the soft blue color and silently thanking Sarah once again for talking her into buying it that morning. She'd curled her hair; it was longer now and had actually cooperated with her intentions.

She had no idea where they were going, but could hardly wait to be alone with Tanner. She still couldn't believe he'd shown up for Christmas. But somehow she had a feeling Tanner Collins would never cease to surprise her.

Her cell buzzed on the dresser and she glanced at the message. Come to the barn.

The barn? What in the world was he up to?

Natalie went downstairs in search of her parents, Grandpa Hal, Sarah, or Uncle Jeff, but the house appeared deserted. Laughter from the direction of the patio drew her attention. She crossed the living room and stood at the window. They were all sitting outside, chatting, laughing like old friends. Natalie couldn't recall when she'd last seen her parents so relaxed. She breathed a silent prayer of thanks, watched them a minute longer, then left the house, closing the door with a quiet click.

Natalie parked Grandpa Hal's truck off to the side of the large structure, hopped out, thankful for her flats, and looked around. "Tanner? I'm here." The doors to the barn were closed and she didn't see anyone around. She took a few steps forward, checked her phone again.

The doors to the barn swung open and Tanner stood between them. "About time. I was starting to think you stood me up."

Natalie smiled and walked toward him. "Now why would I do that?" The sight of him took her breath away. "You're wearing a suit," she squeaked, smothering a giggle. "Oh my."

Brand-new by the looks of it. Heather gray, with a slim royal blue tie. His usually unruly hair was cut and combed back neatly, his jaw void of any stubble, and the smile he wore made her heart beat a little faster.

"Well, I must say, you clean up well, Mr. Collins."

Tanner laughed and held out a hand. "C'mon, gorgeous."

Natalie stepped into the barn after him, and let out her breath in a rush. "Oh my gosh."

The entire place had been given a makeover. Whitewashed walls replaced the old rotting slats, fans spun in lazy circles from the beams, the dirt floor now hidden by new wood planks, a few colorful rugs thrown here and there. Twinkling fairy lights hung everywhere, giving the place a magical feel. A lone linen-covered table sat in the center, set with silverware, stemware, and china. Two white Chiavari chairs with gold cushions waited for them.

"Well?" Tanner bounced on the heels of his shiny black loafers, grinning like a kid.

Natalie turned in a slow circle. "When did you do this?"

"Hired a guy before I left, and your uncle oversaw the project. Had them on double-time last week. We still have to put in proper facilities out back, bar and kitchen and probably air-conditioning . . . but . . . is this what you had in mind for a wedding venue?"

"Oh yes." Tears burned as she stared at him. "This is exactly what I had in mind."

"Good." He moved into her space and put his arms around her. "Did I tell you how much I missed you?"

"Practically every day."

"Mmm." He kissed her forehead and drew back. "Well, I did."

But the time spent with his family in Seattle had been good for him. He'd told her how he and his brothers were already making plans for a long week of hiking in the mountains. Tanner had been blown away by how similar they were, how many interests they shared. Said his baby sister seemed to be a little in awe of him, but she messaged him every day. And he'd even succumbed to Facebook for the sake of keeping in touch.

"Oh, I got you a Christmas present," Tanner said.

"I thought *you* were my present." She giggled at the look he gave her.

"Hush." Tanner fished in the breast pocket of his jacket and pulled out a small box. Flipped the lid and presented it to her.

Natalie pulled air into her lungs and stared at a small silver charm on a slim chain. The Maoilios emblem was carefully carved inside an intricate circle. She touched it with a trembling finger, meeting his questioning gaze. "Tanner. It's perfect."

"I designed it myself, actually." He placed the box on the table and fastened the necklace for her, his hands coming to rest on her shoulders. "And that's just the beginning. But you should probably sit down."

Natalie let him propel her to a chair, in a daze. It was all so amazing. Fresh cut peach and pink roses interspersed with lavender overflowed from a glass vase in the middle of the table and permeated the air with a pleasant scent. Tanner pulled his chair close, tapped an envelope that sat between their place settings, and raised a brow. "You want to guess what's in here?"

"No clue." She shook her head. She had to be dreaming.

Everything about this moment was more than she had ever allowed herself to imagine.

"Open it."

"Okay." Natalie managed a small smile, pulled out papers, and scanned them. Almost dropped them. "What in the—" She clapped a hand over her mouth and stared at Tanner. He sat forward with a satisfied grin, wiping a tear off her cheek.

"Don't smudge the ink, Mouse."

"He did this?" Natalie blinked and studied the legal documents once more.

"Gave them to me today. I'm still a little stunned."

Laughter rushed out of her, startling her. But it was all she could do, that or blubber like a baby, and she wasn't about to go that route. "My dad *gave* you his shares in Maoilios? For real?"

"Looks that way." Tanner took the papers from her and pushed them back into the safety of their envelope.

Natalie took deep breaths, her heart racing and her mind tracking even faster. "I did not see that coming."

"Neither did I." Tanner moved around the table and fiddled with a serving dish. Checked out the open bottle of wine and gave a satisfied nod. "He, uh, told me he wanted to keep it in the family." He met her eyes and waited for the words to sink in. Before they could, he'd moved to the side of her chair and dropped to one knee.

"Right after I'd asked his permission to marry his daughter." Tanner took her hand in his and brought it to his lips. "He was pretty sure you'd say yes."

"Tanner," Natalie breathed out, her shoulders shaking with laughter and tears.

"I love you, Natalie Grace Mitchell." Tanner sniffed, his eyes shimmering. "I think I've been in love with you forever. At least it feels that way. And I know I don't want to live another day without knowing you'll be there beside me for the rest of my life."

"I love you too," Natalie whispered. "Since forever."

He nodded, pulled another box from his pocket, and revealed a beautiful marquise cut diamond. "So I guess all that's left is this. Will you marry me, Mouse?"

"Yes." Natalie let him slip the ring on her finger and pull her to her feet. She put her arms around his neck and waited for his kiss. "Tanner, I said yes. I'll marry you."

"I know." He grinned and touched his nose to hers. "I just want to stay here a minute."

"Okay." She nodded, traced the side of his face with a finger, and willed her heart to quit pounding.

"Did you see what's on the table?" he asked.

"Is that our new wine?"

"It is." Tanner held her closer. "I hear it's pretty amazing. Could be the one."

"It is, Tanner. I'm sure of it."

"Jeff said you were waiting for me to name it."

"Well, we thought it only appropriate."

"Thank you." His smile lit his eyes and his embrace felt like home. "I have the perfect name picked."

Natalie arched a brow. "Which would be?"

"Kismet." His smile broadened, his eyes shimmering under the tiny lights.

Perfect, indeed.

Happy laughter tumbled from her as Natalie shook her head, delighting in his mischievous grin. "Did you just say 'kiss me'?"

"No," Tanner slid his hands around her face, his breath warm and inviting as he filled the space between them. "But I don't mind if you do."

Acknowledgments

OUR FIRST TRIP TO CALIFORNIA TOOK PLACE ABOUT FIVE years ago. My husband and I were celebrating our twenty-fifth wedding anniversary, and I was completely captivated by the area from the moment we crossed the Golden Gate Bridge and I caught my first glimpse of the rolling brown hills, tall cypress trees, and rows upon rows of lush grapevines. It was a trip we both cherish and one I was still thinking about that following summer. My in-laws weren't doing well at the time, and we were spending a lot of time in Canada driving back and forth to visit them. The route we took from our cottage in northern Ontario to their home was scenic, the road winding around lakes and forests. In some way it reminded me of that magical trip to Sonoma, and in all the driving time, the idea for this story was born.

If you've read any of my previous books, you know I love writing about family. As *The Memory of You* began to take shape, I realized this one would be perhaps a bit more challenging. The story of sisters, secrets, loss, and fractured families began to play out on the page, and I was reminded of how complicated our lives can be. And once again, God began to whisper, *"Grace."*

Isn't it astounding that no matter what we've done, how far we run, God is always there, just waiting for our return? And His grace is sufficient for all our needs. I love this story for so many reasons, but the biggest takeaway for me is exactly that: God's grace. My prayer is that you, my reader, will also know this wonderful gift.

Once a story is complete, much hard work and dedication from many other people go into the making of a book, and I must thank everyone who played a part to get this story into your hands.

Rachelle Gardner, my agent and friend, your godly wisdom and guidance and support over the years mean more than I can ever adequately express. Thank you for always being there.

To the amazing team at Harper Collins: Becky Monds—when I signed my contract, I was told that you were "the best" and that I would love you. So true. Thanks for everything you do to make me a better writer. Thanks to everyone else on the team—Daisy, Amanda, Becky, Jodi, Karli, Kristen, Paul, everyone in marketing and sales, and all those who work behind the scenes to give the world great fiction. I can't thank you enough for your support, encouragement, and enthusiasm. Natalie Hanemann, it was wonderful to work with you again. Your insight and editing skills are always so much appreciated.

To my community of writing friends, you make me a little less crazy. It's a beautiful thing when friends feel like family. I thank you for doing life with me, getting real, and more importantly, letting me get real (actually I think you insist on it), and for talking me down off those ledges when necessary. This journey wouldn't be nearly as much fun without you.

And to all the wonderful book bloggers and reviewers who have become friends along the way, you have my sincere gratitude and humble thanks for all you do to make getting the word out about a new release just that much easier.

My family and friends in Bermuda and abroad, thank you for your continued support of my writing. Thanks as always to my Dad and Vivian, for reading and sending my books to your friends! To my amazing and talented kids for always believing in me. Sarah and Randy, I can't wait to read books with my first grandchild. We are so excited for you.

Chris and Deni, your love and laughter keep me going. You inspire me always!

And of course to Stephen, my own knight in shining armor— thank you for continuing to love me through this crazy writing journey and for believing in me, and for being mine.

And to you, my readers, I thank you for reading and supporting me, and for loving my characters as much as I do. I truly love writing books for you to enjoy!

Discussion Questions

1. In *The Memory of You* we see how Natalie struggles with the secret she has kept for so many years. Keeping secrets can be so damaging. Have you ever held on to a secret for longer than you should have?

2. Natalie's relationship with her parents has been fractured since the death of her sister. Have you experienced a fractured relationship? How do you cope with that kind of pain, and if the situation was resolved, how did that come about?

3. Tanner has put the blame on his father for breaking up their family and basically abandoning him. Have you ever felt abandoned by a family member or friend?

4. Tanner and Natalie both have to face incredible loss. Do you think this played a part in their reconnecting? How do you think shared experiences shape our relationships?

5. Sometimes people make poor decisions with often tragic results. Have you ever been in a situation where you made a wrong choice and regretted the outcome? Or did you make the right choice and see what could have gone wrong had you not?

6. It's often easy to blame ourselves when things happen that are out of our control, like Tanner and Natalie do. How do you think they could have handled their guilt differently?

7. Which characters in *The Memory of You* did you most relate to and why?

8. Natalie makes the hard choice to go against her father's wishes

to fight for what she believes in, regardless of how it might affect their relationship. Do you think she made the right choice?

9. What themes (grace, forgiveness) did you pick out from the story, and what spoke to you the most?

10. Letting go of the past is often the hardest challenge we face. Have you ever had to release something and allow God to heal you? What was the outcome?

11. Facing the reality of a loved one's illness is always difficult. Did learning the truth about how Sarah handled Marnie and her marriage so many years ago change your perception of her?

12. What scene or overall impression from the story will stick with you, and why?

About the Author

CATHERINE WEST WRITES STORIES OF hope and healing from her island home in Bermuda. When she's not at the computer working on her next story, you can find her taking her Border collie for long walks on the beach or tending to her roses and orchids. She and her husband have two grown children. Visit her online at catherinejwest.com.

Facebook: CatherineJWest
Twitter: @cathwest